BIG IDEAS FOR GROWING

YOUR SMALL BUSINESS

How to build profits and manage growth

FRANCES McGUCKIN

McGraw-Hill
Ryerson

Toronto Montréal Boston Burr Ridge, IL Dubuque, IA Madison, WI New York San Francisco
St. Louis Bangkok Bogotá Caracas Kuala Lumpur Lisbon London Madrid
Mexico City Milan New Delhi Santiago Seoul Singapore Sydney Taipei

McGraw-Hill
Ryerson Limited
A Subsidiary of The McGraw-Hill Companies

ISBN: 0-07-087874-9

1234567890 GTC 01234567890

Printed and bound in Canada.

Canadian Cataloguing in Publication Data

McGuckin, F.
   Big ideas for growing your small business: how to build profits and manage growth.

(SOHO solutions for Canadians)
Includes index.
ISBN 0-07-087874-9

Small Business—Management   I. Title.   II. Series.

HD62.7.M227 2000   658.02′2   C00-932383-X

Publisher: **Joan Homewood**
In-house Editor: **Carrie Withers**
Production Co-ordinator: **Susanne Penny**
Editor: **Tita Zierer**
Interior Design: **Dianna Little**
Electronic Page Composition: **Bookman**
Cover Design: **Matthews Communications Design**

To my incredible ninety-one year-old mother,
Emilie Gisela Shaw,
whose strength and determination,
courage and sheer stubbornness,
persistence and perseverance
have been an inspiration, not
just to myself, but to
friends and family
universally.

I love you mom.

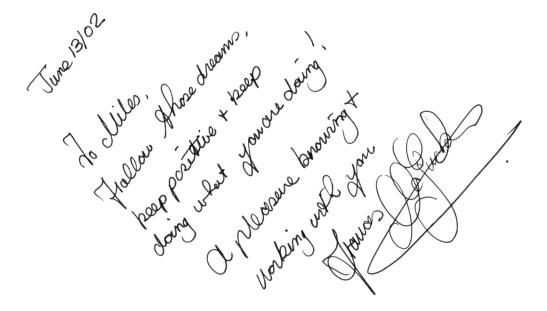

Foreword

I'm sure you have heard the following comment:

Q. "How do I run a small business?"
A. "Start with a big business."

There's more truth than humour in that statement. As a business owner for the past 25 years, I've grown Canada Wide Magazines & Communications Ltd. from gross sales of $76,000 in 1976 to today's gross sales of $25 million. And then along comes this book *Big Ideas for Growing Your Small Business* by Frances McGuckin. Where were you when I needed you the most?

Her easy-to-read "how to" book on growing your business is a refreshing, insightful step-by-step process for all who seek the elusive success formula and "ah-hah" ideas that bounce off every page of Frances McGuckin's second book.

This very practical book will show you how to identify the "Top Ten" mistakes and avoid them; how to find your customers; how to sell; how to control your finances; develop a team; achieve extraordinary results; and develop important communications skills, plus much, much more!

Buy this book, read this book and improve your performance, productivity and profitability. You'll be glad you did and you will turn your small business into a successful big business. And it won't take you 25 years like it did me.

Peter Legge, MA, CSP, CPAE
President & Publisher
Canada Wide Magazines & Communications Ltd.
Author/Publisher/Professional Speaker

Table of Contents

Chapter 1: So You're Open for Business—Now What? / 4

Owning a small business is exciting, yet it presents many challenges that affect positive growth. YOU are your business and the key to its success. Excellent customer service and avoiding the Top Ten Mistakes in Growing a Business are good starting points.

Chapter 2: Do Your Entrepreneurial Skills Need Fine-Tuning? / 19

A true entrepreneur has to develop many multi-faceted talents and wear 60 hats. Growing a business requires that you develop the Eight Essential Entrepreneurial Skills, identify strengths and weaknesses, and learn to delegate tasks that waste time or burn you out.

Chapter 3: Are You Organized—Or Out of Control? / 35

Overwork and disorganization creates chaos and inefficiency, so you need to establish simple daily, weekly and monthly systems and learn some time-management. Your files, administrative systems, computer, yourself and your home-office need to be organized.

Chapter 4: Are You in Control of the Financial Reins? / 52

Thorough accounting records are crucial to your financial health and give you valuable management and future planning information. Using a case study with easy-to-understand terminology, learn how to use accounting records to monitor financial progress, calculate a break-even point and increase gross profit margins.

Chapter 5: How Else Can You Increase Your Profits? / 78

Operating inefficiently easily fritters money away, yet instigating some basic systems can prevent this erosion of profits and increase cash flow. Fine-tune your administrative systems, inventory control, costing and monitoring, and credit and collection procedures.

Chapter 6: Are You Ready for Growth? / 100

While planned growth is productive, uncontrolled growth causes the demise of many promising businesses. Have you planned for growth? Are you ready for it? Do you want "more" or "bigger"? Use the Six-Step Growth Analysis Plan to decide whether growth is for you. Incorporation may be a viable consideration, so understand the pros and cons.

Chapter 7: How Do You Find Good Help? / 123

Growing a business usually requires delegating work. You can't do it all yourself. Know how to find and hire that perfect person. Be sure you are boss material and that you understand an employer's responsibilities and the additional costs involved.

Preface

HOW WAS THIS BOOK WRITTEN?

I'm the first one to admit that I am a dream maker. No different from anyone else, I spend some time dreaming about what I want from life. Perhaps different from some, I spend a lot of time making those dreams become a reality.

This book started as a dream. It became a reality because I made it a focussed goal with a time limit of completion for the end of summer 2000. No later. Regardless of whether it was to be published commercially or self-published, after nearly three years of puttering on the keyboard, it *would* be finished. It happened. How?

Simply by setting a goal, focussing on that goal, and working day, night and weekends to meet the publisher's deadline. You see, dreams are only dreams, but they have to become goals to make them happen. No one can make those dreams happen except you with your own hard work.

WHY WAS THIS BOOK WRITTEN?

Still on the subject of dreams and goals, four years ago my goals were to write books and give seminars to help reduce the small business failure rate—and to earn enough income to semi-retire to do what I most enjoy. These too were focussed goals involving more hard work, sometimes too much.

But those goals gave birth to my first book, *Business for Beginners: a Simple Step by Step Guide to Start Your New Business*, which I self-published in September, 1998. That book is now a best-seller with over 35,000 copies sold. From the age of 11, when I wrote my first book, *Teens and Horses* (still collecting dust), my dream was to publish a book. It's an amazing feeling to have made it happen.

I have also achieved my second goal—to become a successful speaker, and I am passionate about delivering my keynote addresses and seminars. While travelling throughout the lower mainland of B.C and the western provinces, often visiting remote locations, I realized the need for "the sequel." The more seminars I delivered to new and not-so-new entrepreneurs, the more I recognized the need for information on how to plan for and overcome growth problems. Many said, "Now that I'm already in business, I need a book on how to grow my business." Sorry it took so long, but here it is.

WHOM IS THIS BOOK WRITTEN FOR?

If you have just started a micro-business, or are experiencing "getting it off the ground" problems, or are growing too quickly or too slowly, or want to make more profit, or learn more, this book is written for you. On my travels, I have had the pleasure of meeting many enterprising, talented and dynamic micro-business owners experiencing all stages of growth. Many can't yet afford professional help or don't know where or how to find it.

Some are doomed to fail while others will succeed with commitment, learning and help. There are plenty of topic-specific reference books on the market, but I couldn't find one addressing the unique challenge of growing a micro-business, written in a down to earth, easy to understand style. So I decided to write one.

My message to you is simple. You have your entrepreneurial dream and no one can take it from you—except you. If you set your goals, give them time limits, focus, learn, be open to change, and use the information in this book, nothing can stop you from growing your dream into a dynamic and profitable business. You *can* do it.

I would love to hear from you with your comments or questions. Please visit my Web site at *www.smallbizpro.com* for more business information, or e-mail me at contact@smallbizpro.com.

Frances McGuckin
Langley, B.C.
Summer, 2000

Acknowledgements

"I get by with a little help from my friends," says it all. This book would not have been what it is without the help, support, encouragement, input and output of close friends and associates, many of whom are successful entrepreneurs.

One may author a book, but it takes teamwork to complete it. There are many people to thank, so starting from the beginning, my deepest respect and thanks to Carolyn Swayze, my literary agent. Carolyn had the faith and patience of a saint with this manuscript (which I believe finally encroached into her living space) to persevere in offering it to publishers.

Thank you Joan Homewood, publisher for McGraw-Hill Ryerson. Your insight and direction turned a good idea into a Big Idea. The support and expertise of the McGraw-Hill Ryerson staff has been invaluable.

A special thank-you to Cal Purcell, who contributed much of the information for the sales chapter. Cal has that true entrepreneurial spirit and a passion for sales, with twenty years' professional experience. Not only is he the Provincial Director of Government Services for Sprott-Shaw Community College in Vancouver, B.C., but he is also busy developing his own software company in his spare time.

To a long-time special friend, Christina Severin-Henriksen, who contributed valuable information on hiring employees in Chapter 7, my special thanks. Christina started Christina Personnel Ltd. in Vancouver, growing it over fifteen years into a well-respected business with a staff of fifteen. She now enjoys early retirement. Thanks also to Diane Wiley, General Manager of Eastleigh Personnel Ltd., for her valuable input into this chapter.

Unknown to Peter Legge, who kindly and readily wrote the foreword for this book, I have been his long-time admirer. Peter is an outstanding role model and the epitome of a truly inspirational and successful entrepreneur. He devotes countless hours to community and charitable organizations.

Not only did Peter build his business to become the biggest independently-owned magazine publishing company in Western Canada, he is also an internationally acclaimed, award-winning speaker. His awards include Toastmasters International's "Top Speaker in North America." A special thank-you Peter, for being an important part of this book.

Then there are those close entrepreneurial friends who read reams of manuscript and gave their most valuable input; Meredith Miller of M.J. Communications and Ken Smith of Fastforward Marketing and Communications Co. Ltd. Thank you for your time, commitment and most valued friendships.

A special thanks to Ken Baker, Managing Partner of B.D.O. Dunwoody L.L.P., Chartered Accountants and Consultants, Fraser Valley Regional Office, for sparing his staff Shawn Ganz and Agatha Cluff, to review and give input into the insolvency information in Chapter 14.

My thanks to the Royal Bank for their permission to use information on bank financing options in Chapter 6, and to *Business in Vancouver* for allowing me to use quotes from their inspiring May 2000, "Success" issue in Chapter 15.

To all those very special entrepreneurs who appear in the "Real Life" stories, particularly my "dream buddy" and inspirational friend, Barb Rees—thank you for being a very special part of this book. You are why this book was written.

To my very special eleven-year-old daughter, Katrina, sorry we missed another summer together because mom was "book-writing" again. Your understanding and perception often amaze me. Yes, the trip to Disneyland or Tahiti is still on.

And finally, to my dear partner, friend and husband, Michael, what can I say? I have to write. Thank you for understanding this stubborn writing maniac who continued on well into the midnight hours, week after week, to meet the publishing deadline. I love you too.

Introduction

SMALL BUSINESS IS BIG BUSINESS

Literally millions of entrepreneurs across Canada are self-employed, chasing the great entrepreneurial dream of self-sufficiency, being their own boss, and making lots of money—or so they hope. Those who follow the formulas for success usually achieve their aspirations, and more. Those who wing it on a whim run the risk of failure.

Self-employment has skyrocketed in the last decade. To quote recent statistics, British Columbia leads the way with a 70 percent increase, followed by Ontario at 47 percent and Alberta at 43 percent. Changing technology and economic conditions have both contributed to the proliferation of small and home-based businesses. Small business is indeed big business in Canada.

While many organizations offer help at the start-up, there doesn't seem to be enough ongoing, affordable support available to new, struggling and growing micro businesses. Hence, the high failure rate, generally quoted at 80 percent for those not trained in operating a business. This book was written not only to help reduce these sad statistics, but also to help entrepreneurs realize their dream. Let me help you realize yours.

WHAT DOES "GROWING A BUSINESS" MEAN?

You don't have to set a goal to own a large corporation to grow your micro-business. Growing a business means learning all aspects of profitably managing, marketing, operating and administering your business. Once the doors are open, you are faced with a myriad of unexpected challenges that no one told you about.

The first few years are always difficult. Too many businesses fall through the cracks because owners don't know what steps to take to rectify problems. This book lists the 60 jobs that an entrepreneur is responsible for. How do you cope with all these chores and generate a profitable income? Let me show you.

GROWING SUCCESSFULLY MEANS WORKING SMARTER, NOT HARDER

By learning how to circumvent operational stumbling blocks, your business has a better chance of success. The secret is to make the time to learn how. Most proprietors are "too busy" working *in* their business to work *on* their business. This book is designed to teach you how to work smarter, not harder, thereby increasing your profits while decreasing your stress level.

"MORE" OR "BIGGER"?

Many people have the misconception that growing means "more." More sales, more employees, more overhead expenses—and more headaches. Not so. Who needs these stresses? However, if you aren't generating the expected profits, then there are reasons why. The answers are in this book.

Then there are those entrepreneurs with aspirations of "bigger." To take your business to the next level, you must stop first to con-solidate your ideas by assessing where you are now and where you want to go. Bigger is only better if you do it right. Do you want a big-ger business generating bigger profits, or do you just want to retain your micro-business and make it more profitable?

WHAT WILL YOU LEARN?

By reading this book thoroughly and using the worksheets, you will have a better understanding of the hard work that growing a business takes. It will guide you step-by-step through the necessary steps and in a nutshell, it:

* helps you assess where you are now and where you are going
* teaches you the important entrepreneurial skills
* identifies common growth problems
* offers workable and practical solutions
* helps you get organized and operating efficiently
* shows you how to increase profits
* helps you assess whether you are ready for growth

- guides you through operating in crisis
- includes many self-assessment worksheets and checklists.

The first chapter addresses how important you and service are to your business. It explores the most common mistakes that precipitate growth or operational problems. Take the "Where Am I Now?" questionnaire at the end of Chapter 1 to assess both your emotional and physical business health.

If you use the information found in this book and complete all the questionnaires, worksheets and checklists, you will be well on your way to understanding your strengths and weaknesses and formulating your success plan. The rest is up to you.

CHAPTER 1

So You're Open for Business—Now What?

YOU ARE YOUR BUSINESS

We all dream of owning our own business sometime during our life. Perhaps opening a business was not a dream, but the only solution to a financial nightmare. Perhaps you were laid off, downsized, capsized, retrenched, cut-back, computer-replaced, too young, too old, too expensive, too good—or not good enough. Whatever the reason, you are here now, on your own in a highly competitive, business-eat-business marketplace.

Your Dream or Reality?

For many, the dream turns into cold reality all too soon. What you thought would be an exciting experience has become a daily grind of managing dozens of chores at once and tackling mountains of paperwork with not enough time to do it all. Your family and loved ones are complaining that you are always working and grumpy. For some strange reason, the dollars you expected to make so easily just aren't materializing. "Why is it happening like this?" you ask yourself. "What am I doing wrong?"

Don't feel alone with these thoughts. Most new entrepreneurs experience these same feelings, but are usually reluctant to admit that "my business is a giant headache." Who honestly wants to admit that it is nothing like they dreamed of or that they are afraid of failure and need help? No one. We all have our pride.

Success Takes Hard Work

Don't let pride stand in the way of succeeding in your business—after all, no one was born a professional. These skills are learned over a period of years. So why should you expect to be a hotshot business expert when you have never owned a business before? That is why you are reading this book.

You have taken the first step toward making your business work for you. The second step is to work on the necessary skills to make you a confident, competent, successful business person. The third step is to put some of the ideas and information offered here into practice. The final step is to constantly monitor your business.

Grow With Your Business

Some of the information found in this book doesn't apply just to business. As you work on improving your skills, you will gain confidence and be pleasantly surprised at how the rest of your life becomes more fulfilling. Every time you learn a new skill, you gain more self-esteem. When you gain more self-esteem, you gain more confidence. More confidence enables you to overcome the fear of tackling something new.

The learning process is exciting and self-rewarding. No longer held back by doubts and fears, and armed with new knowledge and confidence, your goals are within reach. It's a wonderful feeling to reach those goals because *you* made it happen. What could be better?

Never forget these four important words:

YOU are your business.

You may have the best product since the invention of the Internet, but if you can't market and manage your business it will just putter along. Many small businesses are operated by one to five people, but most are only one person—the sole proprietor—you. What's the use of having a beautiful store or wonderful technical talents if you can't relate to people or have few business skills? It just won't work.

Are You in Top Entrepreneurial Shape?

Before you start thinking about growing your business, you have to make sure you are in top entrepreneurial shape. You need to be multi-faceted like a polished diamond, with all-round business skills. You gradually transform into a smooth business machine with well-oiled cogs, all synchronized and working together. You are a combination of sixty different employees (more about that in

Chapter 2) and this book will help you to identify where you need advice and offer workable solutions.

BUSINESS IS ALL ABOUT SERVICE

Because you are your business, you are responsible for finding and keeping customers. People expect service these days, and if you don't give it, your competitors will. Have you ever gone into a store and been ignored or treated rudely by a staff member? How did you feel? You probably felt angry and vowed "never to pass through these doors again." Your feelings were hurt, because you were the customer, a Very Special Person.

IDEA   **BIG**   **COMPLAIN ABOUT POOR SERVICE**

If you have been treated rudely, tell the management. If they don't know there is a problem, they will lose your business and won't be afforded the opportunity to apologise. You are doing a business a favour by complaining. We always remember what it's like to be at the receiving end of poor service, so vow to treat your customers the way you expect to be treated.

REAL LIFE: Cleaning Up with Service

Recently I turned the house upside down in readiness for a new carpet cleaner (who offered an irresistible deal) to arrive. He didn't. On calling, he said that he had called the house two hours earlier and no one answered, so he didn't bother coming. I had previously pointed out to him that I would be out until an hour before the appointed time.

He had not listened and didn't apologise, making no effort to come. As my house was in total upheaval, I needed someone—now. I called a cleaner that I had used previously, and he came that same afternoon, re-organizing his schedule to do so. Now *that* is service! Someone lost a new customer that day, and someone else gained their old one back.

IDEA

BIG

- •
- •
- •
- •
- •

MAKE ALL CUSTOMERS VSPs

Your best cost-free advertising is good word-of-mouth referral. Customers make you money, build your business and pay your bills. This makes them VSPs—Very Special People. Treat each one as if they were your only client. They deserve your undivided attention. Not only will you keep clients, they will refer others to you. It's the most effective form of advertising, and it's free. The real bonus? You will make some wonderful friends and experience the satisfaction of making clients happy.

RULES TO KEEP YOUR CUSTOMERS HAPPY

1. The *customer* is always right.
2. The customer is *always* right.
3. The customer is always *right.*

THE TOP TEN MISTAKES IN GROWING A BUSINESS

Here are the 10 most common mistakes made by entrepreneurs as they impetuously plunge into their first business. As time passes, making any of these mistakes will cause serious operational problems or hinder growth. Can you identify with any of these?

1. No growth plan

You wouldn't sail across the ocean without first plotting your course and knowing how to sail, or build a house without blueprints. Similarly, a business cannot operate or grow without a practical, well-researched plan. Successful businesses use and revisit their plan before making any growth decisions. If you don't have one, this book will guide you through the process.

2. Wrong business, wrong location

You may have opened a retail store, only to find that the long hours and hard work don't add up to a profit, let alone an acceptable wage. Perhaps you chose a service business, only to find that you are technically good at your work but not so good at administering your business. You may have found the competition too tough, or the demand for your service not what you had envisioned. You now have to decide whether to make a concentrated effort and continue, or try your hand at something else.

Location, location, location makes or breaks a retail store. "But the rent was cheap!" you say. "Why is the rent so cheap?" I ask. Retail stores should plan to pay for a prime location with good visibility, walk-by traffic, and ample, accessible parking. Otherwise, you will spend a fortune in costly advertising or lose money by being forced to hold regular, low-profit sales to draw in new customers.

Growing Pains

If you chose too small a location, you may have to move within the first two or three years, a costly exercise. You will be leaving expensive renovations and fittings behind. Some people move to a location far too big for their needs, and can't maintain the overhead. Two local businesses recently declared bankruptcy for this very reason. They both moved to larger locations, thinking bigger was better. It wasn't. The only things that increased were their square footage and debts.

3. Lack of technical skills

Without the necessary technical expertise, you have little to offer your customers. Consider taking night-school courses if you need to accelerate your learning. Once you open a business, clients look to you as the expert.

Learning a new trade takes years, as does learning to manage a business. Most successful owners choose a field in which they have expertise. They then only have to cope with learning the management functions. If you have chosen a business that dictates learning new technical skills, your frustration level must be high.

4. Lack of sales and marketing skills

Selling is not everyone's strongest point. For many, the thought is quite scary. A true salesperson is a professional who has worked over the years to develop the necessary skills. But have hope as selling can be learned, especially as you develop more confidence in yourself and knowledge in your field. Chapter 13 explains how to improve sales skills.

Many people have trouble knowing how to market their business, so don't feel alone. If you have prepared a business plan, your market research would have revealed where and who is your market. It's amazing just how narrow your true market is when you start to research. Chapter 8 will help you to grow your customer base. Chapters 9 through 13 will help you to better market your business.

5. Lack of financial skills

You are the CEO of your business, so you have to learn about accounting, financial figures and cash flow—not everyone's favourite subjects. If you don't have financial knowledge, you probably won't succeed. Never hand the financial reins to someone else. The good news is, you can learn these skills as well. See Chapter 4 and learn how to increase your financial control.

6. Undefined financial resources

Staying solvent from start-up through the first few years requires a stable cash flow. Too many businesses start on a shoestring budget, hoping for enough sales to produce healthy profits. In most cases, growth is a slow process taking years. You should work with a cash flow forecast and monitor it closely. It will indicate where and when you may experience cash shortages.

7. Lack of market research

Most people don't spend enough time learning the demographics of their market—that is—where and who their market is, or if there is a market at all for their business. Competition is fierce, so you need to offer something better or unique to customers. This requires regularly researching your competition: their pricing, customer service policies and marketing strategies. To you, your widget is the best invention since Eve, but it isn't if no one wants it, needs it, or can't afford it.

8. Investing in trendy businesses

Many people jump on the bandwagon of trendy businesses without researching their potential longevity. A business should have a projected life of at least 10 years. By the time some trends are established, they are already on their way out. How many coffee

> **IDEA**
>
> **BIG**
> •
> •
> •
>
> ### CATER TO LONG-TERM TRENDS
>
> One key to growth is diversification. As an example, what could you do to service all the home-based businesses springing up in abundance—a long-term and growing trend. Most self-employed people don't have much time to shop, wash and maintain vehicles, fix computers or go to the hairdresser. Be creative. Think of ways to diversify and cater to a growing trend.

shops will still be operating in one to three years? Study future trends to ensure you are filling a long-term niche.

9. Over-projecting sales, under-projecting marketing costs

Over-projecting sales or under-estimating expenses may look good on paper, but you are only fooling yourself. It takes many months—usually up to three years to generate steady and consistently profitable sales. Business plans should project a realistic sales growth for the first two years. Initial losses are common, so make your projections realistic. You should also know your break-even point—that is—the gross sales required to meet all monthly overhead expenses. This subject is explained in Chapter 4.

Operating on a shoestring budget leaves little for effective marketing. Plan to spend a minimum of 10 to 15 percent of projected sales in the first two years. Some businesses spend even more.

Research the marketing techniques that work best for your type of business, rather than spending valuable dollars on ineffective methods.

10. Professionals are not consulted

Once operational, few people budget to regularly meet with an accountant, business consultant, or lawyer, so unless you are all of these, you need help. Accountants are trained to recognize financial problems, and lawyers are necessary to review leases, employment contracts, loan agreements, franchise, partnership and buy-sell agreements. If you are experiencing problems, please turn to a professional for help.

WHERE ARE YOU NOW?

Perhaps you have been in business only a few weeks and are still very confused. You may have been operating several months or a few years, but your business expectations are not being met. Perhaps you are experiencing rapid growth and feel out of control. There are numerous facets of your business requiring solid strengths and knowledge and much of this knowledge comes from experience—as with any job.

With a microbusiness, there is no one to train you, watch over you, or tell you what you are doing wrong. The old adage, "you learn by experience" is fine in some situations, as in learning to ride a horse. You can take a few falls from a horse and probably survive, but you can't afford to have too many falls in business. More often the general rule is: "Learning by experience will cost you nothing but money." A small business—in fact any business—can't afford to lose money.

TAKE THE TEST: "THE WHERE AM I NOW?" QUESTIONNAIRE

Now is a good time to seriously address where you stand with your business. Documenting facts will bring to your attention situations that you may not have previously noticed—or ignored.

Admitting to yourself that there may be a few problems is a giant first step in the right direction. Writing the problems down makes you face reality. Read Figure 1.1, The "Where Am I Now?" questionnaire, think carefully about your answers and answer honestly.

HOW DID YOU RATE?

This questionnaire is designed to draw your attention to the areas that cause operational problems. It will indicate where you went off track at start-up and assess your current enthusiasm for your business. Don't be too discouraged if you obtained a low score, as addressing these problems will allow you to develop a sensible and cautious plan of action. If you have identified critical operational problems, your score could be extremely low, if not a minus.

For example, if you started because you were laid off and couldn't find work, you probably started the business feeling pressure to bring in an income—and fast. In this state of mind, most people start out tired and depressed. Poor decision-making and bad judgements often occur. You may have seen your friends succeed and were tempted to emulate their successes. You could have started the wrong business or not had the necessary skills to make it work smoothly.

Many people act impetuously at the thought of owning their own business, rushing into it with their blinders on and a sense of "I must do it now!" Usually, the groundwork and research are not completed. Business opportunities appear to be just that—wonderful money-making machines that can be started with minimum capital and maximum, immediate returns. There are not too many of these opportunities available.

If you consulted professionals with your plan and researched the market, you started out right. Give yourself a big pat on the back. If you financed most of the business yourself from savings and a small bank or family loan, this is another big point in your favour (as long as the family loan didn't create a family argument). If you used money from credit cards, extended mortgages or funds from loan sharks, this was dangerous money.

Commit to Overcoming Obstacles

Many problems can be overcome by learning. You won't succeed without learning how to organize and administer your business and yourself. Growth creates problems for most businesses. Some grow too fast and are undercapitalized. Some are located in poor locations, whereas others can't keep up with the administrative "stuff." Most of these problems can be overcome.

Most importantly, you must have the right attitude toward your business. Keep motivated and positive, and start each day feeling charged. Once you operate in a negative mode, the business will start to fail. Remember—*YOU* are your business. Goal-setting

IDEA **CHART YOUR PROGRESS**

In six months to a year, take the "Where Am I Now?" questionnaire again and compare the two results. If you have worked hard to grow your business, you should be pleasantly surprised at the results.

enables you to measure your progress, and attainable goals are what will keep you motivated when the going gets rough. You now have an initial guide to prepare your plan of attack.

Chapter 2 focusses in detail on developing the necessary entrepreneurial skills. It highlights the many jobs a sole proprietor is responsible for and analyses your current workload, with suggestions of how to think about working smarter, not harder. Be sure to complete the Figure 2.3 "Where Am I Going?" questionnaire.

Figure 1.1	The "Where Am I Now?" Questionnaire

First test: **Second test:**

Date completed: _____   **Date completed:** _____

1. I have been in business for:
    a) _____ weeks   b) _____ months   c) _____ years.

2. I started because: **(Circle only the most accurate response.)**
    a) I was laid off and couldn't find work.
    b) I no longer wanted to work for my employer.
    c) I was not getting enough recognition or pay for my work.
    d) I was worried about job security.
    e) My work was boring and posed no challenges.
    f) My goal has always been to own my own business.
    g) I have planned this for years, and now I am ready.
    h) My family owns its own business.
    i) All my friends seem to be self-employed.
    j) Owning my own business seemed like an attractive idea.
    k) Other: _____

3. I chose this business because: **(Circle only the most accurate response.)**
    a) I have worked in this field for more than five years.
    b) I have excellent technical skills in this area.
    c) It was a challenge that drew on my strengths.
    d) It required start-up capital of less than $10,000.
    e) I could work from home.
    f) I saw an advertisement which really appealed to me.
    g) The business proposal promised an immediate income.
    h) I always wanted to own a business like this one.
    i) I thought I could learn how to operate it quickly.
    j) I have had a business before and this appeared to be a profitable concern.

4. Before making the decision to start this business, I: **(Circle each applicable response.)**
   a) consulted an accountant or consultant with my idea
   b) researched the current and future market
   c) researched the competition
   d) researched the product or service
   e) prepared a business plan
   f) prepared projections and cash-flow sheets for two years
   g) had an accountant review my business plan
   h) had a lawyer review contracts and leases
   i) checked local government bylaws and licencing agencies
   j) had enough money on hand to operate for a minimum of six months
   k) set short-term and long-term goals.

5. I financed the business with: **(Circle only one applicable response.)**
   a) my own capital
   b) my partner's and my own capital
   c) a small business loan from the bank and 1/3 my own capital
   d) money from my family
   e) cash from my retirement savings
   f) a small business loan and little capital
   g) my own capital plus d or e
   h) my own capital plus a line of credit
   i) a line of credit
   j) money obtained mainly through credit cards
   k) an extension on my home mortgage
   l) a higher-interest loan, not from a bank.

6. I am experiencing difficulties with my business in: **(Circle each applicable response.)**
   a) making enough profitable sales to pay the bills
   b) knowing how to reach my market
   c) finding effective methods of advertising
   d) selling, and closing potential deals

e) understanding the necessary paperwork

f) understanding the bookkeeping and accounting requirements

g) keeping on top of the paperwork

h) motivating myself to work

i) keeping organized

j) not having enough recreation or family time

k) keeping a positive attitude

l) drawing business away from the competitors

m) keeping my prices competitive but profitable

n) getting my clients to pay me on time

o) finding the right employees

p) keeping inventory turning over quickly

q) knowing how to manage my inventory.

7. At this time, I know the following about my business: **(Circle each applicable response.)**

a) the seasonal sales trends

b) my average gross sales each month

c) my average monthly gross profit

d) my monthly break-even point

e) how much my clients owe me

f) how much I owe to suppliers and tax departments

g) my approximate personal tax situation for year-end

h) the correct balance in my bank account

i) my estimated sales in the next six months

j) how much I can safely draw from my business each month

k) how I am going to market in the next three months.

8. My current state of mind in relationship to the business is: **(Circle only the most accurate response.)**

a) I am still very excited about the future.

b) I am always planning ahead and thinking of innovative ideas.

c) I love what I am doing and am very content.

d) I can foresee great potential for the future.

e) I am uncertain about the future.

f) I am not sure if I made the right decision.

g) This was not what I expected it to be.

h) It's hard work and the glamour has worn off.

i) I get tired and have trouble motivating myself.

j) I am depressed because I don't earn enough money.

k) I don't think I am an entrepreneur after all.

l) I think I'd prefer to be an employee again.

m) I could close the doors tomorrow and walk away.

9. At this time, my future plans for the business are: **(Choose the one item which best describes your future plans.)**

a) to learn everything I can and to work on making it succeed

b) to locate my problem areas and try to resolve them

c) to be profitable, to diversify and grow

d) to build this business to help support my retirement

e) to build the goodwill and sell within the next few years

f) to seriously analyse where I stand before I go much further

g) I don't have any future plans as yet

h) I'm having enough trouble surviving day-to-day, never mind the future

i) to sell it for what I can and get out.

Total your score for questions two to nine by using the following formula and writing your points scored (or lost) in the space provided.

Score

Scoring:

Question 2: 1 point for a-e; 5 points for f-g; 2 points for h-k _____

Question 3: 5 points for a-c; 3 points for d-e; 2 points for f-j _____

Question 4: 15 points for all items circled; 7 points for
              7-9 circled; 5 points for 4-6 circled;
              1 point for 1-3 circled   _____

Question 5: 5 points for a-c: 4 points for d-g; 3 points
              for h-i, 0 for j-l   _____

Question 6: Deduct 1 point for all items circled in
              this question   _____
              Bonus: add 10 points if no items are circled

Question 7: Add one point for each item circled

            Bonus: add 5 points if all items circled

Question 8: Add 5 points for a-d; deduct 1 point for e-f;

            deduct 3 points for g-j; deduct 5 points for k-m _____

Question 9: Add 10 points for a-e; 3 points for f;

            no points for g-i

Total Score _____

Score analysis

71 points: You are obviously an excellent entrepreneur who is doing everything right. Congratulations! Keep on doing what you are doing.

60-70 points: Well done and bravo! You have made a successful start and have pinpointed a few areas where you know you need to improve. Work on these areas with proper guidance, and you will definitely build or improve on a fine business.

30-59 points: There are some important areas you should address. For the most part, you have made a valiant effort to "do it right." Don't ignore problems or shortcomings as they can likely be overcome.

10-29 points: The warning bells are sounding. You have to evaluate what you are doing wrong or not doing at all. It's not too late to work on the areas of concern, but it will require your dedicated commitment.

(–) to 9 points: Perhaps you should consider letting the business go before you get deeper in debt and more depressed. Entrepreneurship is not for everyone. Some of the most successful people have quit or failed multiple times before eventually succeeding. If you are willing to accept professional guidance, you could get your business back on track. If it is the wrong business or you have lost interest, let it go.

Do Your Entrepreneurial Skills Need Fine-Tuning?

WHAT IS A TRUE ENTREPRENEUR?

A true entrepreneur has the ability to learn and develop a multitude of abilities and talents. Entrepreneurs are risk-takers, dream-makers, visionaries and decision-makers. They are often creative and impulsive, driven and tireless in working toward their goals. Many people are self-employed, but only a few are true entrepreneurs. If you better understand what makes an exceptional entrepreneur, you can improve on the areas that are holding you back from truly realizing your dreams.

Being your own boss is not as glamorous as it first seems. Who do you blame when things go wrong? Who looks after the business when you are ill? Who makes decisions? Who has to fire employees? Who is responsible for paying the bills? You—that's who. Were these distasteful tasks a part of your dream? Do you have the human resource skills to handle delicate situations? Learn-as-you-earn, hands-on experience is not necessarily the best way to operate a business.

THE EIGHT ESSENTIAL ENTREPRENEURIAL SKILLS

To cope with the many daily challenges, you need a positive attitude. Although technical skills are necessary, a true entrepreneur develops the Eight Essential Entrepreneurial Skills and uses them daily. You have to be *SCCOPPED*—an all-round people person with these following skills and qualities. When you have read this section, ask yourself this question: Am I *SCCOPPED?*

A SCCOPPED PERSON HAS:

Self-motivation and discipline
Confidence
Communication skills
Organization
Passion and a positive attitude
Persistence and perseverance
Expertise
Dreams and goals

Self-Motivation and Discipline

If business looks a little grim and there are no foreseeable solutions to problems, it's difficult to face the day—let alone feel motivated. If there are orders to fill and work to complete, motivation is usually not a problem. So how do you become motivated? Working positively and seeing results is motivational. Developing confidence, organizational skills and a positive attitude will help. In other words, self-discipline will evolve from developing the other entrepreneurial skills.

Confidence

When your confidence is low, life can seem overwhelming. By becoming an expert in your field, maintaining a positive attitude and keeping organized, you gain confidence just knowing how you are going to tackle each day. If you are passionate about your business, you automatically radiate confidence.

Excellent technical skills will feed your confidence. Have you ever experienced a salesperson trying to sell you something he or she obviously knew little about? Did you buy from that person? Probably not. In business, knowledge and confidence are what convinces the customer to buy from you.

Confidence comes from trying something new and succeeding. When you close a sale or customers refer you to others or send a thank-you card, confidence builds. When you draw a hard-earned pay cheque or you try a new winning advertising strategy, your confidence is strengthened.

To gain and maintain confidence, you have to work hard at your business. For most, it evolves over time and with experience. If you do it right, confidence is one of the lasting rewards.

Communication Skills

Communication is the ability to convey your message clearly, concisely, and confidently. In business, communication skills are a must. You must sell yourself before you can ever sell your business. You will need to compose a variety of professional correspondence, so effective written skills are essential. In many instances, they are your only foot in the door.

We can't survive in this e-society without telephones, voice mail and electronic communication gadgets, so telephone skills and the art of conversation are important integral components of doing business. Whether speaking one-on-one or to a group, if you can't get your verbal message across clearly, who is going to speak for you? These skills can all be practised and learned. Chapter 10 is devoted entirely to the art of verbal communication.

Organization

What is organization? It is the ability to plan and execute a series of tasks in an orderly fashion. It is the ability to find any piece of paper within twenty seconds, or to arrange a cupboard so that you aren't buried in junk on opening the door. It's the ability to arrive at appointments, complete work on time despite emergencies, and to allocate your priorities, working through them in sequential order. It is the ability to complete all of the above—and more—without losing your cool.

How can an unorganized person learn to be organized? Through discipline and practise. First, you must want to be organized. By being more disciplined and motivated, your desire to be more organized will increase. The busier you get, the more organized you need to be. Chapter 3 is devoted entirely to becoming more organized.

Passion and a Positive Attitude

Passion! Described in the dictionary as meaning appetite, desire, ardour and hunger, these words aptly define the very essence of what drives an exceptional entrepreneur. You need to have a love affair with your business. Enthusiasm will allow you to play the game well, but passion will score you the goals.

Without passion for your business, what will positively motivate you? Money, desperation or the competition will only motivate you for the short-term. If you started your business without passion, you could be in serious trouble, because if you don't have it, you won't find it doing what you are doing now.

Passion inspires your creativity and motivates you to reach for your goals. It builds confidence and gives you the determination to persevere. Passion helps to close a sale. It creates a hunger to improve your skills. There are no books written about "How to get passionate about your business." If you ain't got it, you can't learn it—you are probably in the wrong business.

One multi-level manager I met informed me that the company refused to recruit any person who doesn't have a passion for their business. Their philosophy is that other skills can be taught, but passion can't. It has to be there from the beginning.

Positive attitude

At times, a positive attitude may be the only lifesaver that keeps you afloat. It's easy for the stress of our "progressive" society to drag you into depression. I'm sure you have asked friends: "How are you today?" only to be regaled with stories of deaths, debts, disaster, divorce and despair. If you wanted macabre entertainment, you could watch a soap opera. Do you feel inclined to approach or associate with depressing people? Of course not. We can all be depressed without help from our friends.

In business, the principle is no different. Is the glass half-empty, or is the glass half-full? Project a positive attitude as you deal with the day-to-day assortment of people you meet through your business. They will not remember you favourably for your negative attitude, but they will remember you for your positive and upbeat approach to life. If you possess a sense of humour, all the better. These two qualities go hand-in-hand.

No one can teach you how to have a positive attitude. As you develop confidence in your abilities through perseverance and learning, so your positive attitude will develop. If you are the eternal pessimist, you shouldn't be in business. To feel more positive, work on the other skills and read some books on positive thinking.

Persistence and Perseverance

Highly successful people don't use the words "I can't" or "I quit." They have learned that you learn by your mistakes, and that setbacks are only challenges. It is not a crime to fail, but it is a crime not to learn from failure.

Persistence takes over where passion leaves off. Where passion gives you the hunger to set goals and succeed, persistence and perseverance will keep you going through the long and sometimes tedious process of reaching those goals. Some call it stubbornness or "stick-to-itness." Whatever term you use, perseverance is the quality that ensures the task is completed properly and that your goals are attained.

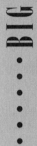

IDEA **LEARN THE PERSISTENCE PRINCIPLE**

This gem from an old Toastmasters' magazine is yellow with age from living for years on my refrigerator. It has guided me through many difficult times. The message is universally famous. "Simply stated, the persistence principle says: 'It's too soon to quit.' Highly successful people pursue their goals relentlessly. They know that perseverance is a key ingredient for success. Patience and diligence, like faith, can remove mountains. Successful people overcome mountains of rejection, dismissal and repudiation by operating on the persistence principle."

Expertise

Quite frankly, if you are not an expert in your chosen field, you should not be in business. In a service business, you are often responsible for peoples' lives and safety, so learn all there is to know about your profession. You should never stop learning and keeping abreast of changing technology.

When you are sure of your advice to others, your confidence will continue to build. The more you know, the more your clients will have confidence in you, and will refer you to others. Become an expert before you hang out your shingle.

Dreams and Goals

Operating a business without having dreams and goals is rather like sailing without a rudder and compass. Use a business plan that incorporates both your short- and long-term goals. Without goals, you will flounder, so never lose sight of them.

Long-term goals obviously take time to achieve, so in the meantime, reward yourself by setting short-term goals, or baby-steps. These can be practical daily, weekly or monthly goals that are achievable. After a few months, you will be surprised at just how far those baby steps have taken you.

Once you have set goals, your passion, confidence and positive attitude will drive you to achieve them. Being the organized, motivated and disciplined expert with fine communication skills, your persistence and perseverance will ensure your success.

IDEA   **DREAM**

Ask yourself: Why did I start this business? Do I want it to grow? How big? How many people will it employ? Do I want to expand into other branches? When? When do I plan to buy a fancy company car? When do I plan to retire, where, and with how much money? How much will my business be worth in 10 years if I work hard at making it a success? Indulge yourself in the luxury of a little dreaming, then write down your goals. See Chapter 6 Figure 6.2 for a goal-setting list.

THE A TO Z ENTREPRENEUR

Your entrepreneurial wardrobe is crammed with a variety of hats which you regularly change each day. Not only do you need to develop the eight essential entrepreneurial skills, you now have to cope with a multitude of tasks, some not particularly to your liking. Figure 2.1 shows a list of some of the hats you will be wearing during your business days.

There are 60 jobs listed, and you may be able to add more. A sole operator has a mammoth task in organizing each day. If you have employees, it can be even more difficult, because now you also have to schedule, train, supervise and pay them. Which priority comes first? It's not easy—this needs careful organization.

Don't Feel Alone

On analysing some "Where are you now?" tests taken at a home business trade show, most entrepreneurs experienced difficulty with marketing, sales, keeping on top of the paper flow, understanding

Figure 2.1   Your Entrepreneurial Wardrobe

Advertising manager, administrator, accounts payable clerk, accountant

Banker, bookkeeper, budget planner

Computer technician, credit manager, controller, customer service agent, CEO

Debt collector

Expert, educator

Finance manager, fixer

Gofer; goal setter

Human resources officer

Investor, insurance planner, invoice clerk

Jack-of-all-trades, janitor, job coster, journalist, juggler of jobs

Keyboard operator, keynote speaker

Legal advisor

Manager, marketing strategist, motivator, mail clerk, media relations manager

Networker

Office clerk

Payroll clerk, personnel manager, president, promoter, problem solver, purchasing agent

Quality control officer

Receptionist, receiver

Secretary, salesperson, shipper

Technician, trainer

Umpire

Vendor, visionary

Writer, warehouse manager

Xmas party planner

Yellow page advertiser

Zoo keeper (organizer of all the above).

accounting requirements, and keeping motivated. They scored 23 to 34 on the test. These results demonstrated the obvious need for entrepreneurs to learn all they can about working smarter in their business and developing the many essential skills.

TAKE THE TASK TEST

Solutions to many operational problems are addressed in this book, however, there is no solution if you are not motivated enough to work on solving your problems. When the above tasks are arranged into more defined categories, you are responsible for all the tasks listed in Figure 2.2.

Instructions

Examine the list of jobs numbered one to ten, highlighting the ones you enjoy and do well. Then with another colour, highlight the ones that you "really hate." Now change colours to highlight the

Figure 2.2	Your Daily Task List

1. **Accounting:** budgeting, paying bills, financial planning, credit management, debt collection
2. **Administration:** purchasing, mail, filing, correspondence, reception, invoicing
3. **Computer:** data entry, word-processing, contact management, learning software, maintenance, upgrades, e-mail, Web page
4. **Correspondence:** advertising copy, letters, press releases, articles
5. **Employees:** hiring and firing, training, motivation, payroll, arbitration
6. **Maintenance:** office and other equipment, tools, vehicles, building
7. **Problem-solving:** trouble-shooting, quality control, customer service
8. **Sales:** marketing, promotion, advertising, delivery, follow-up
9. **Warehousing:** inventory control, shipping, receiving, storage
10. **Your job:** completing all the above in addition to generating income

ones that you don't have time for. Finally, change colours to high-light the ones that you need to develop more expertise in.

You will probably find that many of the jobs you hate are the ones you don't make time for. Most of these are critical to the success of your business. At the end of this chapter is Figure 2.3, the "Where Am I Going?" self-evaluation questionnaire. Transfer this information to questions 8, 9, 10 and 11.

A small business doesn't often have the luxury of staff to help. However, your business growth can be severely impeded by your failure to recognize the need for help.

ENTREPRENEUR OR OPERATOR?

If you want your business to flourish, you can't afford to be bogged down with time-wasting chores. Many talented individuals prefer to work *in* their business, not *on* it. *You* have to make your business happen, but it won't if you are just an operator. A typical operator is someone who is happiest doing his or her chosen job, such as designing Web pages, landscaping gardens, or repairing vehicles. Their day consists mainly of scheduling the income-generating workload and doing it.

Work *on* Your Business

Somewhere along the line, this same person still has to make time to complete the other tasks. Michael Gerber said it best in *The E Myth Revisited*. "The typical small business owner is only 10 percent Entrepreneur, 20 percent Manager, and 70 percent Technician."

IDEA **BIG**

WORK SMARTER

If you are too busy doing your work and not working on what is needed to grow, you will eventually suffer from entrepreneurial burn-out. Many owners burn out after a couple of years. They lose their passion and become unmotivated by all the "stuff" they have to manage, willingly letting go of their business when it becomes overwhelming. This sad ending can be avoided by learning to work smarter, planning for growth, and planning for help.

<u>REAL LIFE:</u> The Resurrected Entrepreneur

Ron worked solidly for three years developing a business magazine. He had prepared a business plan, knowing there was a market for his product. The business was starting to break even and make a small profit—but at what cost?

He was working days, nights, and weekends, with constant deadlines to meet, and worst of all, advertising space to sell, sell, sell. The pressure was terrible and he began to hate it. His wife dreaded talking to him. Although his family life deteriorated, Ron was determined to make it work. He was suffering from entrepreneurial burn-out and something had to give—which it did. He called me one day in a state of excitement.

"Fran, I just have to tell you the news!" he blurted. "I've just spent three days mulling this whole thing around, and I feel absolutely euphoric!"

"What's happening Ron?" I asked.

"I've decided to wind the whole business down and shut up shop!" he exclaimed. "I just feel like a ton of weight has been lifted off my shoulders. I can't handle the pressure anymore, and this decision feels absolutely great!"

"Ron, you can't do that!" I replied, somewhat stunned. "You've spent three years working hard on your business, and it's doing so well!"

"My wife hasn't seen me for three years, and I've been hard to live with. This feels like the right decision," he replied.

"Well; first, when was the last time you bought her some flowers?" I asked.

"I can't remember."

"Then stop at a florist, buy her a dozen red roses and a thank-you card for still being your wife," I suggested. "Now to this other matter. You've created a very saleable business. You've done all the start-up work, developed a fine product, and are starting to make some profit. Why wouldn't you at least consider selling the business—you know—for money?"

"Hey, I never thought of that!" Ron laughed. "Guess I just couldn't see the forest for the trees." We talked about the value of the work he had put into the magazine, and Ron finally hung up, promising he would think carefully about selling the business. He also promised to stop and buy his wife some flowers.

A few weeks later, he called again.

"Fran, I just had to tell you that I have two offers on the business. I'm so glad we talked. I must have been in bad shape not to realize the value of all that work."

"Ron, I'm thrilled! Tell me how you did it."

"Well Fran, I was heading for failure with a capital F. After talking to you, I focussed on a business plan for eight or nine days. I turned off the phones and worked on it until I got the numbers working sensibly. I took time to address all the serious problems, and how to overcome them. There is so much strength in a written proposal—it doesn't fly until it goes down on paper and you work on tightening it up. It's an incredible experience," he continued excitedly, "I have the bounce back in my step now—I know it's going to work!"

Ron chatted on with enthusiasm about his plans, which included interest from potential partners, and I breathed a silent sigh of relief. It would have been such a shame for the magazine to have folded because he burned out.

The Moral

Ron had lost his passion because he pushed himself too far. He was one of the lucky ones, able to regenerate his passion by addressing the problems and getting help. Later, he told me that he had found a partner who brought a sales staff with him, and there were now seven people working on the magazine. Not only was the magazine resurrected, it now has a chance to grow. One person alone couldn't do it all, but many hands made the magazine successful.

GETTING BY WITH A LITTLE HELP FROM YOUR FRIENDS

Ron's story is no different from many others in small business. I'm sure you know of at least one of your friends who has faced a similar situation. Not all businesses fail due to lack of cash-flow or management skills. Many fizzle out because the owner does. This fate can be avoided.

Put a value on your time, realize your strengths, and acknowledge your weaknesses. Let's say as an example, you are a talented printer and own a small printing shop. You love to help your clients design the perfect layout, and take great pride in producing quality work. You meet all deadlines, but in doing so, the accounting and administrative work tend to fall behind. Before you know it, the bank bounces a supplier's cheque. You didn't take time to reconcile your bank account. Now you have a black mark against your credit rating.

You stare at the mountain of paperwork and the unopened mail, wondering what to do. It's year-end, and time to prepare your books for the accountant. They haven't been entered for a year. My, how time flies... You feel depressed, knowing you will hate the task of preparing the books. Besides, you never really understood what you were doing anyway. What is the wisest move you can make now? To get help of course.

Budget for Help

Picture yourself as a huge circus tent. You cannot stay supported without the aid of guy ropes and poles. Your associates and professionals are those poles and guy ropes. We all reach out to others during our lives, and your business needs that help too, or the tent will collapse. You cannot afford *not* to enlist help. Budget for a few hours of help a week for the time-wasting chores or in the areas in which you lack expertise, and consult professionals for advice.

Should You Hire Friends?

In one simple word—no. I have heard only disaster stories from people who hired friends or a friend of a friend. You immediately place a responsibility upon yourself that you don't need. You have to keep this person happy or they will tell tales out of school.

Friendships can be lost, so if you value a friendship, tell your friend thanks, but no thanks. Read more on this subject and use the employment guidelines as set out in Chapter 7. Hire people with the necessary skills and who offer reliable references. You will save yourself a lot of trouble.

Friends and Business

On the subject of friends, be careful of heeding their advice. How many times have you asked a friend for advice, only to realize later that it wasn't such good advice after all? We all ask friends for advice, or for a referral to a "good hairdresser," or a "good lawyer," or a "good mechanic."

If you need professional help, find it yourself by researching and asking questions, or by being referred by a professional association. Friends are wonderful people and we all need them, but when it comes to business, you should be the one who makes the important decisions, not them.

What Do You Really Want to Do?

Reread the questionnaires in these last two chapters and ask yourself these three questions:

1. Where do I want to focus my efforts?
2. Do I want to learn how to work smarter?
3. Do I want to learn how to grow bigger?

Don't make this decision yet, just keep it in the back of your mind as you read on. Whatever you finally decide, you must first ensure that your business is stable enough and operating at peak efficiency. The next three chapters will show you how to work smarter and help you to increase your profits and efficiency. We shall start with everyone's favourite subject—getting organized.

THE "WHERE AM I GOING?" QUESTIONNAIRE

The information in these first two chapters is designed to make you take a good look at yourself and your business at this moment. By completing this self-evaluating questionnaire you can target the key areas that you need work on.

Put the Plan Into Action

Now you have taken the time to write down your goals and concerns, you are already on the road to building a more profitable business. Make a commitment to work enthusiastically and with dedication on these areas.

Don't expect miracles right away. Problems take time to resolve and new skills take time to learn and put into practice. With a plan of action and a concentrated effort, you will overcome many of these problems, gaining more confidence as you gain more knowledge, skills and control of your business.

Figure 2.3	The "Where Am I Going?" Questionnaire

1. I think I have made the following mistakes as listed in The Top Ten Mistakes of Business Planning (page 7):

    _____

    _____

    _____

    _____

2. Of these mistakes, the following ones are causing me serious concern:

    _____

    _____

    _____

    _____

3. As per question 6 in Figure 1.1, the "Where Am I Now?" questionnaire, I am experiencing difficulties in these areas (page 15):

    _____

    _____

    _____

    _____

4. As per question 7 in Figure 1.1, the "Where Am I Now?" questionnaire, I need to improve my financial knowledge in these areas (page 16):

    _____

    _____

    _____

    _____

5. My score for the "Where Am I Now?" questionnaire was:_____

6. Of the eight essential entrepreneurial skills, I need to improve my:

_____

_____

_____

_____

7. My current goals for this business are:

_____

_____

_____

_____

8. Of the 60 A-Z entrepreneur's jobs (page 25) I can competently handle _____ of them.

9. The jobs I don't like doing are:

_____

_____

_____

_____

10. The jobs that I need to develop more expertise in are:

_____

_____

_____

_____

11. The jobs I could delegate to someone else are:

_____

_____

_____

_____

12. My customer service could be improved in these areas:

_____

_____

_____

_____

Are You Organized— Or Out of Control?

OVERWHELMED AND OVERWORKED

No doubt there are times when you feel overwhelmed at the number of jobs you have to tackle. It's often difficult to define which priority should come first—completing a client's job or phoning for those outstanding cheques. Attending to 60 different jobs is sometimes impossible, so hiring help is the most practical solution. But for many fledgling businesses, paying for help isn't yet an option as the money isn't available. What to do?

GET ORGANIZED

Simply stated, you have to become organized. "Oh that's easy for you to say," you think, "but how?" One young lady who started a retail fish store with her partner complained one day, "No one told me it would be like this! I have to be up at the crack of dawn to go to the fish market, I'm open six days a week, there's so much to do in the store that I never have a moment to even think of writing up my books, let alone do anything for myself. It's a twelve-hour day or more just in the store!"

Many challenges can be overcome by learning to be more methodical in your daily routine. If the small jobs are attended to in an orderly fashion, they cease to become overwhelming mountains. All business functions can be organized into a monthly cycle, which in turn can be broken down into weekly, and then daily cycles.

THE CYCLE OF BUSINESS

Reread the section in Chapter 2 about the 60 different integral functions involved in operating a successful business. The most necessary functions that cannot be ignored on a daily and monthly basis include:

- attending to telephone calls, faxes, e-mail and correspondence
- regular follow-up and marketing
- billing clients
- banking
- paying the bills
- calculating and paying GST, provincial taxes, payroll and personal tax installments
- filing
- updating accounting records
- collecting outstanding receivables
- purchasing and job quotations
- reviewing your financial situation, planning cash flow
- keeping abreast of news, industry information, and learning
- networking.

Let one of these areas become unorganized or neglected and the business will suffer. As a business grows, systems must change and become more sophisticated. This means getting rid of the shoebox system. Successful growth rarely happens from a shoebox.

START WITH A SYSTEM

If you are currently sitting in an office piled high with junk and papers, you will need some basic organizational equipment, so be prepared to spend a little on these valuable tools. Use Figure 3.1 as a shopping list for the unorganized office to determine what you will need to purchase.

There is a huge assortment of organizational products available and you will have the option of economical to high-end products to suit your budget and personal taste.

THE 20-SECOND FILING SYSTEM

Once you have purchased the right tools, you can get down to organizing your office. Here are some suggestions for setting up your filing system.

Figure 3.1	Operation "Clean-Up" Shopping List

ITEM	USED FOR	$ COST (approx)
❏ Organizer or daily planner	Appointments and notes	$25 – 100
❏ Four-drawer filing cabinet	Filing paperwork	$100 – 800
❏ Suspension frames	Hanging files with tabs	$18 each
❏ Coloured hanging files	Holding file folders	$25 box/25
❏ Manila file folders	Filing paperwork	$22 box/100
❏ Coloured file folders	Filing paperwork	$42 box/100
❏ 2" metal fasteners	Securing papers in files	$7 box/50
❏ Three-ring 2"–3" binders	Filing invoices	$4-6 each
❏ Graduated file holder	Files used regularly	$15 – 25
❏ Letter trays	In and out baskets	$2 – 10
❏ Acco binding cases	Filing past bulky records	$27 box/6
❏ Desk pad	Protect desk and doodling	$22
❏ Magazine holders	Filing magazines	$10 – 20
❏ CD-ROM holder	Storing CD-ROMS	$5 – 25
❏ Disk holders	Storing floppy disks	$5 – 25
❏ Database program	Contact management	$79 and up
❏ Recycling box	Waste papers	$0 (available from most municipalities)
❏ Three-hole punch	Filing papers	$10 – 20
❏ Two-hole punch	Filing papers	$5 – 20
❏ Eight-column pad	Priority list	$5

COLOUR-CODE FILES

To easily locate files in your cabinet, use the colour-coding system. Use different coloured suspension files to house the various categories of paperwork (e.g. projects, marketing information, accounts etc.) with tabs to index them. They are easier to find than shuffling through a drawer full of the same coloured files. To keep individual files organized, use a two-hole punch at the top of each folder. Fasten the papers in chronological order with metal fasteners. This prevents papers from getting lost or out of order.

Accounts payable: When bills are received, check them for accuracy and attend to any anomalies. Then file them alphabetically in an "accounts to be paid" file. If you have a large volume of monthly accounts, you can use either an expanding file or a separate folder for regular suppliers. File accounts payable in the top drawer of your cabinet as you will refer to them regularly, and it saves bending down.

File paid accounts alphabetically and then chronologically. Use a separate folder for the suppliers you use the most and a "miscellaneous" file for occasional suppliers. File the last-paid invoice at the front. If you ever need to refer to an invoice for pricing or payment queries, the supplier's invoices are all together. These files can be cleaned out at year-end, archived for seven years for Canada Customs and Revenue Agency (CCRA) and then reused.

Business and tax information: You will need separate files for the following:

- **GST:** information and remittances
- **Provincial taxes:** information and remittances
- **Workers' Compensation:** information and remittances
- **Payroll:** one folder for tax guides and one for monthly payroll book, T4 summaries and remittances
- **Incorporation documents:** share certificates and incorporation documents
- **Asset register:** All asset purchase invoices should be kept for the life of the business. Always keep this file in your current records.
- **Insurance policies:** liability, fire and theft policies

- **Shareholder's loan:** Every transaction to a shareholder's loan should have back-up paperwork—you will need it for audit purposes.
- **Contracts:** Telephone, equipment leases and loans for asset purchases should each have a file.
- **Business number:** Keep all business number and tax information bulletins from CCRA in one file.
- **Licencing agencies:** Maintain a file for each licencing agency that you deal with.

Banking and financial: Keep your banking and financial records in good order by using files for the following areas:

- **Bank statements:** reconciled statements, cancelled cheques and cheque stubs
- **Credit card information:** credit card facility contracts and information
- **Bank agreements:** all agreements or bank loan papers
- **Financial statements:** Keep a few years' financial statements and tax returns on hand in case you have to apply for a loan or decide to sell the business.
- **Posting:** for all accounting information to be posted to your books
- **Cash or petty cash expenses:** Keep paid cash expenses and paid expense reports in a separate file. If you use an expense report system, keep some spare ones in another folder.

IDEA **KEEP CLIENT FILES**

It may be helpful to keep client information files. You can keep quotations, correspondence and invoices together. Because you need to keep a numerical copy of each invoice, you may have to print invoices with an extra copy to use in this file. It can be beneficial to have a client's history in one place for reference, purchasing, marketing and statistical purposes.

Sales invoices: If you bill just a few invoices a month, they can be stapled together after posting to your accounting records and filed numerically. For a large volume of invoices, use either the Acco binding cases or a 3-inch file binder. To save time and money, have the printer drill the invoices to suit your needs.

Voided invoices must be filed so don't throw them away. All invoices should be numbered to provide an audit trail for both you and the tax audit department. Stamp all invoices "posted" when they are entered to your books. Keep unpaid invoices in a file for collection purposes.

Marketing: Efficient marketing stategies are made easier with the help of the following files:

- **Follow-up files:** Handy follow-up files allow you to keep contact with "work in progress." Keep this information on your desk as you should use it daily.
- **Company profiles**: These can be broken down into corporate and personal profiles, any relevant press cuttings for media or promotional use, and testimonials.
- **Advertising copy:** Keep all your past advertising copy for reference.
- **Contact lists:** Never throw out relevant contacts or mailing lists.
- **Correspondence:** Keep advertising and marketing correspondence of interest.

UTILIZE YOUR FILING SYSTEM

Make your filing cabinet work for you. Use the top drawers for files that you use regularly, and store less-used documents in the bottom drawers. Follow-up and current client files can be stored either on your desk or close to your regular work area by using the graduated file holder. This enables files to be an arm's length away and the tabs easily read.

As files and drawers become full, start the good habit of cleaning out each file as you use it. You will never find time to clean them all out at once, and it is a job that is usually difficult to delegate, so clean-as-you-go.

If you use the above filing system, making additions or deletions where necessary, you should be able to find any piece of paper within twenty seconds. When a client calls for information and you need to refer to your files, they will be impressed that you don't waste their time by shuffling through drawers. Efficiency in these situations can only be a positive in your client's perception of how you operate your business.

IDEA | CLEAN OUT YEAR-END FILES

At year-end, you can empty the fiscal year's files into storage boxes. Clearly identify the contents on the box before storing them. Store accounting records for seven years as the tax department could spring a surprise audit. Recently, shareholders' loans claimed as business investment losses have been the subject of detailed audits, often three years after taxes have been filed. Keep scrupulous records of these loans, or they will be disallowed as a deduction, with penalties and interest charged accordingly.

ORGANIZE YOUR COMPUTER

How many times have you heard of hard drives crashing? It's becoming a regular and annoying occurrence. I have recently experienced this expensive setback twice. With the amount of viruses circulating in cyberspace and the unpredictability of software, regular backup is essential. Learn to back up and perform regular, basic computer maintenance, because in most cases, no computer equals no office and often, no work.

Here are some tips to help to keep your computer information in order.

- **Back-up:** Your wisest investment is a zip drive. You can back up every file daily in a matter of seconds. If a hard drive crash occurs, the files are easily restored from the disk. A 250 megabyte disk is ample for most personal computers and costs about $30. The zip drive will cost approximately $175, a worthwhile investment. Store the disk safely, and preferably, keep another copy out of the office in case of fire or theft.

- **Word files:** The Windows Operating System is known to shut you down at times with the infamous words "illegal operation." This is highly frustrating as the written word is often lost forever—it's difficult to recapture original thoughts. With most word processing programs, you can set your back-up timer to your desired time. I keep mine set at two minutes to ensure I don't lose pages of writing. You can change your back-up time using Help under the Windows menu.

- **Floppy disks:** As an added security measure, use floppy disks to back up after entering your accounting or other important information. They are portable, and a must for opening e-mail attachments. Use the appropriate options on your computer to give you the option of saving Internet information to disk before you open or download anything. Don't risk a virus or system crash.

- **Cache memory:** If you are an avid Internet or e-mail user, your cache memory becomes clogged with GIF and other large graphics files. Your system should be set to empty the cache every few days as it takes up hard drive room, eventually slowing the system down.

  You can also go to Windows Explorer, click on "program files," click on "Netscape" or the browser you use, click on "users," click on your name, then click on "cache." Go to edit and click on "select all." Then go to "file" and click on delete. This will empty your files to the recycle bin, which you should also empty.

- **Regular maintenance:** There are a few basic regular maintenance checks you should perform to keep your computer healthy and trouble-free.

  - **Defragment the hard drive:** Once a month, go to "Help" and type in "defragment hard drive" or install Norton Utilities. This process will reorganize your hard drive to optimize space and efficiency. A large hard drive will take two hours to defragment.

  - **Utilities:** A program such as Norton Utilities will continuously monitor the health of your CPU and hard drive. It reminds you to perform certain checks during the month and you can monitor your computer's health at any given time from an on-screen icon. A red light appears when maintenance or virus updates are required or when a problems arise. Disable this program when you install new software.

  - **Virus updates:** Most programs, including Norton Utilities, will have the facility to update your virus protection system. Use the live update once a week or program the system to remind you regularly.

  - **E-mail trash:** Print any pertinent correspondence and file it in the appropriate file. Always keep a hard copy of important e-mails. Clean out sent messages, your in-box and trash at least once a week. They use valuable hard drive space, particularly e-mails with attachments. Use the control key to select multiple items for deletion then empty the recycle bin.

- **Contact management:** Use a contact management system to dispose of that drawer full of business cards you can never find. It may be as simple as using your Address Book in Microsoft Works, or a more refined system such as Maximizer or Goldmine. When you return from a networking event, take a few minutes to record new contacts. Print a hard copy of contacts for ready reference.

If you make a point of performing these simple functions weekly and backing up daily, your computer will operate more efficiently and down time will be kept to the minimum. Now you have to find the time to do all this, so the next thing to organize is you.

ORGANIZE THE MANAGER

Organization starts with feeling in control of your life and knowing what you are doing from day to day and week to week. You cannot be organized without using a daily planner, so if you use a calendar or scraps of paper, change these bad habits immediately. Organizers range in price and size, so purchase one that you can work with. It's advantageous to use one small enough to carry with you. If you attend meetings or make appointments, you can instantly refer to your organizer before making a time commitment.

Because you are the boss, you have to make the time-management decisions. You will undoubtedly work evenings and weekends until you can employ help. Even then, the unpaid overtime doesn't stop.

Developing a daily routine is important for feeling in control and able to cope with unexpected situations. Many home-based operators have great difficulty in maintaining a "work mode" from the home-office, so developing a routine is a necessary component of organization.

Ten Tips to Keep Your Day Organized

1. For home-office operators, start each day at a regular time as though you were preparing to leave for work. Dress neatly and

forget working in your robe or pajamas—you cannot function in work mode sporting slippers, stubble and sloppy clothes.

2. Quickly tidy the house first thing in the morning or in the evening. If your home is untidy, you won't work efficiently. Don't even think about performing household chores during a working day. They are not a priority.

3. At the end of each day, clean off your desk and make a list of things to do tomorrow in order of priority. If you start the day with messy desk syndrome, you will not function at peak performance. As you work, keep your desk organized.

4. Check your e-mail regularly and return those requiring an answer within twenty-four hours or you'll forget. You can do this in your pajamas in the evening or when you are preparing your list of things to do.

5. Review your follow-up file daily and make any phone calls after 9:30 a.m. Allow people time to settle in at work. Avoid follow-up after 3:00 p.m. when sugar and concentration levels are low. Forget follow-up on voice-mail Friday—most people are in TGIF mode and are not receptive or not there.

6. Keep a "things to do" list close to you on your desk or in your organizer. Or, use "Post-It" notes, transferring the information to your list once or twice a day.

7. Open your mail and attend to it immediately to stop a pile-up of papers. Note important account payment dates, check accounts and file them to be paid. File or attend to other correspondence. If you can't attend to something immediately, note it on your "to do" list and place it in your "in" basket. Review your in basket once a day.

8. Write up the bank deposit and attend to payment discrepancies. Review your organizer and accounts to be paid file.

9. Work to a structured routine. Stop for lunch, catch up on the news, and finish at the same designated time each day. Take a short walk to recharge the batteries. Spend quality time with your family and return to the office in the evening if necessary.

10. Refer to Chapter 4 under "What are source documents?" to learn how to organize your accounting information.

WORK WITH A PRIORITY LIST

No doubt you have looked back on certain days and asked yourself, "Whatever did I do that was constructive today?" It seems that Murphy's Law often rules, leading to nothing but frustration at not completing designated tasks. These are the negative experiences that contribute to stress and burn-out, so working with a priority list is a must to keep yourself sane and on track.

IDEA   **USE AN ACCOUNTING PAD**

Make a priority list at least once a week. An eight-column accounting pad is an excellent tool for preparing it. If you are diversified and involved in many activities, divide the pages in half and make a heading for the different aspects of your life, such as family commitments, phone calls, letters, volunteer committee duties, business functions, and marketing.

Write down the various tasks to be completed under the applicable headings, along with a deadline date or time, in the next column. Then classify the task as an A+, A, B or C priority. In the morning, review only the A+ priorities and start working on the earliest deadline. As each one is completed, cross it off with a highlighter. Add to the list during the week. When you have completed the A+ column, start on the As, then Bs.

Review the list each week and re-write it, reclassifying your priorities. You often find that "C" priorities don't need doing. Cleaning filing cabinets is usually a "C" priority that I tend to neglect until I eventually set aside a morning to start the dastardly chore. Organizing the files as I use them definitely works better for me. Figure 3.2 gives an example of a priority list with deadlines.

Develop a Monthly Routine

Business is cyclic, so certain monthly tasks have to be completed. The more you work to a routine, the easier time management becomes. New habits take a while to adapt to, yet once they are established, you will feel more in control and able to focus on growing your business. Incorporate the above suggestions to develop a

Figure 3.2	Things To Do: Week Ending July 24, 20__				
THINGS TO DO	**DEADLINE**	**A+**	**A**	**B**	**C**
Phone bank re: loan application	July 21	✓			
Call overdue accounts	July 20	✓			
Order business cards	July 31			✓	
Prepare mail-out	July 24		✓		
Clean filing cabinet	July 31				✓
Register for trade show	Aug.10			✓	
Write thank-you cards	July 23		✓		
Mail samples to Mrs. Johnson	July 20	✓			
Complete committee report	July 22	✓			
Book car for brake repair	July 30		✓		
Research leads on Internet	July 31			✓	
Lunch appointment with Jill	July 30				✓
Complete AllPure's job	July 24	✓			

daily routine. Figure 3.3 gives one outline of some of the necessary monthly functions, along with a suggested time frame.

THE HOME-OFFICE CHALLENGE

No doubt the thought of operating from a home office initially sounded like the best idea since cyberspace, but as many have experienced, it's not really that glamorous. Once again the eight essential entrepreneurial skills must be harnessed to make a home office a practical place to do business.

Once you start, countless problems that you hadn't thought of surface, often presenting very real and irritating situations. Let's look at some of the common problems that home operators experience, along with some suggestions to keep you better organized and motivated.

| Figure 3.3 | Monthly Administrative Functions | |

FUNCTION	SUGGESTED TIME FRAME	BENEFIT
Ordering stationery and supplies	Beginning of the month	Extends credit period by nearly 30 days
Billing clients	Beginning of new month	Increases cash flow
Collections	Once a week	Keeps cash flowing
Payroll reconciliation	By end of first week	Avoid overdue penalties, plan cash flow
Paying accounts	Twice a month	Avoid interest, plan cash flow
Provincial taxes	Beginning of new month	Plan cash flow
GST remittance	Beginning of new month	Plan cash flow
Accounting	When bank statements arrive	Monitor progress immediately
Review financial situation	When accounting completed	Tax and future planning, catch errors
Marketing and follow-up	Each morning	Generate income
Staff meetings	Once a week, Mondays	Start week positively

Family

Family may have to be trained to leave you alone during working hours. This takes time and patience, so you must take your business seriously or your family won't. Sit down and explain that it is a great benefit to have you at home, however, you are unavailable—excluding emergencies—during working hours when the door is closed and the "do not disturb" sign is showing.

Children usually adapt to these rules and understand them quite well once they are aged seven. As the mother of a pre-teen, I speak from experience. If you are the person picking them up from school, make time in the afternoon to have a "coffee break" with them, organize the children and go back to work. As they become older, ensure they organize their after-school social life the previous evening so that you can plan your day accordingly.

Stress to your partner or spouse the importance of having uninterrupted quality work time. If you say you'll finish at five o'clock, avoid making exceptions so that the family doesn't build resentment towards the business. There is always the evening to complete any urgent work.

Growth

Many businesses start in a small office, only to find that they need more room. There is no easy answer to this problem if you didn't do some planning at start-up. Look in furniture catalogues to see how you can utilize floor-to-ceiling storage shelves, computer and desk organizers, bookshelves and filing cabinets. Throw away "stuff" and keep the office bare-bones and efficient.

IDEA **SEEK ALTERNATIVE SPACE**

It's a common dilemma for your business to be too small to move to commercial premises, yet the residence has run out of room. If local bylaws permit, you may be able to utilize accessory buildings or build an addition. Another option is to rent a mini-storage warehouse or a small workshop. My son exchanges shop rent for use of his tools, paying only for a portion of hydro.

If the situation becomes unbearable, prepare some projections of the required sales volume in order to profitably move to commercial premises, and make this your goal. Of course, you could move house, although that is a family decision.

Other Diversions

Some neighbours don't understand that you are working from home, so they have to be trained. When they call, comment that you would love to chat and will return their call after five. Stress that you have work to finish. Don't fall into the trap of "taking a break" with your neighbour. You wouldn't do it if you were working for someone else so don't do it now.

IDEA **PLAY A LITTLE**

It's difficult to work during fine weather. You can hear the neighbour's lawn mower or chainsaw and would dearly like to be out there with them. Considering that the fine weather season is relatively short in Canada, it's not such a bad idea to play a little. You need your rewards, and often, home-based self-employed people don't take enough relaxation time.

So plan to play during the fine weather. Make it a goal to achieve certain priorities, and when that work is completed, turn on the answering machine and go out to play. You will achieve far more returning feeling refreshed, exercised and energized. There has to be some benefits to being home-based, but don't play at the expense of letting your clients down.

Shift Workers

There couldn't be a worse combination than trying to operate a home-based business and living with a shift worker. You may have started a business when your spouse was working a day shift, only to experience a change of jobs and hours (it happened to me). The two are not compatible if you entertain clients or work with noise-generating devices, particularly telephones.

If this situation arises, you and your spouse will have to work together to meet each other's needs. You shouldn't have to downsize your business operation because of this, but finding workable solutions takes time (earplugs work). Telephone and fax ringers have to be turned down, and you may have to visit clients instead of them coming to you.

Geographic Isolation

On my seminar tours to remote locations, I have met many entre-preneurs and have been impressed at how people manage under adverse circumstances. One couple live in a remote British Columbia interior location. They operate two craft businesses and face the challenges of generator-powered electricity, a radio phone, and no Internet access. Their property is a two-hour drive from the nearest town on pot holes surrounded by road.

Yet they have overcome these challenges by utilizing a local answering service and checking messages once a day. This information is printed on their business cards. They are in the process of having a Web page designed and hosted by a local company. They keep in touch with the business world by subscribing to trade magazines and regularly attending seminars, conferences and trade shows to maintain their presence and networking contacts. There is always a way if you are determined to succeed.

PLAN TO STAY ORGANIZED: A CHECKLIST

This chapter has discussed many areas of your business requiring astute organization. You may already be a well-organized person who is in control of all facets of the operation. If you are, then feel proud of yourself and keep up the good work. If you need some organizational help, complete Figure 3.4, a checklist which will guide you through the process.

Now You're in Control

Once you are physically and mentally organized, you will feel better able to control both your business and your personal life. The next step is to gain control of the financial aspect of your business. You can't do one without the other, so Chapter 4 will show you how.

Figure 3.4	Operation "Get Organized" Checklist		
AREA TO ORGANIZE	**Needs Work**	**Already Organized**	**Completed**
1. Purchase equipment for filing system	❏	❏	❏
2. Organize business and tax files	❏	❏	❏
3. Organize banking and financial files	❏	❏	❏
4. Organize client files	❏	❏	❏
5. Organize sales invoices	❏	❏	❏
6. Organize marketing information	❏	❏	❏
7. Organize accounts payables	❏	❏	❏
8. Install a zip drive	❏	❏	❏
9. Change back-up timer to two-minutes	❏	❏	❏
10. Know how to clear cache memory	❏	❏	❏
11. Know how to defragment hard drive	❏	❏	❏
12. Install utilities program	❏	❏	❏
13. Update virus protection weekly	❏	❏	❏
14. Update contact management program	❏	❏	❏
15. Clear e-mail files weekly	❏	❏	❏
16. Clean desk each evening	❏	❏	❏
17. Start a priority list system	❏	❏	❏
18. Attend to mail daily	❏	❏	❏
19. Attend to bank deposits regularly	❏	❏	❏
20. Develop a structured daily routine	❏	❏	❏
21. Use a daily planner	❏	❏	❏
22. Use a monthly administrative routine	❏	❏	❏
23. Delegate time-consuming chores	❏	❏	❏
24. Do follow-up calls each day	❏	❏	❏
25. Monitor business monthly	❏	❏	❏

CHAPTER 4

Are You in Control of the Financial Reins?

WHY IS ACCURATE ACCOUNTING SO IMPORTANT?

Just as historians have recorded the evolution of the world in writing, so must you record the evolution of your business from conception. Words are not enough. The progress of your business is recorded in figures using an age-old system devised many centuries ago called double-entry bookkeeping. This system is universal—only the tax implications change.

Mention the words "accounting, books, records, and taxes" and the average entrepreneur shudders. Oh! To be left alone to run their business without this time-wasting, hateful chore. Those who fly by the seat of their pants and are not diligent in monitoring their business through their financial records often experience an untimely financial demise. See Chapter 14 for an intimate discussion on this subject. The astute entrepreneurs who utilize their financial information to monitor progress and in decision-making are usually successful.

WHAT DOES ACCOUNTING TELL YOU?

Accounting records serve multiple purposes and act as a financial barometer for your business. An accurate set of accounting records transferred into financial statement format and carefully analysed can tell you the following about your business:

- whether projected gross profit margins are being met
- where expenses are contributing to losses
- whether actual results are meeting projected results
- what percentage each overhead expense is costing in relation to sales

- which products or services are selling the most
- which products or services are profitable or losing money
- how much is collectively owing in accounts receivable and payable
- how much each client owes and how much you owe each supplier
- the dollar cost of asset purchases from start-up
- the accumulated depreciation of assets and their book value
- how much the business owns in assets
- how much the business owes in liabilities
- the accumulated profits or losses
- the working capital situation
- your current tax situation, personal and corporate
- whether you are financially ready for growth
- whether wages and management salaries are too high (or too low)
- invaluable for making future projections based on past history.

Shoebox or Common Sense?

Even if you prefer to operate in the dark, the sad fact is, the government requires that you maintain accurate accounting records and prepare financial statements at year-end to assess both the business and your personal tax situation. You have the option of throwing everything into a box and presenting it to your distraught accountant at year-end and crossing fingers as the end results are crunched. Or, you can be sensible about the whole thing and realize that accounting is an important and integral part of growing a successful business.

How Does Accounting Work?

If you understand how the accounting puzzle fits together and the logical reasoning behind it, organization of your records becomes easier to learn. Accounting dictates that you maintain careful records. These records are compiled from all those everyday pieces of paper you deal with: invoices, bank deposits, cash receipts, paid accounts, credit card statements and cheque stubs. If the information is transcribed incorrectly from these documents, then your accounting records will be wrong.

THE SIX-STEP ACCOUNTING CYCLE

Accounting records start from the first day you spent money on your business, so hopefully, you kept all the receipts and entered them into your records. Information from these papers is entered into an accounting journal, which has both a control and descriptive entry. One is a debit and one a credit.

Debits and credits follow a formula which is more easily understood once you learn a few basic principles. If you use an accounting program, enroll in a course on manual bookkeeping to ensure you understand how to make correct entries. Otherwise your records will be wrong, and often, mistakes are never found.

The accounting cycle follows six steps, which are shown in Figure 4.1.

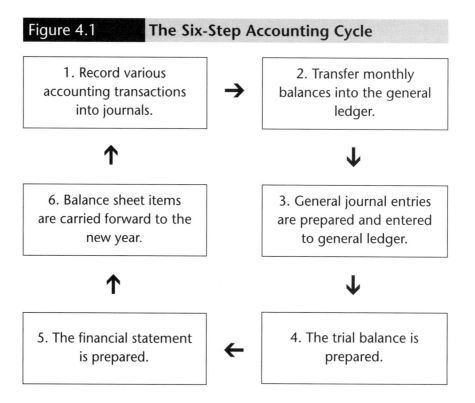

Figure 4.1	The Six-Step Accounting Cycle

1. Record various accounting transactions into journals.

2. Transfer monthly balances into the general ledger.

6. Balance sheet items are carried forward to the new year.

3. General journal entries are prepared and entered to general ledger.

5. The financial statement is prepared.

4. The trial balance is prepared.

Step 1

Each transaction is recorded into the appropriate columns in the correct journal monthly. The columns are totalled both down and across, with debits equalling credits.

Step 2

The monthly balances are transferred into a general ledger, which is organized by account names in the format of a financial statement. When the monthly totals from all the ledgers are entered and the new ending balances in the general ledger added, the debit entries should equal the credit entries.

Step 3

Any entries that cannot be recorded into the general ledger through the normal journals are prepared in a general journal, then entered to the general ledger, usually by your accountant at year-end. Many businesses use monthly journal entries to keep their reporting precise. These entries consist of depreciation, prepayments, bad debts, and expenses that have not been billed but belong to that fiscal year (for example, an accountant's year-end fees are included as an "accrued expense" to the fiscal year).

Step 4

A trial balance is prepared from the general ledger in order of the assets, liabilities, equity, income and expenses for that period. It lists all the debits and credits with both totals agreeing.

Step 5

Financial statements are prepared from the trial balance. The difference between the income and expenses represents either a profit or loss, which is transferred to the "retained earnings" account on the balance sheet. The financial statement is then prepared in a standard format.

Step 6

The income and expense accounts are reversed out to zero balances. The balance sheet items are carried forward to the next year. If interim financial statements are prepared, the income and expense accounts are not closed off until year-end.

WHAT ARE SOURCE DOCUMENTS?

Keeping the daily paper flow organized will be a tremendous help in maintaining accurate accounting records. Accounting records are a compilation of the following source documents—those papers that seem to breed on your desk into large piles. To organize your accounting, here is a list of the documents you will need, their purpose, and the journal they are entered into:

- **Sales invoices, cash register tapes:** Used to record monthly sales plus provincial tax and GST. These are recorded into a **sales journal,** which can be designed to give you useful sales information. Invoices are entered numerically with cancelled invoices entered as "void" to ensure an accurate audit trail.

- **Bank deposits:** Monies deposited into business bank accounts are recorded into a **cash receipt journal**. These deposits should itemize the client, invoice number paid, the amount, and discount taken. It also provides for an itemized accounting of cash deposits, loans or other income. This journal is reconciled monthly to the bank statement.

- **Cheques:** Cheques are recorded into a **cheque disbursements journal**, which is used to itemize costs by expense category, and for reconciling to the bank statements monthly. Each cheque should detail what the expense is for plus the GST amount. Columns are used for more frequent expenses. Less frequent expenses are entered into a "miscellaneous" column with a description of the expense written beside it.

- **Credit card expenses:** Credit card transactions related to your business need careful organization. Keep all receipts attached to the original purchase invoices. When the statement arrives, highlight the business expenses, calculate the GST and the net expense amount. These expenses are considered accounts payable.

- **Cash expenses:** Expenses that you pay for on behalf of the company are entered into a **cash expense journal** with a description of the expense. This allows the accounting system to keep a record of the money you put into the business. The cheque disbursement journal records the money you draw from the business.

- **Accounts to be paid:** Referred to as accounts payable, if you monitor your business and prepare regular financial statements, you need to use an **accounts payable journal** to record all unpaid trade accounts. These are listed in the month of purchase with a description of the expense. When the account is paid, the payment is recorded in the "Accounts Payable" column in the cheque disbursement journal.

- **Other information:** Transactions often occur that cannot be recorded in any of the above journals. An example is trading services or products with a supplier. If you don't have accounting knowledge, keep details of these transactions for your accountant. These entries are recorded in the **general journal**.

IDEA **KEEP ORGANIZED AND INFORMED**

By keeping your source documents well organized and detailed, putting your accounting together to prepare financial information becomes easier. A financial statement or a trial balance can be produced quickly when you need it. With the source documents correctly entered to the journals, ready for entry to the general ledger, or correctly coded and ready for entry into your accounting program, the worst job is over.

THE GENERAL LEDGER—YOUR BUSINESS BIBLE

The general ledger is a record of all your business' financial transactions since its inception. It is your most valuable asset, as it can be used to give you financial information at any period in time. It is also a necessary component of your accounting records, as financial statements are prepared from these records. A number and a name is assigned to each account.

As the six-step accounting cycle demonstrates, all source documents are recorded into the various accounting journals, which at month-end are totalled. The monthly balances of all the columns are transferred into the general ledger, which is organized into individual asset, liability, equity, income and expense accounts, based on the format of your Chart of Accounts (see a detailed explanation on page 59). If you are using an accounting software program, each source document is recorded both into an accounting journal and then posted to the general ledger.

THIRTEEN TIPS FOR TIDY ACCOUNTING

The key to making the accounting process smoother and less of a headache is to be organized and practise good daily habits. Here are some tips for keeping your records organized.

1. Keep completed sales invoices in numerical order in a binder or folder marked "current month invoices."
2. At month-end, check the numerical order for missing invoices.
3. Record retail cash till tapes daily into the sales journal—it's a five-minute job but becomes a chore if you only do it once a month.
4. Detail bank deposits carefully, because if other income is not recorded correctly, it can be mistaken for sales income and you'll pay tax when you shouldn't—and your records will be incorrect.
5. Never leave a cheque stub blank. Record cheques in numerical order, including void ones.
6. Reconcile the bank account monthly and correct the balance in your cheque book.
7. Use a ring-binder (available at banks) for cheques. It's easier to enter data and for reconciling the bank account.
8. Don't use debit cards or cash withdrawals through bank machines. It makes for complex, time-consuming accounting, and increases the chance of errors. Write cheques where possible.
9. Keep credit-card receipts and invoices in the plastic wallet found in most cheque binders. This keeps them safe and easy to find when the statement arrives.
10. Attach a sheet to each page of your credit-card statement, detailing the account code, expenses less tax, and the GST. This makes entering credit-card charges an easier task.
11. When bills arrive, check them for accuracy. Note any important payment dates in your planner so you don't forget to pay them.
12. Keep accounts payable in a "current payables" folder in alphabetical order for easy access.
13. Empty wallets and purses regularly and keep an envelope in the office and vehicle marked "cash expenses" so you don't lose them.

FINANCIAL STATEMENTS—YOUR HEALTH BAROMETER

With the amount of competition from small business, only the financially fluent will successfully grow their business. To plan for this growth, you need to use your financial statements regularly as a management tool in decision-making.

Accounting programs make data preparation and monitoring results simple in comparison to the days of hand-written ledgers. Entries that took days to complete are finished in a matter of hours, and financial statements printed at the touch of a keyboard. So there is no excuse *not* to take control of the financial reins and learn what your figures are telling you.

Understand Your Financial Statements

Financial statements are broken down into two sections—a balance sheet and statement of income and expenses. Countless business owners have no concept of what these documents mean, except that they do or don't have to pay income tax at year-end. Not paying taxes means no profit, so don't jump for joy when your accountant tells you there is no tax to pay. Rather, be extremely concerned that there is a real problem. Financial statements will indicate where problems lie, so spend time with your accountant until you understand how to interpret them.

DESIGN AN INFORMATIVE CHART OF ACCOUNTS

Accounting follows a standard format using a Chart of Accounts which can be specifically designed for your business. It is set out in financial statement format and allocates a universal number to each general ledger account. Your general ledger should always be set up in the order as explained in Figure 4.2 to keep it in correct financial statement order, for ease of comprehension and statement prepara-

IDEA **BIG**

REVAMP YOUR CHART OF ACCOUNTS

How your Chart of Accounts is designed can make the difference between basic or more detailed reporting. More information allows you to closely monitor expenses and profit margins. Information can be incorporated into updating your business plan, enabling you to make more accurate decisions and projections. As you experience growth, you will need to refer regularly to your business plan and financial statements. Review your current Chart of Accounts to see where you can break it down into more informative groupings.

tion. Familiarize yourself with these numbers and ensure that data is entered to the right account. Your accountant will help in designing an informative Chart of Accounts.

CASE STUDY: SNAPPY LAWN EQUIPMENT SERVICES LTD.

Figure 4.2 shows an example of the income and expense accounts for a small business that repairs lawn mower equipment and sells new and used equipment and parts.

How to Use Costing Information

By designing the Chart of Accounts, the owner can monitor individual sales categories, along with their associated costs. By breaking down the opening and closing inventory for each sales category, the gross profit can be calculated and compared to projected returns.

If this exercise is completed quarterly, seasonal fluctuations can be monitored. This information helps in ordering inventory, comparing actual profit margins to projected ones, and for planning future cash flow. Figure 4.3 gives an example using Snappy Lawn Equipment Services Ltd.

HOW TO ANALYSE AN INCOME STATEMENT

You would be surprised at the detailed information accounting figures can provide. By breaking down each section of the figures and comparing the performance in each area, you will learn to better understand your business and pinpoint its strengths and weaknesses. From here, you can make informed management decisions based on past and recent history. You will need to analyse these following areas:

1. **Sales:** product lines, their profitability, seasonal peaks and lows
2. **Cost of sales:** materials, labour, freight and production expenses
3. **Gross profit margins:** actual versus projected, why they have increased or decreased
4. **Overhead expenses:** what is necessary, what can be reduced, how to increase efficiency and profitability

Figure 4.2	**Chart of Accounts—Snappy Lawn Equipment Services Ltd.**

Revenue:

4000   Sales, new equipment

4010   Sales, used equipment

4020   Sales, new parts

4030   Sales, used parts

4040   Sales, shop labour

4050   Other income

Cost of sales:

4400   Opening inventory

4500   Purchases, new equipment

4510   Purchases, used equipment

4520   Purchases, new parts

4540   Purchases, used parts

4550   Purchases, oil and gas

4560   Labour, shop

4580   Equipment repairs

4590   Shop supplies

4600   Closing inventory

Overhead expenses:

5000   Accounting fees

5010   Advertising

5020   Bad debts

5040   Bank charges

5050   Casual labour

5060   Depreciation

5070   Employee benefits

5080   Fees, licences

5090   Insurance

5100   Loan interest

5110   Legal and professional fees

5200   Management fees

5210   Marketing and promotion

5220   Office supplies

5230   Office wages

5270   Promotion — meals

5280   Rent and taxes

5290   Repairs & maintenance — store

5300   Seminars & trade shows

5400   Telephone, fax, Internet

5410   Travel & accommodation

5420   Utilities

5430   Vehicle gas

5440   Vehicle repairs, insurance

5450   Wages, sales

5460   Workers' compensation

5500   Corporate taxes

5999   Suspense account*

*items that need explanation at the time of entry; once resolved, this account will be zero.

Figure 4.3	Snappy Lawn Equipment Services Ltd.

SALES AND COST ANALYSIS
SIX MONTHS JANUARY TO JUNE 20__

	Jan.-March	%	April-June	%	Total	%
Sales:						
New equipment	$3,250	14.5	15,720	18.0	18,970	17.5
Used equipment	1,110	5.0	3,790	4.5	4,900	4.5
New parts	4,030	18.0	14,160	16.5	18,190	17.0
Used parts	1,760	8.0	4,640	5.5	6,400	6.0
Shop labour	12,320	54.5	47,950	55.5	60,270	55.0
Total sales:	$22,470	100.0	86,260	100.0	108,730	100.0
Cost of sales:						
New equipment	$1,950	8.7	8,640	10.0	10,590	9.7
Used equipment	390	1.7	1,140	1.3	1,530	1.4
New parts	2,420	10.8	7,790	9.0	10,210	9.4
Used parts	620	2.8	1,620	1.9	2,240	2.0
Shop labour	5,890	26.2	28,090	32.6	33,980	31.3
Total costs:	$11,270	50.2	47,280	54.8	58,550	53.8
Gross profit:	$11,200	49.8%	38,980	45.2%	50,180	46.2%

Following is an analysis of Snappy Lawn Equipment's first six months.

SNAPPY LAWN EQUIPMENT— ANALYSING THE FIRST SIX MONTHS

1. Sales

By analysing the sales for a six-month period, the first quarter reflects the winter drop in sales. New and used equipment account for 19.5 percent of sales and parts 26 percent. Shop labour at 54.5 percent of sales reflects the largest source of income. In the following quarter, sales increase by nearly 400 percent as spring is traditionally the season when customers have their equipment repaired or replaced.

New and used equipment sales have increased proportionately during the second quarter and constitute 49 percent of gross profits. It is evident that repairing equipment should remain the focus of this business. The owner should compare the sales percentages to projected figures. Perhaps he envisioned more new or used equipment sales. If so, the figures should be studied and the reasons for lack of sales established.

Is it lack of target marketing, or competition from chain stores? How could the business increase sales? Should money be spent on diversification? Should the owner focus on growing the repair division? This detailed sales analysis provides enough information to help make informed decisions.

2. Cost of Sales

Because shop labour constitutes a large percentage of sales, labour costs should be scrutinized. The labour income of $12,320 in the first quarter was generated by one employee working full-time for February and March at a cost of $20.00 per hour, with a shop charge-out rate of $45.00 per hour. The shop billed 274 hours in two months although the employee was paid for 346 hours, or 79 percent of actual paid time. Therefore, 21 percent of his paid time was not billable.

In the second quarter, two full-time employees were paid $20 and hour and one part-time employee was paid $16 an hour. In addition, one part-time shopworker was hired at $12 an hour. The shop billed $47,950 or 1,065 hours at $45.00 an hour and paid wages for 1,560 hours. Therefore, the employees were 68 percent productive. The owner should monitor labour productivity to ensure it meets projections, planning for a 32 percent non-productive factor. If more billable hours were projected, now is the time to find out why productivity has decreased.

The purchase price of new parts and equipment normally fluctuates as suppliers offer specials. Better discounts are offered on larger orders. Therefore, the cost of new equipment and parts will vary, and this is reflected in the cost of sales percentages. These costs should be watched to ensure they remain consistent with projections.

3. Gross Profit

Gross profit is calculated by deducting direct costs from sales before overhead. Cost of sales is the key area to a profitable operation as gross profits pay for all other expenses. The gross profit of $50,180 for six months reflects an average of $8,363 per month. In the first three months, the gross profit totals only $11,200, hardly enough to pay the rent and owner's salary. This is common with seasonal businesses, so an astute owner will have a contingency plan for the quiet season.

In the second quarter, gross profit has dropped from 49.8 percent to 45.2 percent, a decrease of nearly $4,000. The six month's average reflects a 46.2 percent gross profit. In this case, the owner was assuming a gross profit of 50 percent, so he should study the messages the figures are telling him to evaluate why gross profits have dropped four percent.

IDEA   **CATCH COSTLY ERRORS QUICKLY**

BIG :

Use your financial figures not only to review past performance, but to plot future profits. The more accounting figures are reviewed, particularly the cost of sales, the sooner the reasons for unprofitability can be pinpointed, before valuable profits are frittered away.

4. Overhead

On reviewing the overhead expenses for Snappy Lawn Equipment Ltd. in Figure 4.4, you will find that with operating a retail location and being both a service and retail business, overhead costs are high. Snappy's owner is running a fairly tight ship and understands the need to spend money on advertising and promotion. Although a minor reduction could be made in overhead costs, the most viable solution is to work on increasing sales, productivity and profitability.

Higher wages because of inefficient administrative systems contributed to lower productivity. Because the business deals in thousands of parts, copious time was spent searching for suppliers in the various catalogues and microfiche records. The solution was to find an efficient inventory program and supplier database. Once in place, employee productivity increased dramatically, with unproductive paid hours reduced by 10 percent. In six months, this increased gross profits by over $5,000.

KNOW YOUR BREAK-EVEN POINT

Most businesses experience seasonal peaks and lows that affect cash-flow. There are times when you need more capital to purchase inventory and times when work is either too slow or too busy. To operate efficiently, you need to know how much it costs to open your doors. Even a small home-based business incurs monthly costs that have to be paid for from gross profits.

How Do You Use This Information?

Documenting your break-even point is essential for comparing actual expenses to projected ones and for upgrading your business plan. Even if you don't use a business plan—although we shall assume that you do—knowing your break-even point allows you to monitor daily, weekly and monthly sales.

If you don't know what your monthly overhead expenses are, you could be spending money that you shouldn't. Many businesses have been closed down by federal and provincial agencies for not paying the various taxes because the money was spent on increased overhead costs.

In the case of a seasonal business, owners must know monthly operating costs. Reviewing overhead costs will reflect the months when cash-flow will be tight. Astute financial planning is necessary to survive these difficult months. Figure 4.4 shows an example of how Snappy Lawn Equipment Services Ltd. calculated its break-even point.

Figure 4.4	Snappy Lawn Equipment Services Ltd. Break-Even Point Calculation

	Six-months actual		One month average		First quarter actual	
Sales:	108,730		18,121		22,470	
Less cost of sales:	58,550		9,758		11,270	
Gross profit:	50,180	46%	8,363	46%	11,200	50%
Overhead expenses:						
Accounting fees	900		150		450	
Advertising	3,150		525		1,575	
Bad debt allowance	600		100		100	
Bank charges	510		85		255	
Computer supplies	330		55		165	
Employee benefits	6,000		1,200		2,400	
Freight	390		65		195	
Fees & licences	210		35		105	
Insurance	450		75		225	
Loan interest	1,980		330		990	
Management fees	8,000		2,000		2,000	
Marketing & promotion	1,350		225		675	
Office supplies	720		120		360	
Office wages	2,250		450		900	
Promotion — meals	450		75		225	
Rent & taxes	6,600		1,100		3,300	
Repairs — equipment	600		50		150	
Repairs — store	600		50		150	
Security system	210		35		105	
Seminars, trade shows	600		50		150	
Sign rental	390		65		195	
Small tools	600		100		300	
Shop supplies & gas	600		100		300	
Telephone, fax, cell	1,500		250		750	
Utilities	1,050		175		525	
Vehicle — gas	1,380		230		660	
Vehicle — insurance	600		100		300	
Vehicle — repairs	600		100		300	
Vehicle — lease	2,100		350		1,050	
Workers' compensation	850		170		340	
Overhead:	45,570		8,415		19,195	
Average gross profit:	50,180		8,363		11,200	
Shortage/surplus	**4,610**		**(52)**		**(7,995)**	

Break-Even Point Analysis

Snappy needs to generate sales of $18,300 a month to pay all expenses. The business is currently operating at a break-even point. The first three months reflect sales of $22,470, with monthly overhead costs of $8,415. The overhead factor alone costs $25,245 for three months, plus $11,270 for the cost of sales. This means a shortfall of $14,045 in cash-flow. This shortage is remedied within the next three months but a contingency should be in place to finance the quieter months.

The six-month figures show net profits of $4,610, but only because employees were laid off during the quieter months and management reduced their salaries by $4,000. Without this salary reduction, the business would not have made a profit as many costs cannot be reduced, such as rent.

Possible Solutions

If this business operates at break-even point for the first six months of the year—which traditionally are the busiest—it is quite feasible that the next six months will reflect a loss. The owner needs to take a serious look at the business to find ways to remedy this situation. Here are some suggestions:

- review marketing strategies to see if current methods are generating sales
- review the staffing structure to ensure each employee is working to maximum efficiency
- review overhead costs and trim unnecessary expenses
- research ways to diversify the business or to increase sales
- continue to reduce the owner's salary during quieter months
- review administrative and shop systems to pinpoint inefficient or time-wasting tasks.

Could Snappy Diversify?

The owner will have to use some creative marketing strategies to increase sales. Perhaps a pick-up and delivery service could be offered, or some used mowers stocked for clients to use as a replacement while theirs is being repaired. These service-oriented incentives could help to increase business.

A customer database could be established and customers phoned to remind them to bring in their equipment for service. Landscaping companies could be contacted by Snappy to submit bids to repair their equipment. Perhaps an investment in some snow removal equipment would pay off. Services could then be contracted out to businesses with customer car parks. Of course, this idea would first require some market research.

SERVICE BUSINESSES: BREAK-EVEN POINT

Service businesses usually generate most of their income through billable hours. The misconception with these businesses is that you can bill eight hours a day—which you can't—unless you work long days and eventually become a burn-out candidate.

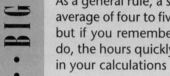

IDEA **BIG** : **USE CONSERVATIVE CALCULATIONS**

As a general rule, a service business should calculate to bill an average of four to five hours a day. It doesn't sound like much, but if you remember the long list of other jobs you have to do, the hours quickly disappear. It is better to be conservative in your calculations than to over-project your income.

To calculate the break-even point of your service business, list the monthly operating overhead costs. Once these figures are established, make the following calculation, which allows for 20 working days a month. This exercise demonstrates that two hours a day must be billed to cover overhead costs, and four hours a day to make a profit of $2,900. Any hours billed over this amount are a bonus as shown in the example in Figure 4.5.

OTHER BUSINESSES: BREAK-EVEN POINT

Retail, manufacturing or distribution businesses that rely on fixed gross profit margins can easily establish their break-even point. For example, a bookstore works on an average of a 40 percent gross profit margin. Snappy, as both a service and a retail business, would make the calculation as shown in Figure 4.6.

Figure 4.5	Example of Break-Even Point Calculation: Service Businesses

Monthly overhead costs:	$2,730 divided by
Hourly billing rate:	$65
Equals hours to pay overhead:	42 per month
Minimum hours a day to bill:	2.1

$65 per hour x 4 hours a day x 5 days a week x 4.33 weeks =

Gross sales	$ 5,630
Monthly overhead	2,730
Net profit and owner's wage:	$2,900

Knowledge is Motivational

Knowing your break-even point is not only essential, it is motivational. By dividing the required monthly sales by 4.33 weeks, you now have a weekly sales target. You can break the figure down even further into a daily goal. If you are experiencing regular days when the break-even point is not being met, ask yourself: "Why am I opening the doors? To pay the landlord? How can I increase sales on these slow days?" A retail store should at least cover overhead costs and management salaries each day.

Now is the time to calculate or review the break-even point for your business. Use either the last financial statement or tax return information, reviewing the overhead to ensure it is up to date. List the current monthly overhead costs of your business as shown in Snappy's example and complete Figure 4.7.

Figure 4.6	Break-Even Point: Snappy Lawn Equipment Services Ltd.

Projected gross profit margin	46%
Projected overhead costs per month:	$ 8,415
Divide $8,415 by 46% =	$18,293

To check:

Gross sales to break-even = $18,293 x 46% =	$ 8,415

Figure 4.7	Exercise: Calculate Your Break-Even Point

Retail, manufacturing or distribution:

Gross profit margin percentage:	_____	
Monthly overhead including owner's wages:	$_____	
Divide overhead by ____ percent	$_____	
Gross sales to break-even:	$_____	A
Weekly sales: divide A by 4.33	$_____	B
Daily sales: divide B by 5 or 6 days	$_____	

Service industries:

Monthly overhead including owner's wage:	$_____	
Hourly billing rate:	$_____	
No. hours monthly to pay overhead:	$_____	A
No. hours weekly: divide A by 4.33	$_____	B
No. hours per day: divide B by 5 or 6 days	$_____	

HOW TO DECIPHER A BALANCE SHEET

An income statement tells only one side of the story. To get the complete picture, you have to understand the components of a balance sheet. This lists the assets, liabilities and equity of the business at the time the statements were prepared. A business may have many assets, but if the liabilities are high and profits low, then you need to know the reasons why.

Snappy's six-month balance sheet as shown in Figure 4.8 tells us valuable information that couldn't be found on the income statement. Banks take particular interest in balance sheets as they reflect the overall management and performance of the business.

THE BALANCE SHEET SHOWS...

Current assets (*any item that can be converted to cash within twelve months*): The **bank account** is not healthy considering the trade suppliers that need to be paid. Fortunately, much of Snappy's business is cash and the account is replenished daily. If each of the

Figure 4.8	Snappy Lawn Equipment Services Ltd.

BALANCE SHEET
AS AT JUNE 30, 20__
(Unaudited)

ASSETS

Current assets:		
Cash at bank	$4,280	
Accounts receivable	17,900	
Inventories	62,300	
Prepaid expenses	2,100	$86,580
Fixed assets:		
Computers	$6,200	
Vehicle	2,000	
Equipment	18,200	
Furniture & fittings	8,300	
Leasehold improvements	4,900	
	39,600	
Less accumulated CCA:	(19,300)	20,300
Other assets:		
Incorporation fees		750
TOTAL ASSETS:		$ 107,630

LIABILITIES

Current liabilities:		
Accounts payable	44,700	
GST payable	3,800	
Withholdings payable	2,450	
Current portion long-term debt	10,450	61,400
Long-term liabilities:		
Bank indebtedness	32,350	
Shareholder's loans	36,470	68,820
		130,220

SHAREHOLDER'S EQUITY (DEFICIENCY)

Capital stock		100
Retained earnings:	(27,300)	
Net profit (loss for period)	4,610	(22,690)
TOTAL LIABILITIES & EQUITY:		$107,630

accounts receivable customers were analysed, they would show that over 60 percent of the money is over 45 days due and that many accounts are over 90 days. Attention is not being paid to collections.

Most of Snappy's cash is tied up in **inventory**, which is not moving as fast as was planned. It is important to keep fast-moving items in stock and to closely monitor increasing inventory levels. The **prepaid expenses** *(expenses paid in advance of the current fiscal period)* consist of a lease deposit and insurance.

Fixed assets *(assets owned by the company, not for resale, value per item over $200)*: Although the books show a purchase value of $39,600, the assets have depreciated to half their original worth and now have a **net book value** after accumulated depreciation and leasehold amortization of $20,300. The **total assets** of the business are valued at $107,630.

Current liabilities *(any debt due and payable within twelve months)*: The **accounts payable** represent unpaid trade suppliers. Many of the accounts are slipping into 90 days because of high inventory levels and poor collections. If the suppliers' terms are not met, the business could endanger its credit rating. The **GST** and employee **withholdings** are payable in July, so cash should be made available by then.

The **current portion of the long-term debt** represents the principal portion of the bank loan due to be paid within twelve months. This loan was incurred to purchase equipment and to help finance the inventory.

Long-term liabilities *(debts due to be paid over a term longer than one year)*: The **bank loan** must be repaid in full in four years, with principal and interest payments amounting to nearly $1,200 a month. The capital injected by the shareholder is recorded in the **shareholder's loan**. Banks would be pleased to see that the shareholder has put a substantial amount into the business.

Shareholder's Equity *(capital shares, accumulated profits or losses)*: The shareholder has issued **capital stock** of 100 shares at a par value of $1 each. The business has been operational for two years and the **retained earnings** show accumulated losses of $27,300.

Some of this is attributed to start-up costs and some to operational losses. The profit for the period reduced the losses by $4,610.

Summary: The **working capital** (*current assets less current liabilities*) seems healthy at $25,180, however the business is operating in a loss situation and has too much money tied up in accounts receivable and inventory. There are many factors that would concern a bank on reading these statements. At this stage, an allowance has not been made for depreciation, which will reduce profits when the statements are prepared at year-end. The management should be concerned as it will take some sound business management to find ways to keep the business viable. Following are some suggestions as to how this can accomplished.

INCREASE YOUR GROSS PROFIT MARGINS

Without healthy gross profits, there isn't enough left in the pot to cover overhead costs. Many operators make the mistake of not watching their cost of sales or performing some simple and regular job costing. The main factors that slowly erode into profits are listed in Figure 4.9; check those that apply to you—these areas need attention.

Figure 4.9	Gross Profit Erosion Factors

COMMON PROBLEM	REVIEW?
1. Starting with low prices to attract customers	❏
2. Not increasing prices when raw material costs increase	❏
3. Wage increases	❏
4. Freight, duty and brokerage increases	❏
5. Offering too many specials or discounts	❏
6. Too much slow-moving inventory	❏
7. Fear of losing customers if prices increase	❏
8. Not increasing prices because of competition	❏
9. Inefficient production equipment	❏
10. High wastage or spoilage factor	❏

What is the Solution?

There is often no easy solution to increasing profit margins. If you started in a highly competitive business or if more competitors moved into the area, you have your work cut out for you. Using effective marketing techniques to improve sales and exposure is necessary, as is recalculating costings when raw material or other costs increase.

Having a panic attack and spending fruitless dollars on a huge advertising campaign is not the answer. Spending $2,000 on advertising at a 40 percent gross margin means that $5,000 in sales must be generated to cover this cost. Start by looking in-house and take Figure 4.10, the Twenty-Question Profitability Checklist.

How can you improve? Sometimes you just need a gentle reminder to stop and take a long, hard look at your business. Our economy is always changing; it is constantly affected by the international, national and local economy, consumer trends and changing technology. Are you keeping up with the times?

IS YOUR OVERHEAD OUT OF CONTROL?

As competition increases and technology changes, overhead becomes even more difficult to control. We used to manage with just telephones; now we need faxes, voice-mail, extra phone services, e-mail, pagers, cellphones, Internet service providers, Web pages and hosting, to name a few. Time and money are spent replying to these communications, learning new programs and upgrading or fixing computer equipment.

IDEA — BIG | REVIEW YOUR CURRENT OVERHEAD

If you haven't made a habit of perusing your financial figures, why don't you start now? Waiting until year-end is too late. Get your figures up to date then sit down with your accountant and review your current overhead costs with a fine tooth comb. Your general ledger lists each expense, when it was incurred, who to and the amount. Particularly review expenses where you do have control — you can't control rent, but you can control marketing, office and telephone costs. See where you are being frivolous and trim those unnecessary expenses.

Figure 4.10	Twenty-Question Profitability Checklist

	Yes	No
1. Am I purchasing raw materials at competitive prices?	❏	❏
2. Are there suppliers who can offer better prices?	❏	❏
3. Could I streamline production or distribution costs?	❏	❏
4. Is inventory slow-moving and often unprofitable?	❏	❏
5. Could I afford to replace inefficient equipment?	❏	❏
6. Could employee productivity be increased?	❏	❏
7. Would an employee incentive program help?	❏	❏
8. Could I diversify my products or service?	❏	❏
9. Could I offer better service to my customers?	❏	❏
10. Is my discount structure too high?	❏	❏
11. Could I lower discounts without losing customers?	❏	❏
12. Am I monitoring my marketing efforts carefully?	❏	❏
13. Am I using unproductive marketing techniques?	❏	❏
14. Is it time to change marketing strategies?	❏	❏
15. Is the competition becoming too powerful?	❏	❏
16. Can I afford to offer something that the competition doesn't?	❏	❏
17. Am I effectively networking?	❏	❏
18. Am I keeping up with technological changes?	❏	❏
19. Am I monitoring increasing costs carefully?	❏	❏
20. Are consumer trends adversely affecting my business?	❏	❏

Marketing efforts have to be stepped up to stay competitive and production equipment upgraded to increase efficiency and keep prices competitive. No wonder people have difficulty coping with change—it is the only thing that remains constant in our lives. Often, overhead costs are incurred without first calculating whether the business can sustain the extra cost. Before committing to extra expenses, answer questions in Figure 4.11, the Twenty-Question "Do-I-Need-It?" checklist.

Controlling the Financial Reins

This chapter is designed to increase your financial knowledge and to show you how to put it to work for your business. Once you understand and utilize financial information, you will feel in control of the financial reins. Chapter 5 shows you how to apply this knowledge to streamline other areas that may be eroding away at your profits.

Figure 4.11	Twenty-Question "Do I Need It?" Checklist

	Yes	No
1. Will this expense help increase efficiency?	❑	❑
2. Will it save the business money?	❑	❑
3. Have I calculated how much money it will save?	❑	❑
4. Do I know how long it will take to produce profitable results?	❑	❑
5. Am I committing to a long-term lease or contract?	❑	❑
6. Can I make the payments if sales do not increase?	❑	❑
7. Am I currently operating over and above break-even point?	❑	❑
8. Will this expense help to generate more sales or profit?	❑	❑
9. Will time be needed to educate staff?	❑	❑
10. Will any transition downtime be needed?	❑	❑
11. Can I manage without it and still maintain efficiency?	❑	❑
12. Will I be uncompetitive without it?	❑	❑
13. Is this just a status symbol purchase?	❑	❑
14. Will it need to be upgraded in the next few years?	❑	❑
15. Is the product covered by satisfactory warranties?	❑	❑
16. Am I aware of all the ongoing maintenance costs?	❑	❑
17. Will we incur serious downtime if the equipment breaks down?	❑	❑
18. Can I keep this new employee fully productive?	❑	❑
19. Is everyone working at maximum capacity before hiring new staff?	❑	❑
20. Will this new employee contribute to the bottom-line profits?	❑	❑

CHAPTER 5

How Else Can You Increase Your Profits?

INCREASE PROFITS BY INCREASING EFFICIENCY

Have you ever reviewed your year-end financial statements with your accountant, only to be told that the profits were less than you had expected? "How can this be?" you ask. "Sales have been good and I'm trying to keep my overhead down. What else could be wrong?" An analysis of your accounting records will reveal where many problems lie. The key to an efficient operation is of course to work smarter, not harder.

The dollars are usually indicative of internal or inefficiency problems. Although the expenses shown on the statements may be acceptable, if you investigated all your current administrative and operational systems, you may well find room for improvement.

Is Your Paper-Shuffling Productive?

A business needs informative reporting and administrative systems. At the same time, these systems shouldn't drown you or your employees in paperwork. Wasted time is wasted profit. Some businesses don't use detailed enough systems, while others overload themselves with time-wasting paper trails. The secret is finding a balance that gives you the necessary information with a minimum of fuss.

Although the advent of computers has sped up a multitude of tasks, learning new software and organizing the extra paperwork frustrates many people. Some find change difficult and prefer to use time-consuming manual systems that leave more margin for error. Whatever the size of your business, there is always room for more efficiency.

TAKE A SYSTEMS INVENTORY

There are some areas where efficiency can be easily achieved. Chapter 3 showed you how to organize your time and filing systems. Figure 6.5, a checklist in Chapter 6, highlights operational areas that may need reevaluating. All other aspects of your operation need to be revisited to see where time or money is being wasted. Here are some simple suggestions for streamlining your administrative system.

Accounting system: Chapter 4 explained how to use your accounting to increase profit margins and financial efficiency. If you are using a manual system, consider changing to a computerized one. If the system is well designed, it will give you all the information you need in less time with less errors.

Billing: Accounting systems can be designed to accommodate either computer-generated or manual invoices. For a service business such as plumbing, writing an invoice on the job is far more practical. Before any data can be entered into the system, invoices have to be coded with an account number. To eliminate this time-waster, redesign your invoices so that account codes are pre-printed on invoices.

Collections: Update your accounts receivable weekly, then print a new receivables ageing list and call the overdue accounts. This gives you immediate cash flow information for budgeting purposes. See later in this chapter for more detailed collection information.

Accounts payable: Use an accounting program that produces an aged analysis of accounts payable. Update the payables weekly so that you have a current payables and receivables list. This saves time shuffling invoices and you can allocate your bill payments based on the receivables information.

IDEA **BIG**

RECONCILE PAYROLL MONTHLY

If you use a manual system, reconcile the payroll monthly and maintain accumulative totals. This saves you adding pages of figures once a year and potentially making time-wasting errors. It also allows you to catch any errors made during the month.

Cheques: Note the GST and net expense amount on each cheque stub. Keep a chart of accounts in the front of the cheque book and code the cheques as you write them. This saves you forgetting what the cheque was for and shuffling through the filing cabinet to find the invoice. If you regularly update your accounting, the cheques will be correctly coded.

Payroll: Using a software payroll program is efficient as it calculates the pay cheques, keeps a record of vacation pay, prints monthly payroll summary reports for CCRA remittances and prepares year-end payroll requirements.

IDEA	PRE-CODE ACCOUNTS PAYABLE
BIG	Design a rubber stamp with space for date received and a few blank expense account codes. When you have checked the invoice, break it down into the various expense categories and code the invoice. When it comes time to enter it to the payables ledger, the preparation work is completed. Provincial sales tax should be proportionately added to each expense.

SAMPLE STAMP

Date received:	10/29/00
5250: Office	152.78
1400: Furniture	698.68
2235: GST	52.70
2000: Payables	904.16

IS YOUR INVENTORY UNDER CONTROL?

No matter how efficiently you run your operation, if inventory isn't under tight control then your financial figures won't be accurate. Inventory management seems to be one of the biggest headaches for small businesses. Many operators don't realize how crucial this area is to profitability. Any business carrying an inventory relies on regular movement of goods sold at a certain gross profit to maintain the overhead expenses and generate a net profit.

Where inventory maintenance should be a top priority, it's often allocated to the bottom of the list. By the time the problem is pinpointed to mismanaged inventory, thousands of dollars of profit can be lost. Inventory is a key factor to cash-flow. If it's too large or not turning, cash-flow is seriously reduced. Here are the secrets to efficiently managing inventory:

- prudent purchasing
- avoiding overstocking
- efficient stock control systems
- regular inventory turnaround
- minimal damages and wastage
- correct inventory costing at year-end
- close monitoring of theft
- regular checks of actual to theoretical inventory stocks.

How Does Inventory Dictate Profits?

Quite simply, if your year-end inventory count is incorrect then the financial statements are wrong. Inventory is equivalent to cash in the bank—you wouldn't consciously throw money away, yet when it comes to inventory, this is exactly what happens. If you are not correctly accounting for wastage, damaged goods or samples, your material purchase costs will appear inflated in comparison to actual sales. This directly affects your gross profits.

By breaking down these other costs, you can carefully monitor such expenses. If they are lumped in with your material purchase account, that cost will be inflated. Put systems into place to control these costly factors. Figure 5.1 gives an example of three common scenarios contrasted with the reality.

What happened?

1. **Inventory overvalued:** By incorrectly overvaluing inventory at year-end, gross profits are overstated by $5,000.

2. **Inventory undervalued:** By undervaluing the inventory, gross profits are understated by $4,000.

3. **Purchases inflated:** By not separately accounting for damages, wastage, theft, personal use goods and samples, the cost of goods in relation to gross sales is $10,000 higher and there is no way to monitor these costs.

Figure 5.1	Inventory Error Comparisons			
	1 **INVENTORY** **OVERVALUED**	**2** **INVENTORY** **UNDERVALUED**	**3** **PURCHASES** **INFLATED**	**4** **CORRECT** **FIGURES**
Sales	152,000	152,000	152,000	152,000
Cost of sales:				
Opening inventory	32,000	32,000	32,000	32,000
Plus purchases	<u>102,000</u>	<u>102,000</u>	<u>112,000</u>	<u>102,000</u>
	134,000	134,000	144,000	134,000
Closing inventory	(52,000)	(43,000)	(47,000)	(47,000)
Cost of sales	82,000	91,000	97,000	87,000
Gross profit:	(46%) <u>70,000</u>	(40%) <u>61,000</u>	(36%) <u>55,000</u>	(43%) <u>65,000</u>

Common Mistakes in Inventory Control

The worst mistake is to have no control. I have seen retail stores place goods directly on the shelves without checking packing slips, pricing, or recording the shipment into inventory. Errors become lost profits, so review your system to see if you are making any mistakes. If you are, correct the situation, as each error will affect the accuracy of your inventory. Common errors include:

- not checking packing slips for shortages or damages when goods are delivered
- not checking supplier invoices for correct quantity and pricing
- not having an inventory control system to record receiving and shipping
- not making allowances for damaged goods, wastage, personal use and samples
- not performing regular spot checks to compare theoretical inventory to actual
- using only a computer-generated theoretical inventory tally at year-end
- not regularly reviewing computer inventory records to adjust any minus quantities

- not counting inventory correctly
- not costing inventory correctly
- not writing off obsolete or unsalable inventory
- carrying goods that do not turn over.

Which System Will Work For You?

Each business has different inventory management requirements, but the principles remain the same. Goods received are recorded into stock and goods shipped are recorded out of stock. A manufacturer working with raw materials such as lumber has to use a more detailed system than a retail store receiving finished goods. Various raw materials are used in manufacturing, so inventory will move from raw materials to finished goods. Business such as florists, restaurants or garden nurseries should make an allowance for spoilage and wastage.

Manual or Computerized Systems?

Manual system: A business dealing with small quantities of products may manage well using an index card system. These cards are designed to record inventory movement, the date, who the product was shipped to, invoice number, and whom goods were received from. The cost price of the item should be recorded on the card for costing purposes. It's not a difficult task to perform spot checks by taking the card and comparing its balance to actual stock.

Computer system: There are a variety of software programs available that incorporate inventory control. Many tie into accounting programs and other administrative functions. Be careful in your program selection as the wrong choice will create more work and frustration. Most programs automatically reduce inventory when an invoice is generated. There are industry-specific programs available, such as Book Manager for retail book stores.

Whichever system you use, it all boils down to one basic fact—garbage in, garbage out. If your data entry is inaccurate, the resulting information is wrong. Imagine the embarrassment if a client calls for an urgent product, the records show plenty of stock, and there is nothing on the shelves. Part of your administrative system should include a regular review of inventory reports for errors.

HOW TO COUNT INVENTORY

An inventory software program will theoretically count and cost inventory for you, as long as the prices and quantities are entered correctly. However, at least once a year, a physical inventory count must take place. No one loves this job. It's probably the worst part of owning a business—next to paying taxes. There are some simple steps you can take to ensure that the final figure is as accurate as possible.

Using an Inventory Program

1. At year-end, ensure that all sales invoices are processed and that invoiced goods awaiting shipment are not counted.
2. Close the premises or count at the end of a working day, always at month-end.
3. Always have two people count inventory together.
4. Print a full inventory report, ready to compare theoretical inventory to actual.
5. Design a sheet to record items that do not agree with the theoretical count. These need to be rechecked or recounted before the inventory is completed.
6. As each item is counted, if it agrees with the theoretical tally, check the item off.
7. If there is a problem, highlight the item and enter it on the checking sheet, writing the item description, theoretical tally, physical tally, the difference, and a column for the correct amount.
8. When the correct amount has been established, transfer this information to the inventory sheet.
9. Correct your computer inventory records before the next trading day.

Using a Manual System

The manual process is similar to the one above. Prepare an inventory tally sheet as shown in Figure 5.2, showing product description, theoretical quantity, physical quantity, a discrepancy column, the item price and total value. When the physical count is complete, go back and adjust your manual records.

Figure 5.2	Sample Inventory Count Sheet

GLORIOUS GIFTS AND CANDLES: DECEMBER 31, 20__

Department: *Candles*   Counted by: *John McKenzie*   Checked by: *Sue Taylor*

ITEM	THEO-RETICAL	PHYSICAL	DIS-CREPANCY	PRICE	TOTAL
8" taper candles, blue	48	52	+4	.25	13.00
8" taper candles, green	46	46	—	.25	11.50
9" rainbow candles	25	32	+7	.51	12.75
9" white candles	66	61	-5	.40	24.40
3" ball candles	15	15	—	.95	14.25
2" ball candles	12	13	+1	.75	9.75
PAGE TOTAL:	212	219	+7	—	85.65

Accurate Counting

The rule of counting inventory is to use two people. It's easy for one person to become bored or distracted and make errors. With small screws, these errors could be negligible, but with larger or more costly items, one error may represent many dollars. Inventory sheets should be set out to ensure legibility, as this often causes miscalculations as in the Real Life example, 'What's in a Decimal Point?'

REAL LIFE: What's in a Decimal Point?

While working as an office manager for a food manufacturing company in Australia, part of my job was to complete the inventory sheet calculations. They were completed and the accounting information sent to the accountant. He called, sounding most distressed. The gross profit was definitely incorrect—it seemed to be understated by nearly twenty thousand dollars.

The accounting was thoroughly checked. All seemed in order. The last resort was to check the inventory sheets. The plant supervisor didn't have the neatest of handwriting, and on closer scrutiny, a glaring error surfaced. The stock remaining of product that cost $25.00

a kilogram had been written as 90.0 kilograms at the count. Luckily, the boss who ran the factory realized that the stock would never run that low. The correct count was 900 kilograms. The error had made a difference of $20,250.00 to the gross profit.

HOW TO COST INVENTORY

Accurate Costing

The above example shows how important attention to detail is with an inventory count. The same applies to correctly pricing inventory. Each item should be recorded at purchase price. Additional costs such as freight or duty are accounted for in other expense accounts. Check the pricing for each item, as suppliers' costs increase during the year and prices may not be correct. Once the sheets are extended, have the calculations checked by another person.

Accounting for Obsolescence

The smart operator tries to sell slow-moving or obsolete items through clearance sales before the inventory count. There are still bound to be items that are taking up valuable shelf space and tying up cash-flow. These should be recorded on a separate inventory sheet. The decision then has to be made; should they be completely written off as a loss and disposed of, or their cost value reduced and then sold at a discounted rate?

Discounting is a common practice with items such as discontinued wallpaper, paint or clothing. When this decision has been made, total the amounts to be written off in full and the amount to be devalued, and by what percentage. Give this information to your accountant who will then make the appropriate journal entries.

How to Record Non-Sale Items

A portion of your inventory will never be sold. If these items are not accurately recorded, you will not be able to monitor your true operational costs. Each non-sale item becomes an overhead expense, and it isn't difficult to apply simple systems as explained following to record these expenses.

1. **Samples:** Whether you manufacture chocolates or CDs, you will offer samples to potential customers. These should be recorded as items coming out of inventory at cost and be charged to a "sample" account.

IDEA **KEEP A RECORD OF SAMPLES**

If you regularly give samples away, keep a monthly sample list, itemizing the product and cost. You now have a monthly dollar total for your accounting records. Promotional give-aways should be taken out of inventory and charged to a "marketing" account. Now you can review these costs to ensure that you are not going wild with the freebies and blowing the budget.

2. **Damaged products:** You have two options in handling damaged products. You can reduce the price or dispose of it. If you reduce the price, start a "discount sales" account to monitor these occurrences. If you are writing off the full cost of the product, take it out of inventory and charge it to a "damaged product" account.

3. **Personal use items:** Sometimes management takes products for personal use or to give to employees. For personal use, deduct these products from inventory records and charge either your shareholder's loan or capital account. The same principle applies for products given to employees, only the expense should be allocated to the promotion account. If products are exchanged for wages, the value is deducted from net wages payable.

4. **Waste and spoilage:** Recording each spoiled item—such as food or flowers—is time-consuming. You should know the approximate amount of wastage and use a set percentage to be calculated when your financial statements are prepared. Manufacturing businesses use this method. Tell your accountant this percentage so that an adjustment can be made. Material costs will be reduced by the dollar amount and the spoilage account increased by the same amount.

5. **Theft:** Because inventory theft affects many businesses, strict internal control and security monitoring for retail stores is

necessary. I have known of businesses where "trusted" employees have been responsible for thousands of dollars worth of theft. Retail stores also have to cope with shoplifting. It's often difficult to establish a dollar amount for theft. Where possible, estimate the amount, document the information for tax or court purposes, and give this information to your accountant.

Keeping the Records Straight

Figure 5.3 gives a few examples of the accounting entries to be made for the above situations. They are called journal entries and are first manually documented for audit purposes and then entered to the general ledger. Because you are recording the exact dollar value

Figure 5.3	Accounting Journal Entries

INVENTORY ADJUSTMENTS

ADJUSTMENT	ACCOUNT	DEBIT	CREDIT
1. January samples to clients	Purchases		346.00
Sample product from inventory	Samples	346.00	
2. January promotional product	Purchases		225.00
Promotional product from inventory	Marketing	225.00	
3. Damaged SnoozeKing 6' queen	Purchases		155.00
January damaged mattress	Damages	155.00	
4. 26" television taken by M. James	Purchases		379.00
Shareholder's loan, M. James	Shareholder	379.00	
5. 1 – Boomcity stereo to employee	Purchases		145.00
Wages, Terry Johnstone	Wages payable	145.00	
6. January 5% spoilage allowance	Purchases		975.00
5% of $19,500 purchases	Spoilage	975.00	
7. January theft allowance	Purchases		400.00
2% of $20,000 gross sales	Theft	400.00	
8. Sharp Shot 35mm camera stolen	Purchases		125.00
Missing from front display, 05/07/01	Theft	125.00	

of these costs, you can monitor them as a business expense and include them in your budgets and projections. If any areas are of real concern, they will come to your attention as you read your financial statements.

ARE YOUR CLIENTS PAYING YOU?

When a business first opens, the average entrepreneur pays little attention to setting and enforcing credit policies. It's exciting enough that you have new clients. You don't want to upset them by discussing money—they may choose to go elsewhere. As time passes, outstanding receivables mount, cash-flow fluctuates, and you are unable to keep suppliers paid on time. Perhaps you are too busy to focus on collections until it's too late and a client goes out of business overnight. It happens all the time.

If you are a retailer, most of your receivable income is paid by cash or credit card, although you may carry some trade or customer accounts. Other businesses usually have little choice but to extend credit to align themselves with industry standards.

SET CREDIT POLICIES

As you grow, cash-flow becomes an essential lifeline. If you haven't already set credit policies, now is the time to start. Discussing terms with clients is not a distasteful subject—it's what business is all about. Customers prefer to know the cost and your payment terms, in fact, they will respect you more if these terms are clearly stated.

Don't jump into extending credit without reviewing all the factors and consequences. Too many small businesses have gone bankrupt because they trusted one large client or didn't monitor their accounts closely enough. If you haven't any formal credit policies, answer questions in Figure 5.4, The Thirty-Question Credit Questionnaire to help you decide whether extending credit is a viable proposition for your business.

HOW TO USE CREDIT APPLICATIONS

Few small businesses bother to use credit applications because it involves another "time-consuming" chore. Don't take this attitude—

Figure 5.4   The Thirty-Question Credit Questionnaire

1. Can you afford to extend credit?
2. What percentage of sales income can you afford to have tied up in accounts receivable?
3. Are you currently experiencing problems with slow-paying clients?
4. Are you currently handling your collections efficiently?
5. Are your methods successful?
6. Is there room for improvement?
7. What is the most credit you can afford to extend to a single client?
8. Do you have a line of credit or other arrangements with your bank if needed?
9. Will your bank finance accounts receivable if necessary?
10. Have you discussed credit policies with your bank manager?
11. Are you conversant with standard industry credit policies?
12. Will extending credit affect payments to suppliers?
13. Is your current cash-flow situation healthy?
14. What credit policy will you set? Thirty days from invoice date or 30 days from the month of purchase?
15. What action will you take when accounts exceed your credit terms?
16. Will you charge interest on overdue accounts?
17. Is your accounting software capable of automatically adding interest to accounts?
18. Will you reverse unpaid interest if a client pays an account without paying the interest?
19. At what point will you hold shipments?
20. Will you ask for C.O.D. payments until an account is up to date?
21. Who will handle collection calls?
22. Will you send monthly statements?
23. Do you have the staff available for these extra accounting chores?
24. Do you have a lawyer to handle letters to overdue accounts?
25. Are you willing to go through the small claims process?
26. Do you understand the small claims process?
27. Will you offer a discount for payment in seven, 10 or 14 days?
28. What discount percentage can you afford to offer?
29. Do you currently offer credit-card or debit-card facilities?
30. Can you afford to offer the same discount percentage to receivable clients who pay promptly?

look at it as income protection. You would be amazed at the information you will discover when you start talking to trade references. A client may have had an excellent credit history until the last few months when payments have slowed down. This is always a warning signal, and credit references will tell you this information.

When a new client requires credit, tell them you would be pleased to extend credit subject to a credit application being completed and approved. This will take no more than two days. Explain your credit terms and any discount structure for timely payments.

A credit application will ask for the following information:

- how long a business has been operating
- its corporate structure and owners' names
- three trade references
- client's banking information
- the names of signing officers
- the credit limit the customer is seeking.

Questions to Ask Trade References

Businesses are usually quite happy to supply trade credit references. When you call, ask for the person responsible for accounts receivable. Politely introduce yourself and your business and ask if it would be convenient to request a credit reference on one of their clients. When you have the information, don't forget to thank them. The main questions you need to ask will be:

- How long has the client been trading with the supplier?
- How regularly do they purchase from them?
- On average, what do they spend each month?
- Do they pay within the stated terms of credit?
- Are they consistently late or on time?
- Have purchasing levels noticeably increased or decreased in the last six months?
- Have payments become noticeably tardy within the last six months?
- Have any of their cheques ever been returned NSF?
- Does the supplier have any particular concerns with this client?

 **IDEA** **JOIN A CREDIT REPORTING AGENCY**

The client's bank will confirm the client's bank account status, but most of your decision-making will come from conversations with suppliers. Because business can be so volatile, a wise investment is to join a credit reporting agency such as Dun and Bradstreet Canada. You then have access to regularly updated client credit information, history and reports.

Setting Credit Limits

You can now set a credit limit based on all this information. This is the maximum amount of credit that you are prepared to extend to your clients. If a client applies for a higher limit and you don't feel comfortable, discuss the matter. Explain that your company sets limits based on current credit information. Assure the client that you will be happy to review this limit in the near future. You then have time to assess their payment performance.

MONITOR ACCOUNTS RECEIVABLE

The key to monitoring credit limits is to review and update your receivable ageing list daily and the receivable ledger regularly, as last month's list doesn't take into account current purchases. Monitor current orders before they are filled to ensure they don't exceed the limit. If a new order exceeds the credit limit, call the client and let them know as was done in the Real Life example, 'Cutting Off the Credit.' Perhaps they could deliver a cheque to update the account?

Develop a Daily System

Keeping the cash flowing depends on your vigilance. The more accounts you carry, the more crucial that you use a daily system to keep the cheques arriving. Collections should become part of your daily administrative routine. Here is an example of an effective daily routine.

1. Write up the bank deposit daily.
2. Note and follow up any anomalies, such as short-payments or discounts.
3. Mark each cheque off your aged receivable list.

4. Review the aged receivable list for overdue accounts.

5. Phone clients with a gentle reminder.

6. On the aged receivables list, note the date that they promised to send you payment.

7. If the cheque has not arrived by that date, make another phone call.

8. Note any comments or promised payment dates on the aged receivable list.

9. If there appears to be a payment problem, start a collection file for the account.

10. If you are concerned, notify shipping to put a hold on all orders.

11. Notify the client that shipments are on hold until the account is brought up to date.

12. If it is obvious that the account is not being paid, be prepared to take further action.

REAL LIFE: Cutting Off the Credit

In the early 80s, companies came and went overnight due to the economy's recessive conditions. I was employed as an office manager for a distribution company with 500 accounts. One of my main jobs was credit control and the above system was most effective. By carefully monitoring the receivables daily, they were reduced from an average of sixty days to forty-five days, which represented a substantial dollar value.

On one occasion, I had no choice but to put the largest client's shipment on hold. Their account was well overdue and the promised cheque had not arrived. Meanwhile, their truck arrived to pick up an order and was sent away empty. It returned in the afternoon with the cheque.

The funny side to this story was that I later became a victim of the recession and applied for a job as a credit manager, which turned out to be at that same company whose order I'd held. The interviewer was the boss to whom I had refused to ship the order. We laughed in retrospect and he commented that he had respected me for making that decision. No—I didn't get the job but came a close second.

MONTH-END RECEIVABLES PROCEDURE

1. Close Off the Month

Your aim is to complete month-end procedures as soon as possible. Regular posting throughout the month will speed up this process. On the first of each month, all debts become a month older. Be sure that all sales invoices, credit notes, bank deposits and journal entries are posted, then run your month-end reports.

2. Update the Aged Receivable List and Send Statements

Prepare the aged receivable list, itemizing each unpaid invoice by customer and amount into current, 30, 60, 90 days and over. Review any bank deposits received since the first of the new month. Cross these payments off both the aged analysis and the clients' statements. Before mailing the statements, check each one for accuracy and account status.

3. Prepare Account Reminders

If clients need a gentle reminder, use a self-inking stamp with the message "this account is overdue." Personally signed, hand-written messages to clients you know seems quite effective. They should be polite and to the point. "Dear Steven, I noticed your account is a little overdue. Is there a problem? Please let me know. Jeff." Or, "Steven, your promised cheque didn't arrive. Have you sent it yet? Thanks, Susan." Remember the squeaky wheel.

Occasionally, you will receive a cheque after you have just sent out a reminder statement. Prepare for this by having a thank-you message printed on your statements. It could read: "If you have sent payment that is not yet credited to your account, please accept our thanks." It's no use upsetting the customer. Monthly statements help both parties keep better records and often alert clients to missing invoices or account problems.

4. Start Collections

Once the statements are mailed, review the aged receivable list, starting at the 90 days and over columns. Call each account, discuss the overdue amount and note any promised payments or other information. If clients request invoice copies, fax them immediately and note this on the list. Work your way through to 60 and 30 days overdue until everyone is called.

WHAT IF YOUR CLIENTS DON'T PAY?

Unfortunately, there will be clients who experience cash-flow difficulties. If they are honest about their situation, you can discuss an alternative payment plan. If messages are being ignored or you are worried about the financial stability of the business, send a first "account overdue" letter as set out in Chapter 9.

Now you have started a paper trail. If there is no response, send a second letter. If you are getting nowhere fast, you may have to resort to a legal letter, using a collection agency, or filing a small claims action. All along, be sure to carefully document conversation details and dates.

Some clients may want to pay but don't have the money. In all cases, don't ship further goods until satisfactory arrangements have been made. It's no use risking further debt. If the client promises to send postdated or regular cheques, and honours their commitment, you call the shots. Do you continue to allow further credit or do you keep them on a C.O.D. basis? Only you can make that decision.

Legal Action—the Last Resort

Any legal action is a tedious, drawn-out, time-consuming, expensive, unrewarding and frustrating process. Having processed a few of these, I can speak from experience. Although each case was resolved, obtaining payment from penniless people wasn't exactly a fun task.

Even if you win the case, collecting the debt is another matter. People with a sound knowledge of the judicial system can stretch payments out over a period of years. You might as well forget the whole thing and write it off as a bad debt and a learning experience.

The art of collections is to heed the warning signs of financial problems, stop supplying further goods, and be persistent in contacting clients for payment *before* their cash stops flowing.

Document All Details

Whichever method you use for difficult collections, start a file and document every detail, promise, conversation and action. Legal

IDEA   USE A THIRD PARTY

If you don't want any more of a client's business, use a collection agency. They work on a percentage of the debt, which increases with the debt's age. Having a third party deal with slow payers is often all the clout you will need. A lawyer's letter usually has even more impact.

cases are won on documented evidence. The more pieces of paper and evidence you produce, the better the odds. For lesser amounts, small claims court is often not worth the bother and time, but for larger amounts, you might as well have your day or two in court.

If you need more in-depth information or are experiencing continual problems with collections, read *What to Say When Your Customers Won't Pay* by Judy Smith and Michael Schulman in the McGraw-Hill Ryerson SOHO Solutions For Canadians series. It is an excellent publication highlighting just about every scenario you will ever experience, giving workable solutions and many examples.

Bad Debts and Your Accounting Records

An account is considered a bad debt when it is deemed uncollectible. Bankruptcies or a business disappearing overnight without paying suppliers are examples of cut-and-dried cases. An account is also considered a bad debt if it has been outstanding for over twelve months. Some debts are dubious because although they are not twelve months old, you know payment is doubtful. Here are three different scenarios to account for bad debts.

1. Bad debt expense: In the case of a bankruptcy, closure, or debt owing over twelve months, the whole amount of the debt is written off. Accounts receivable are credited to clear the amount owing, and a "bad debt" account is debited. This now becomes an overhead expense and is subtracted from net profits.

2. Allowance for doubtful accounts: Most businesses who carry accounts receivables make an annual allowance for bad debts. This is usually a percentage of gross sales, ascertained by a historical average. If you gross $100,000 a year, from experience you may estimate that $2,000, or two percent, will be uncollectible. At year-end, a general journal entry is prepared, debiting the "bad debt" account with this amount and crediting the "allowance for doubtful accounts" account.

3. Recaptured bad debts: If the gods are with you, some of the bad debts may be repaid in part or full during the following fiscal year. If this occurs, your accounting entry would debit "bank" and credit a revenue account called "recaptured bad debts." The expense you deducted last year now becomes taxable income in the year of repayment.

IMPROVE YOUR ADMINISTRATIVE EFFICIENCY

This chapter has been designed to pinpoint many hidden areas that contribute to profit or efficiency reduction. To help you analyse how efficient your current systems are, complete the following checklist, Figure 5.5. Where your answer "needs work," make a point of concentrating on fixing the problems. Then go back and check the "completed" column.

Now You are More Efficient

At this stage, if you implement the systems and advice in the last five chapters, your business will operate at peak efficiency. Now you are working smarter. Next, you must decide whether you are content to remain the size you are or whether you are ready for physical growth. Read Chapter 6 to help you ascertain whether physical growth is for you.

Figure 5.5	Administrative Efficiency Checklist

ADMINISTRATIVE SYSTEM	UNDER CONTROL	NEEDS WORK	COM-PLETED
Accounting system:			
1. Producing accurate, efficient monthly reports	❑	❑	❑
2. Sales invoices pre-coded for data entry	❑	❑	❑
3. Receivables updated at least once a week	❑	❑	❑
4. Accounts payable updated at least once a week	❑	❑	❑
5. Accounts payable coded on receipt	❑	❑	❑
6. Cheque stubs coded on payment of accounts	❑	❑	❑
7. Payroll cumulatively reconciled each month	❑	❑	❑
8. Paper-flow systems streamlined and efficient	❑	❑	❑
Inventory system:			
1. Supplier packing slips and invoices checked	❑	❑	❑
2. Theoretical inventory system in place	❑	❑	❑
3. All goods received entered to inventory	❑	❑	❑
4. All goods shipped taken from inventory	❑	❑	❑
5. Regular inventory spot-checks performed	❑	❑	❑
6. Computer inventory checked for minus tallies	❑	❑	❑
7. Slow-moving stock regularly cleared on sale	❑	❑	❑
8. Accurate year-end counting system in place	❑	❑	❑
9. Computer prices regularly checked	❑	❑	❑
10. Two people count inventory together	❑	❑	❑
11. Sample product is recorded correctly	❑	❑	❑
12. Damages and waste are recorded correctly	❑	❑	❑
13. Personal goods from inventory recorded	❑	❑	❑
14. Anti-theft systems installed	❑	❑	❑
Credit and collections:			
1. Credit policies established	❑	❑	❑
2. Credit application forms used	❑	❑	❑
3. Trade references always checked	❑	❑	❑
4. Thirty-question credit check completed	❑	❑	❑

Figure 5.5	Continued

ADMINISTRATIVE SYSTEM	UNDER CONTROL	NEEDS WORK	COM-PLETED
5. Joined a credit reporting service	❏	❏	❏
6. Receivables ageing list updated daily	❏	❏	❏
7. Collection calls made at least once a week	❏	❏	❏
8. Contacted a lawyer for collection purposes	❏	❏	❏
9. Contacted a reputable collections agency	❏	❏	❏
10. Aware of small claims court procedures	❏	❏	❏
11. Initiated efficient month-end procedures	❏	❏	❏
12. Initiated efficient daily collection system	❏	❏	❏
13. Use monthly statements	❏	❏	❏
14. Established an annual bad debt percentage	❏	❏	❏

CHAPTER 6

Are You Ready for Growth?

DID YOU PLAN FOR GROWTH?

Growing your small business can be a most exciting experience. You know you are taking positive steps toward success while feeling a sense of accomplishment, increased confidence and self-esteem. You have worked hard to come this far and deserve the rewards. Planned growth is exhilarating—uncontrolled growth is chaotic.

For some, growth suddenly sneaks up on them when they are least prepared. Some people prefer to stay at a certain level of operation, while others plan growth that doesn't happen. Growing a micro business is one of the most difficult goals to achieve, because in many cases, you aren't ready for it.

Too often, a small business is started without any formal business plan, or the plan is not revisited before growth decisions are made. Part of this plan should include provisions for sudden or unexpected growth. How will you handle it? Do you have the resources to expand, finance a larger inventory or hire more employees? What about the cost of relocating to larger premises?

Many owners don't even think about growth when they start, suddenly finding themselves trying to handle those 60 different jobs. This eventually leads to poor decision-making, burn-out, and often the failure of a potentially viable business.

Signs of Uncontrolled Growth

It's easy to bury your head in the sand, immersed in the day-to-day operation without really noticing what is happening. What are the warning signs that your business is growing in a disorderly fashion? Perhaps you can identify with some of the following situations:

- Your desk is a mess, piled with unopened bills and correspondence.
- Suppliers are calling for payment of overdue accounts.
- The money seems to go out faster than it comes in.
- You constantly feel under pressure, tired and worried.
- You can't keep up with all the tedious administrative duties.
- You mutter when the phone rings and don't return calls promptly.
- Taxes and other government payments are falling behind.
- Your books are months behind.
- You don't know how much is owing by clients or to suppliers.
- Your family complains that you are difficult to live with.
- You often find yourself working evenings and weekends.
- You don't take regular vacations.
- You are not enjoying your work.
- You make silly mistakes.

If you can identify with any of the above, then it's obviously time to address some important growth issues. Your business cannot grow if you are uninformed, overworked, out of control and perhaps even depressed. You have to change both your attitude and the way you are operating—*now*.

THE SIX-STEP GROWTH ANALYSIS PLAN

Even if you didn't plan how to grow your business, it's never too late to start—but where to begin? Spend time seriously evaluating where you are, where you want to go, whether you can afford it, and how you are going to do it. Work with your accountant to formulate a structured growth plan.

You can't plan for growth until you set some goals. Have you really thought about what you want from your business? How practical are your goals? How and when can they be attained? As you work through this analysis process, you may discover areas in both your business and personally that need some fine tuning.

The six steps to planning for growth are:

1. evaluating where you are now
2. deciding whether you want to and are ready to grow

3. setting goals
4. planning how you will grow
5. planning how to finance your growth
6. comparing progress to projections.

STEP 1: EVALUATE WHERE YOU ARE NOW

The worksheets and checklists in this book are designed to help you assess and pinpoint your strengths and weaknesses. Your business will not grow or overcome problems without your willingness to do something about it.

Review Previous Worksheets

Chapter 1: The "Where Am I Now?" questionnaire (Figure 1.1) should have indicated whether you are feeling positive about your business. It should have identified areas requiring improvement, or affirmed that you are heading in the right direction. How did you feel you when you answered the questions? Do you still feel that way? Are you mentally ready to objectively tackle growing your business?

Chapter 2: Successful growth needs nurturing with a positive attitude and a determination to overcome all obstacles. Revisit Figure 2.3, the "Where Am I Going?" questionnaire where you noted areas of concern. You should have also noted the jobs you don't like doing, where you need to develop more expertise, and work that could be delegated. Are you willing to take action in these areas?

Chapter 3: Growing requires that you develop refined organizational skills. There will be more of everything to cope with, so organization is critical to save serious errors and confusion. How did you fare on the Figure 3.4 "Operation 'Get Organized' Checklist"? Are you prepared to reorganize yourself, your systems and your business so that all operate at peak efficiency?

Chapter 4: The "Twenty-Question Profitability Checklist" (Figure 4.10) notes key areas that contribute to the profitability of a business. Of those you have checked "no" to, are you prepared to investigate some viable solutions? Have you calculated your break-even point yet?

Chapter 5: You need optimum administrative efficiency to utilize every dollar of revenue generated. For those areas in Figure 5.5, the "Administrative Efficiency Checklist" that you checked "needs work," will you complete the task of streamlining your administrative operations?

Chapter 6: When you have read this chapter and completed Figure 6.5, the "Going for Growth Action Plan," add your answer to the worksheet in Figure 6.1. It's a lengthy and detailed growth analysis. Are you ready for all that is entailed in growing your business?

There are other important checklists at the end of each chapter in this book. They will give you further insight as you work toward growing your skills and business.

If you check "no" under "improvement needed" to all six questions, then you don't need to read this book. Congratulations! You are on your way to becoming another Bill Gates. If you have checked "yes" to most of the six worksheets under "willing to improve," my hat is off to you. You are truly ready and willing to work positively on growing your business and are obviously aware that it will take time, commitment, and hard work. With this attitude and determination, you *will* succeed.

If you have answered "no" more than three times under "willing to improve" and "yes" more than three times under "needs improvement," then perhaps growing your business is not the right

Figure 6.1	**Are You Ready for Growth? Worksheet**			
	IMPROVEMENT NEEDED		**WILLING TO IMPROVE**	
	Yes	No	Yes	No
1. Where am I now?	❏	❏	❏	❏
2. Where am I going?	❏	❏	❏	❏
3. Operation "Get Organized"	❏	❏	❏	❏
4. Profitability checklist	❏	❏	❏	❏
5. Administrative efficiency	❏	❏	❏	❏
6. Going for Growth	❏	❏	❏	❏

decision for you at this time. For those willing and wanting to grow their business, read on to the next step.

STEP 2: DECIDE WHETHER YOU ARE READY TO GROW

In most cases, growth doesn't just happen—you have to make your business grow at a pace that you can physically, mentally and financially manage. If you have completed the Figure 6.1 checklist, then you are aware of the various areas that need work. Some of these take time and money to implement; others can be implemented quickly and at little cost.

If you are suffering from any of the warning signs discussed on page 101, you are definitely tackling too much by yourself and need help. Many people say, "But I can't afford to hire someone, I'm not making enough money." Often it is a "catch 22" situation—if you don't get help to grow, you won't.

To Grow or Stay Small?

Some people don't want to grow. They have developed a lifestyle around their business which complements both their family commitments and personal life. This is particularly true with women-owned home-based businesses which can be operated part-time in-between raising a family.

If you follow this six-step growth analysis plan, you will know better whether you can cope with growth or whether you should just stay small, work smarter, and become more profitable. Let's look at some of the questions you need to ask yourself.

1. Skills: If you refer to the 60 different jobs listed in Chapter 2 and haven't highlighted the ones you hate to do or can't do, go back and complete this exercise. This will help to pinpoint your strengths and weaknesses. You should have solid financial, marketing, sales, communication, technical and administrative knowledge. If you haven't, you either have to learn these skills or delegate them to a more qualified person.

Many of the jobs you highlight will be administrative jobs that are encroaching upon the time you need to concentrate on growing your business. Which ones could you delegate? How long will it take you to learn the other necessary skills? Can you still grow your business as you work on these skills?

2. Relocation: Would growing your business mean having to relocate to a larger premises? Can you afford to move? Make some enquiries about the cost of relocating, as it can be expensive. Many home-based businesses are not ready to take the plunge to commercial premises without the in-between step of hiring one or more employees.

Some local government bylaws prohibit non-resident employees working from your home, so the choice then becomes to operate illegally—which many people do, or to move the business out, which isn't always financially viable. Others are tied into a commercial lease for a building that is now too small. Explore all your options to determine the best solution for you.

3. Finances: Growth often requires some financial injection. Is your business stable enough to apply for a loan? How much income would you have to generate to repay the loan? How will you generate that income? Is your business paying you a satisfactory wage? Is it wise to consider growth if it isn't yet supporting you? Growth may be the ideal solution, but how will you convince the bank of this?

Study your most recent financial statements. Review the working capital situation and the statement of income and expenses. What are your financial statements telling you? Sit down with your accountant and spend some time finding out.

4. Employees: Are you ready to take on the responsibility of hiring and training employees? One of the most difficult tasks is finding the right person. It's even more difficult to fire an incompetent one. Do you have the cash flow to ensure that wages and deductions are paid on time? Are you ready for the responsibility of directing and working with someone else? Being a boss doesn't come naturally to everyone.

5. Time and energy: Are you still enthusiastic and energized about your business? Or are you overworked, depressed, tired, and a little burnt out? Will growing your business put undue pressures on you? Will your family support you? Do you have the time to seriously commit to growing your business? Will a well-thought-out plan which incorporates hiring staff ease some of these pressures, allowing you to move forward?

Think carefully about these five important areas as you continue on to step three. Make notes of those issues which need to be addressed as you set your goals and document your ideas.

STEP 3: SET GOALS

The importance of goal-setting was discussed in Chapter 2, so now it's time to commit them to paper. It's a step that is too often missed on start-up. There is no doubt about it—if you set goals, give them timelines and stay focussed, you will reach them. The only person who puts limits on you is yourself.

IDEA

ELIMINATE FEAR AND LIMITS

I once said to a friend that the sky is the limit. "Oh no it's not," she replied, "why should you limit yourself?" I thought carefully about her words and had to agree—why set yourself limits? The most common reason for not forging ahead and making those dreams a reality is fear of failure. What could you achieve if you took away the fear of failure? Think about it.

Goals aren't all materialistic, nor are they all short- or long-term. You need a variety of goals than will enrich and enhance your life. Here are some ideas to consider:

- **Personal:** increasing self-confidence and self-esteem, feelings of achievement, inner enrichment, peace and happiness, community recognition, retirement

- **Business:** short-term goals, one-to ten-year goals, how long you want to own this business, how big you want it to grow, increasing the goodwill value, "perks" the business can provide, diversification

- **Material:** increasing personal assets and net worth—do you dream of a bigger house, a better vehicle, a boat or more travel?

- **Family:** improving family lifestyle, better relationships, more time together, providing children with jobs in the business, having family support, better education for the children

IDEA	**SHARE YOUR GOALS**
BIG ● ●	Don't rush into setting goals. Talk to successful business people to see how they achieved their goals. Talk to your family to ensure you have their support and that they understand how you feel and what your goals are. Include them in your plans.

As you are sure of each goal, write it down in Figure 6.2. Then either photocopy this worksheet or rewrite it. Put it somewhere highly visible, like the refrigerator or your office bulletin board. Read and affirm your goals daily. When you reach each one, fill in the date that you achieved the goal and highlight it on your list. You will experience an extraordinary and satisfying feeling of power and achievement.

STEP 4: PLAN HOW YOU WILL GROW

This part of your growth plan may take time to develop. A service business or retail store has certain physical and geographic boundaries, unless you plan to open other locations. Unless it diversifies, a manufacturing company may only be able to capture a certain portion of the market due to cheaper exports or larger competitors. The ultimate goal for any business is to make healthy profits. Bigger isn't always better.

Part of planning for growth is to know *why* you want to grow and whether it will be beneficial. You need to answer some vital questions:

1. Am I filling a need and a niche in the market?
2. What will my position in the market be?
3. What marketing methods will I use?
4. What are my competitive strengths and weaknesses?
5. How will the weaknesses be overcome?
6. What is my projected time frame?
7. Will growth increase the net profits of the business?
8. Will I require outside financing?
9. Where will I obtain that financing?
10. Can the business afford to repay the debt?

Figure 6.2	My "Go-Getter Goal-Setter" Plan of Action

GOALS   TIMELINE

Personal: 1. _____

2. _____

3. _____

4. _____

5. _____

Business: 1. _____

2. _____

3. _____

4. _____

5. _____

Material: 1. _____

2. _____

3. _____

4. _____

5. _____

Family: 1. _____

2. _____

3. _____

4. _____

5. _____

Plan to Plan for Change

A business must spend time planning for growth to succeed. Very few businesses remain unaffected by technological changes or consumer trends. Publishing is a classic example of an age-old industry that is currently facing major challenges. People love books, but they are also hooked on the Internet and electronic gadgets. The publishing industry has to adapt to these changes.

Many booksellers are starting to open digital bookstores online. How will electronic sales affect the demand for traditional books? We shall have to wait and see. Even book titles are affected—they should be designed to appear high up on a search list and contain words that are identifiable by search engines. Cute and catchy titles may be on their way out.

STEP 5: PLAN YOUR FINANCING NEEDS

When you have completed the "Going for Growth Action Plan" at the end of this chapter, you should have identified where additional funding is needed to meet your needs. Research these costs and incorporate them into your projections. Planned growth doesn't happen by keeping ideas in your head; write them down.

Many of these exercises are similar to those required in the preparation of a business plan. What you are now preparing is a strategic growth plan that incorporates a research and development component, a marketing plan, cash flow, income and expense projections. No lending institution will entertain the thought of a loan without this information.

FINANCING OPTIONS

There are a variety of financing options available, so the next step is to estimate the amount you will need from your projections, then itemize what it is for. You may need as little as $5,000 or as much as $100,000. Which financing product best suits your needs? You may be able to secure a government-funded loan for expansion or export. Read the publication *Overview of Government Assistance Programs for Small Business*, available through your Canada Business Service Centre. It lists all the provincial and federal funding and loan programs. Most libraries also hold a resource called *Handbook of Assistance Programs* (Canadian Research and Publication Centre), an excellent guide to government funding, which is updated bi-montly.

WHAT DO BANKS OFFER?

As comparable and competitive financing products are available, you will need to do some homework. Try your own bank or trust company first as you should have built a relationship with them and they can put a face and history to your name. Hopefully this is advantageous to you.

Banks are becoming more small-business friendly, with some offering small business loans under $15,000. The Business Development Bank of Canada offers a variety of small business loans, including a mentorship component.

Finding the financing you need can be frustrating, but there are many options. As an example, see the Royal Bank of Canada™ products outlined in Figure 6.3. Note that quoted rates are subject to change.

IDEA | **SEEK ALTERNATIVE FINANCING**

•BIG•

If you go to the bank unprepared or with financial statements that do not look optimistic, you may face rejection. If this happens and you are still determined to pursue financing, read *Where To Go When the Bank Says No* by Gary Fitchett in this SOHO series by McGraw-Hill Ryerson. It is an excellent publication that details many forms of innovative financing.

How do Banks View Your Business?

Be well prepared for your appointment at the bank with a professional presentation. Ask your accountant to review all your information with you and discuss any potentially weak areas in your presentation. Pick his or her brain for any suggestions. The bank is going to look at these key factors on reviewing your application:

- the overall viability of the business
- the viability of the business plan
- the business's ability to repay the loan

Figure 6.3	Financing Products Available to Small Business Owners: Royal Bank of Canada™

TYPE OF LOAN	FUNDS LIMIT	FUNDS USED FOR	COST & TERMS
Overdraft protection	$5,000	short-term financing repay interest monthly	interest at prime + 5% monthly fee $10
Creditline™ for small business	up to $50,000	short-term financing	interest at prime +3%
Expense cards for small business	varying	short-term financing	currently 18%
Business Operating Line™	$5,000- unlimited	flexible financing repay interest monthly	interest at prime to +3% set-up fee $75 monthly fee $15–$25
Canadian Small Business Financing Loan (CSBF) (Government guaranteed) (Business plan required)	up to $250,000	equipment upgrades leasehold improvements land or buildings	interest at prime to prime +1% 1.25% annual govt. fee 2% registration fee
Business Leaseline™	$1,000 to $100,000	leasing equipment	rates vary dependent on term of lease
Term Loan	variable	asset purchases refinancing, expansion acquisitions	interest varies with prime, variable or fixed; secured loan, up to 7 years
Export financing	minimum $100,000	financing receivables from overseas clients	term or floating rates available
Letters of Credit	no limit	short-term financing for international transactions	percentage of borrowed amount, tiered rates

- what security is offered
- how much the owner(s) have invested in the business
- past and current credit history
- available management expertise.

IDEA **BE PROFESSIONAL**

Be well-groomed, positive and well-armed for your loan application appointment. Take your past and most recent financial statements, business plan, a statement of personal net worth (personal assets and liabilities), any promotional material, newspaper articles relevant to your industry, or anything else that will help to inform and project a professional image. Carting in your set of accounting books is not acceptable.

The Three Crucial Questions

Apart from assessing your overall knowledge plus all of the above, the bank wants to be sure they are investing money wisely. They will perform a variety of calculations from your financial statements to find answers to the following three questions:

1. *Is this business currently "liquid?"* If current assets and current liabilities were liquidated, could the assets pay off the liabilities? Are the owners or management drawing a satisfactory wage?

2. *Is this business currently profitable?* Are gross and net profit margins consistent? Can the business absorb growth costs? Does it have the ability to repay the loan?

3. *Is this business relatively stable?* Do the financial statements reflect a financially stable business? What is the debt to equity ratio? Can this business cope with growth? How has it performed during previous growth periods? What would the financial effect of a downward trend be?

If you pass these stringent tests and your growth plan reveals a viable investment for the bank, you should be on your way to obtaining the finances you need to put your plan into action. Good luck.

STEP 6: COMPARE PROGRESS TO PROJECTIONS

Once you have a viable growth plan in place with the available funds to accompany it, review your financial figures and projections each month. If you borrowed money, it's even more important to see if the investment is reaping the expected returns.

Consult your plan, update financial figures and projections before making any financial decisions—that's why you plan in the first place. By regularly monitoring your progress, you can more readily identify items of concern and remedy the situation. Perhaps you didn't achieve your sales projections or your marketing isn't producing the expected results. This information will reflect in your financial reports.

Compare Spreadsheets

The best method for reviewing your progress is to compare actual results to projections. You can study each area of your analysis to find out why the figures vary, and then decide how to resolve any problems. Figure 6.4 shows an example of a one-month comparison for a small wood craft manufacturing business.

What Happened?

Sales were $3,500 below projections and cost of sales increased by six percent as materials and wages both increased by three percent, a gross profit reduction of $655. Why did both these costs increase? The gross profit for the month was $2,205 less than projected.

An increase in marketing, office costs and an unexpected breakdown of equipment increased projected overhead by $760. The business suffered a net loss of $1,495 instead of a projected net profit of $1,470, a difference of $2,965. If projected sales were met with the 56 percent gross profit margin, the business would have only lost $70 for the month. See the Real Life example, 'Creating the Formula for Success' for inspiration in another business scenario.

REAL LIFE: Creating the Formula for Success

How do a couple who were out of work and down on their luck become the proud owners of a 100 percent financed failing menswear store? That story is all about miracles. Turning the store

Figure 6.4	One-Month Financial Comparison Creative Wood Art Ltd. August 31, 20__		

	BUDGET	ACTUAL	VARIANCE
Sales	13,000	10,500	(3,500)
Cost of sales			
Materials	2,600	2,415	(185)
Packaging	260	230	(30)
Labour	1,950	1,890	(60)
Freight	130	110	(20)
	4,940	4,645	(295)
Gross profit: (62%)	**8,060**	**(56%) 5,855**	**(2,205)**
Overhead expenses:			
Accounting fees	150	175	25
Advertising	260	240	(20)
Bad debts	50	0	(50)
Bank charges	45	50	5
Employee benefits	890	880	(10)
Fees, licences	50	0	(50)
Insurance	100	100	0
Loan interest	300	310	10
Management salary	2,000	2,000	0
Marketing & promotion	400	780	380
Office salaries	500	500	0
Office supplies	100	230	130
Promotion — meals	50	75	25
Rent	700	700	0
Repairs & maintenance	100	420	320
Security	50	50	0
Seminars & trade shows	60	90	30
Shop supplies	100	60	(40)
Telephone	150	185	35
Utilities	110	95	(15)
Vehicle — gas	100	120	20
Vehicle — R&M	150	120	(30)
Workers' Compensation	175	170	(5)
	6,590	7,350	760
Profit/Loss for month:	1,470	(1,495)	$ (2,965)
Actual gross profit deficiency			2,205
Overhead increase/decrease			760
Profit/loss variance			$(2,965)

around and growing it by 30 percent in one year wasn't a miracle—this couple has all the right ingredients for a successful partnership.

Ken Thompson's Men's Wear had operated in Nanaimo on Vancouver Island in British Columbia for 42 years. Ken's son Brad had owned the store since 1990, although his real dream was to own a restaurant, which he now does. Derek Rickwood had worked in the mens' clothing industry for 23 years, many of those at the store.

Derek loved to paint, while his talented wife Lisa had seven years' advertising experience, coupled with her passion for fashion and writing. Both Derek and Lisa hold a Bachelor of Fine Art degree. Both are highly creative and artistic, yet possess many of the necessary business skills.

The store was renamed Rickwood's Menswear Ltd. and the revamping and revitalizing commenced. This store would cater to men from head to toe. Expert service was what the customers wanted, and that's what they get. It now offers dry cleaning, shoe and leather repairs, tailoring and alterations, personal after-hour appointments, deliveries to homes or businesses, affordable, quality clothing, exceptional service—and an in-house art gallery of works by Derek. He loves people and is highly service-oriented, with an expert's knowledge of what customers want.

Lisa knew how the media worked and succeeded in having three Nanaimo newspapers publicize the change of management. The couple kept in constant touch with their accountant, who is thrilled as the store reached the break-even point and generated profits in under one year.

Today, Rickwood's Menswear Ltd. employs an experienced book-keeper, two full-time sales staff and Derek and Lisa. Derek wears many hats, including purchasing, fitting and sales. Lisa handles marketing, media relations and deliveries. Their biggest challenge has been to find well-trained staff, especially in fitting suits. This often frustrates Derek as he can only serve one customer at a time.

Derek and Lisa have overcome obstacles that would frighten the average person. As a team, their combined talents, expertise, passion and persistence has turned a struggling store into a success story.

THE BENEFITS OF INCORPORATION

"Should I incorporate?" ask many sole proprietors planning for growth. For those well-organized micro businesses, perhaps incorporation isn't necessary, but in most cases, it is a practical solution to assist in planned growth. Incorporation has considerable benefits, so read this information, then discuss it with your accountant. You may find that you take on a whole new perspective when you become Coastal Charters Ltd.

Read Evelyn Jacks' *Make Sure It's Deductible* in the SOHO series for some excellent tax information on this subject.

Incorporation allows you to:

1. Plan wages and personal finances

Once incorporated, you can draw a regular salary, make CPP contributions, and, dependent on the shareholder's structure, qualify for Employment Insurance benefits. You are an employee of the company, so your wage is a corporate expense—which it isn't in a sole proprietorship—and you receive a T4 at year-end. You can still vary your wage according to cash-flow.

An unincorporated sole proprietor pays both portions of CPP, based on net profits. Your personal tax liability is usually unknown until year-end financial statements are prepared. An incorporated company pays half the CPP benefits, which is tax-deductible.

2. Structure profits, dividends and bonuses

As a sole proprietor, there are only so many deductions you can make from your business. When you are incorporated, your accountant will prepare your year-end and suggest various tax alternatives, including paying more wages, bonuses or dividends.

This puts more money into your pocket and costs less in corporate taxes. Banks understand lower corporate profits when they see healthy management salaries. What they don't like is corporate losses created by top-heavy management salaries or "perks."

3. Project a more stable business image

It's proven that an incorporated business is viewed more seriously by suppliers, clients, investors and banks. It usually indicates that management has thought seriously about growth and profitability. Incorporation projects an image of a "real" business as opposed to a "mom and pop" operation. It is easier to obtain financing with a qualified incorporated business than with a proprietorship.

4. The security of limited liability

An incorporated business is a separate entity from its owners (shareholders). Trade suppliers provide credit with the understanding that if the business bankrupts, they may not recover their money. Shareholders are personally liable for certain debts, such as personally guaranteed loans, provincial and federal taxes and employee withholdings.

If a business bankrupts, the shareholders could start another business immediately. If a proprietorship fails, the owner is personally responsible for all debts, with personal bankruptcy sometimes being the only alternative. This not only leaves a black mark on your credit rating, but also personal assets, including your home, are subject to liens or seizure.

5. Grow in a more structured environment

As your business grows, you may want to add partners or shareholders. You can then have a board of directors who can give valuable input. To keep a controlling interest, you need to maintain at least 51 percent of the shares. If the best option to grow your company is to "go public" on the stock exchange, then the basic corporate structure is in place. If this is one of your long-term visions, talk to your lawyer so that your initial incorporation structure makes adequate future provisions.

6. Benefit from the capital gains exemption

Since the average citizen pays capital gains taxes on certain transactions, so do sole proprietors pay capital gains tax when a business is sold. As of October 18, 2000, if you sell your business and the goodwill portion is $50,000, $25,000, or 50 percent is reported as taxable income. If you have other income which brings your annual taxable earnings to under $61,509, you will pay 22 percent federal tax on the $25,000 plus applicable provincial income tax. Not what you really want to do. Anything over $61,509 is taxed at a rate of 26 percent federal tax. Due to further proposed tax indexing in the next few years, these figures may vary slightly.

Some small incorporated businesses may qualify for the small business capital gains deduction of $500,000 when they sell their business. However, there are many factors to consider, so it is wise to consult with your accountant in advance of a sale. If you are a proprietorship thinking of selling in the future, consider incorporating. Any business with long-term growth plans should incorporate.

7. Take advantage of tax credits

Incorporated businesses are able to take advantage of other tax credits including manufacturing, investment, film, and political contributions, and are generally taxed at a lower rate than personal taxes.

THE DOWNSIDE OF INCORPORATION

Although incorporation is an obvious choice for many growing businesses, you should be aware that it involves more expense and detailed accounting. If you are thinking of incorporating, consider these facts:

1. Incorporation fees

These fees range from $400 if you do it yourself to upwards of $700 through a lawyer, dependent on the complexity of the share structure and whether you register in other provinces.

2. Increased accountant's fees

A roll-over from a proprietorship to an incorporated business is prepared on incorporation. This moves the assets to the new entity and includes the share structure. At year end, a detailed financial statement and corporate tax return are prepared. Depending on how complete your books are, the cost will be $700 and up. Don't be surprised at a $2,000 accounting bill. An incorporated business must maintain a complete and accurate set of accounting records.

3. Payroll deductions

As an employee of the company, you must now maintain payroll records, prepare T4s at year-end, have a business number, and make monthly remittances to Canada Customs and Revenue Agency (CCRA).

4. Extra reporting

Most provinces send you or your registered office an annual corporate report asking for changes in directors' names or addresses.

Filing this form costs approximately $35. Either you or your lawyer should maintain a record of company minutes in the corporate minute book. The share register should be updated with any transactions.

5. **Other costs**

You may wish to print new stationery and business cards or change signs and Web page information to add the incorporated name. If you are rolling personally-owned vehicles into the incorporated business, a transfer of ownership is necessary.

ASSESS THE EFFECTS OF GROWTH

Any change in your operation needs to be carefully analysed to identify the cause, effects and benefits of that change. If you plan to manufacture a new product line, raw materials have to be purchased, extra labour hired, a market niche identified, marketing costs increased, more space made available and extra overhead expenses incurred.

Many questions have to be asked and answered. An integral part of your growth plan is to prepare projections of income, expenses and cash flow, as each move you make will affect another area of operation.

GOING FOR GROWTH ACTION PLAN

When you plan to grow your business, it's not just a matter of generating more dollars. You need to research the following 10 areas to determine the cause, effects and benefits on other areas of operation. Use Figure 6.5 as a guideline to carefully evaluate your plans. Check the areas applicable to your business to formulate a guide for growth. The following chapters will help you with increasing your communication, marketing and sales skills and give some tips on finding the perfect employee.

Are You on Track for Growth?

There is a lot of information to digest here, so you may have to reread this chapter a few times if you are going for growth. Of course, you will need help to lighten your workload, so now read Chapter 7 to learn how to hire the right person, as there are a variety of hiring options. Pay particularly attention to the section on employer responsibilities and theft.

Figure 6.5	"Going for Growth" Action Plan

	ACTION NEEDED	COM- PLETED
1. Research and development: research and know...		
• the time needed to research the complete growth plan	❑	❑
• the time needed to develop new products or services	❑	❑
• the cost and time involved in registering any patents or copyrights	❑	❑
• that you are not infringing on other patents or copyrights	❑	❑
• you have the qualified staff available to complete the research	❑	❑
• how you will market new products or services	❑	❑
• that you have a complete marketing plan in place	❑	❑
2. Revenue: research and know...		
• how revenue will be generated	❑	❑
• in what time frame	❑	❑
• if gross profit margins are acceptable and consistent	❑	❑
• if the pricing structure is competitive	❑	❑
• the life of the product(s) or service(s)	❑	❑
3. Direct costs: ensure that...		
• materials are readily available as needed	❑	❑
• you can meet supplier payment terms	❑	❑
• adequate room is available to store raw materials	❑	❑
• there is enough room to manufacture the product	❑	❑
• equipment meets your production needs	❑	❑
4. Labour: you will need...		
• staff in place for increased production	❑	❑
• to hire the right person with the right credentials	❑	❑
• cash flow to meet extra wage requirements	❑	❑
• to allow for training time and costs	❑	❑
• to factor wage benefits into cash flow	❑	❑
• a contingency plan if employees are absent from work	❑	❑

Figure 6.5	Continued

	ACTION NEEDED	COM- PLETED
• design a reporting system to monitor and evaluate staff performance	❑	❑
• assess productivity level and capabilities of each employee	❑	❑
• assess each employee's potential for promotion	❑	❑
5. Overhead expense increase: plan for...		
• extra help to cope with more paperwork	❑	❑
• potentially upgrading the accounting system	❑	❑
• equipment requiring regular maintenance	❑	❑
• more space for extra staff	❑	❑
• extra telephone lines, cellphones, pagers	❑	❑
• incidental cost increases, such as stationery	❑	❑
• upgrading facilities to house extra staff	❑	❑
6. Asset purchases: analyse...		
• the cost and availability of new equipment	❑	❑
• how you will finance asset purchases	❑	❑
• how each asset will contribute to profit centres	❑	❑
• the life span and maintenance cost of each asset	❑	❑
7. Distribution: be sure you...		
• plan how the product will be distributed	❑	❑
• have sufficient warehousing space	❑	❑
• know costs involved with increased distribution channels	❑	❑
• assess necessary staff to service expanded areas	❑	❑
• assess increased costs involved in packaging or shipping	❑	❑
8. Management: you will need to...		
• review the current management structure of the business	❑	❑
• identify current areas of weakness	❑	❑
• identify whether extra management staffing is required	❑	❑
• analyse who you need to fill in the gaps	❑	❑
• know where you will look to find the right person	❑	❑
• ensure you can offer a competitive salary	❑	❑

Figure 6.5	Continued

	ACTION NEEDED	COM-PLETED
• prepare job descriptions to ensure each person can competently manage the workload	❑	❑
• design a wage increase and incentive bonus system	❑	❑
• list the benefits and "perks" and their cost to the business	❑	❑
• design employment contracts that clearly outline job responsibilities and ramifications of unsatisfactory work	❑	❑
• have a lawyer review and advise on the contracts	❑	❑
• prepare detailed cost analyses for each area of the business	❑	❑
• prepare cash flow, income and expenses projections	❑	❑
• develop a system to monitor marketing strategies	❑	❑

9. **Operational structure: you may need to...**

• design detailed written company policies and procedures	❑	❑
• ensure all insurance policies are upgraded with adequate coverage	❑	❑
• ensure your staff has the necessary technical expertise		
• cope with expansion	❑	❑
• know how to control extra staff and production loads	❑	❑
• develop quality control systems	❑	❑
• know how you will deal with equipment breakdowns	❑	❑
• know where you can find replacement parts	❑	❑
• know the cost of each hour of downtime	❑	❑

10. **Logistics: be sure to...**

• assess your location and how it can cope with growth	❑	❑
• see if your lease allows for modifications to buildings	❑	❑
• analyse the costs involved in expanding current facility	❑	❑
• know when you may have to move to larger premises	❑	❑
• research alternative affordable premises	❑	❑
• research the cost of having to move	❑	❑
• know how you are going to pay for the move	❑	❑
• assess whether you would lose customers if you moved	❑	❑

....

CHAPTER 7

How Do You Find Good Help?

ARE YOU READY TO BE A BOSS?

Recognizing the need for help is a big step toward growing your business. Understanding the skills it takes to become a good employer and then finding the right person for the job are two more giant steps. If you completed the exercise in Chapter 2 identifying the various jobs, you should have a list of the tasks that are time-wasting, or areas where you need increased skills.

You have probably come to the conclusion by now that you can't do it all and grow your business as well. Getting help can be as simple as paying someone to clean your house for a few hours a week or running some errands. You don't have to become an instant employer—there are a variety of options.

Many Hands Help Business Grow

Being "the boss" sounds exciting, but it requires some serious thought. There are many benefits; some tangible, others intangible. You will have someone to bounce ideas off and work pressure will ease. You can now accelerate your work output and growth plans. You will face some unexpected challenges requiring excellent human resource skills, so ask yourself the following questions:

- Am I comfortable with delegating tasks?
- Have I clearly defined the roles and responsibilities of the new employee?
- Can the business financially afford an employee?
- Am I able to reprimand or correct an employee?
- Have I calculated the full cost of hiring?

- Could I fire an incompetent employee?
- Do I understand all my responsibilities as an employer?
- Can I clearly communicate my needs?

Expect the Unexpected

Employees tend to throw employers an array of curve balls. You will be faced with situations that include absenteeism, tardiness, illness, family emergencies, maternal leave, false references, theft, weak excuses, irresponsibility, lying, quitting, alcohol or drug abuse, poor performance and customer service.

As you plan to hire, take all these points into consideration and ask yourself how you would handle these concerns. What if you have an urgent job to complete and your employee doesn't show up? Be prepared to expect the unexpected, because it will happen.

"I CAN'T GET GOOD HELP THESE DAYS!"

Once you have made the decision to hire, you need to find the right person. If you ask growing businesses what their biggest headache is, they will usually reply: "It's finding the right employee! I can't get good help these days!" With the high rate of unemployment some provinces are experiencing, this statement doesn't seem to make sense, so let's look at some of the reasons for this dilemma.

Our Changing Society

Society has rapidly changed, so it makes sense that much of the old work ethic is disappearing. In some provinces, the effects of the 1980s recession are still apparent. Disposable income has decreased as inflation and taxes have increased. Some employers have continually demanded more from employees who have worked long-term in negative environments. Over time, many have lost their enthusiasm and motivation.

Environmental and Technological Changes

Environmental factors have changed many work situations. On both the east and west coasts, people who rely heavily on the fishing industry are affected by fish shortages or reduced quotas. Throughout Canada, whole towns lose their jobs when a mine or a mill closes.

The heady pace of technology demands that employees develop these skills. Technology has replaced countless jobs, eliminated many middle-management positions, and displaced a myriad of talented people, who are then forced to realign their careers. Employees who have only worked at one lifetime job find adapting to change and learning new skills extremely difficult.

The New Generation

Children of recent decades have grown up in a new technological and materialistic world, sometimes reared by parents who couldn't find work due to recessive conditions. They have learned that welfare and employment insurance are income options, so some grow up expecting everything without working for it. It's not surprising that employers experience difficulty finding the right person.

KNOW YOUR EMPLOYMENT OPTIONS

Once you start exploring the available hiring options, you may be surprised at your responsibilities as an employer and the costs involved. If you are home-based, there may be regulations that prevent you from hiring employees (although that doesn't stop some people). A new person requires training and orientation, so you must make this time available. Now you have to learn to delegate, supervise, praise and reprimand where necessary—skills that do not come naturally to some. However you still have a number of options to consider:

Casual Labour

Hiring someone for an occasional few hours is referred to as casual labour. In essence, these people are self-employed, so you agree to an hourly rate in return for services rendered. They should supply you with an invoice for the time worked and you should never pay "cash under the table."

Subcontract Labour

A person such as a plumber, who owns their own business and works for a variety of clients is considered a subcontractor. They should work no more than 40 percent for one employer, supply their

IDEA **PAY BY CHEQUE**

Do not succumb to requests for "cash under the table to supplement my Employment Insurance cheque." Besides being an illegal practice, the cash cannot be reported as a legitimate business expense, as usually, the payee has no intention of declaring the income. Then your financial figures do not accurately reflect your true operating costs. Always write a cheque to the person's name to correspond with the invoice amount.

own materials, and meet other criteria to qualify as a subcontractor. Canada Customs and Revenue Agency (CCRA) will mail you an informative brochure on this subject entitled "Employee or Self-Employed? R CH110."

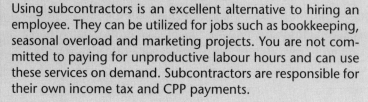

IDEA **PAY ONLY FOR HOURS WORKED**

Using subcontractors is an excellent alternative to hiring an employee. They can be utilized for jobs such as bookkeeping, seasonal overload and marketing projects. You are not committed to paying for unproductive labour hours and can use these services on demand. Subcontractors are responsible for their own income tax and CPP payments.

Self-Employed Commission

If you need sales help, you can hire a self-employed, commissioned salesperson. Bear in mind that these people could be working for other companies and may not devote their full attention to your business. If you are a manufacturer, you could use a distributor or agent to sell your products to a retailer. Distributors work on a percentage of retail price which varies from 10 to 25 percent, so there has to be room in your profit margins to absorb this cost.

Commissioned Employees

If you can find someone who is as passionate and committed about your business as you are, a commissioned salesperson could be the answer for increasing sales. The salary structure is usually calculated on a percentage of sales generated. A base salary or advance on commission is usually paid mid-month, with the balance due dependent on sales volume.

Part-Time Employees

An employee is usually considered part-time if they work less than a full-time week. The benefit of hiring on a part-time basis is that hours can be increased or decreased as needed. Part-time employees are still subject to payroll deductions but rarely receive other benefits. As you become busier, the employee can assume more responsibility and eventually become full-time.

Full-Time Employees

Be sure of the stability of your cash flow before you hire a full-time employee as you are committing to paying them regularly. As you will see in Figures 7.1 and 7.2, hiring is an expensive venture.

HOW DO YOU HIRE THE RIGHT PERSON?

Now that you are aware of the various employment options and where you need help, is it practical for one person to fill these gaps or would two part-time people with different skills be a better option? Your next step is to prioritize the position. As an example, if record-keeping is not your forte, you could prioritize the job description this way:

Priority #1—Necessary skills: Accurate bookkeeping and strong attention to detail work skills are needed. How extensive should these skills be? Do you need bookkeeping up to and including trial balance or just record-keeping with accounts receivable and payables experience?

Priority #2—Salary: What salary are you prepared to pay? Research the classifieds or ask a personnel agency to see what qualified bookkeepers are paid. Can you afford this salary?

Priority #3—Other experience: What other skills should this person have? Perhaps you need a responsible person with all-round small-office experience.

Priority #4—Public relations: Your employees always represent your company. Do you need someone with excellent telephone and customer service skills? In many cases, this priority may move further up the list.

Priority #5—Personality, attitude and motivation: These inner qualities can't be learned whereas skills can. A motivated and optimistic person is a key asset to both the business and to you.

Priority #6—Computer skills: In today's working environment, computer skills are a necessity. Are you willing to spend the time training them on specialized programs or on upgrading their current skills?

Think carefully as you compose your priority list, as these priorities will be incorporated into both your advertising and interviewing. The clearer they are, the easier it is to narrow down the candidates.

HOW TO RECRUIT THE PERFECT CANDIDATE

Although there are plenty of job-seekers, knowing where to look can be an enormous task. Which hiring method you use will no doubt depend on your time and budget.

1. Hire an employment agency

Employment agencies are an excellent, time-saving choice if you can afford the fee, which is usually 10 to 15 percent of the candidate's annual salary. Research the cost and talk to business associates who have used an agency for a recommendation.

Employment counsellors have extensive personnel experience and are trained to identify skills, strengths and weaknesses that you may miss. They will discuss your job requirements in detail, so the priority list will be most helpful. Using their extensive files, a candidate search is performed. If necessary, they will place an advertisement on your behalf. The candidates are thoroughly screened by appropriate testing, interviews, and reference checks.

You are then presented with two or three suitable candidates for interviewing and will usually be able to make a final selection. You are only charged on hiring the candidate and most agencies offer a three-month guarantee to replace unsatisfactory employees at no cost.

2. Contact community employment services

These no-cost agencies are a practical option in your search. Their primary aim is to reduce the number of people on Employment Insurance and welfare assistance. They have taken over in part from the Manpower and Human Resources offices and usually house an extensive on-line applicant base.

IDEA **BIG**

UTILIZE WAGE ASSISTANCE PROGRAMS

Many candidates have taken extensive government-sponsored courses, including retail, nursing, culinary arts, accounting and clerical. There are various provincial and federal programs that pay a portion of salary for hiring these people if you offer some on-the-job training. If you are willing to make the commitment, you may find a well-trained employee and help someone to regain their pride and workplace confidence.

3. Place a classified advertisement

If you are prepared to be inundated with resumés, placing a well-worded classified advertisement in your local or daily newspaper is not an expensive method of finding the right candidate. With your priority list in hand, now consider how to word the advertisement to appeal only to qualified candidates. Put yourself in the candidates' shoes as you compose the script. What would make you respond to this advertisement?

IDEA **BIG**

OFFER BENEFITS

Think about what you are offering besides a job. Can you offer benefits including flexible hours, growth potential, steady employment, a pleasant working environment, team spirit, or incentive programs? In a small-office environment, a bonus or incentive system will attract a motivated "go-getter."

Bold, creative headings will make your classified stand out. For example, instead of using: "Bookkeeper Wanted," which sounds boring, you could try: "Enjoy Figure Work?" This subtle change makes the classified ad immediately sound more personable and will pique the reader's curiosity.

As an example, Sandra needed some staff to expand her small cleaning business. Several advertisements had not attracted the right candidate, so she sought help from a friend who was an experienced personnel consultant. The following advertisement attracted many responses and Sandra found the perfect person for the job.

> **PRIDE IN YOUR WORK?**
>
> Small, independently-owned cleaning service is seeking a person who enjoys cleaning and takes pride in a job well-done. Flexible hours, good wages, opportunity for job security. Call Sandra at 432-9969

4. Surf the Net

Job applicants find the Internet a tremendous help in job-hunting as they can search from their keyboard and e-mail resumés. It's quick, efficient and cheap—isn't technology wonderful? Employers can utilize the many on-line employment agencies and services. Each agency will differ in its payment structure, so ensure you are dealing with a reputable company.

A most comprehensive job search site for both employees and employers is: The Canadian Jobs Catalogue at www.kenevacorp. mb.ca with over 95,000 active job openings via 3,900 Canadian

IDEA   **LINK TO YOUR WEB PAGE**

Most newspapers have an on-line classified service which incorporates both the classified ads and an on-line advertisement. Use this service, as many job seekers use the Internet. The benefits include an on-line, detailed job description and a link to your company Web page or e-mail. This enables candidates to research your business before submitting a resumé, eliminating many unsuitable applicants.

content job-related links. My husband recently landed a wonderful new position within 10 days with all the job-hunting being performed on-line. It was up-to-date, job-specific and informative. You may find that candidates who use the Internet have a progressive attitude and are computer-literate.

Remember—Don't Hire Friends

Chapter 2 suggests that you don't hire friends or relatives, so this is another gentle reminder. **DON'T**. Ask yourself: "Would firing a friend ruin our relationship? Could I feel at ease reprimanding, supervising or correcting a friend?" To reiterate, keep your friendships outside of the workplace or you may regret it as did Marilyn in the Real Life example, 'Friend or Foe?'

REAL LIFE: Friend or Foe?

Marilyn hired a trusted friend to supervise her business during Marilyn's extended absence. All appeared to be going well until another employee called her, asking to speak in confidence. It appeared that the trusted friend was indulging in afternoon-long luncheons and taking her family out on company funds—while delegating her duties to other employees.

Marilyn had no choice but to fire her friend. Not only was a close friendship lost, but Marilyn's "friend" sued her for wrongful dismissal. It was a heart-wrenching and costly experience.

WADING THROUGH THE RESUMÉ PILE

If you advertise for a candidate, wading through piles of resumés is an unavoidable and tedious chore. You can shorten the process, by using coloured highlighters to follow these basic steps:

1. Quickly read each resumé, highlighting each candidate's qualifications that fit your parameters.
2. Change colours and highlight the negative aspects.
3. Mark each resumé with an "A+", "A"," B" or "C" grading.
4. Re-read the "A+" and "A" resumés thoroughly.

You will find that the people with the most positive qualifications will be graded as an "A+." If you are fortunate, you will now have two or three suitable candidates and are ready to start the interviewing process.

THE ART OF SUCCESSFUL INTERVIEWING

To ensure that you cover all the pertinent interview questions, make a list of them by rereading the candidate's resumé and your job description. Highlight areas in the resumé that you wish to question or discuss. You can't remember everything so make notes during the interview.

1. **Fulfilling your job description:** You now have a list of job priorities to discuss with the candidate, so start by outlining the position in order of priority, stressing the most important duties. Then ask the candidate: "Do you think you can handle this job? Does it appeal to you?" Listen carefully to their answer. Did they honestly appear to answer "yes" without too much hesitation? If they hesitate, ask what their concerns are.

2. **Thoroughly review the resumé:** Explore the resumé in detail with the candidate, particularly the reasons for leaving other jobs. You will learn a lot by listening carefully to their answers. Do they blame others or their past bosses for lost jobs? This could be a warning sign. Review qualifications and any certifications. A keen candidate will bring their certificates with them.

IDEA **ASSESS COMMUNICATION SKILLS**

If you require excellent customer service skills, assess the candidate's personality and communication skills. How they interact with you will be indicative of how they will communicate in business. If you sense any negativity in your discussion, the candidate may have an attitude problem.

3. **Personal information:** Although it would be ideal to know the candidate's marital and family status, health, age, and other factors that may affect work performance, human rights legislation prohibits these questions from being asked. If you use

an employment agency, they can ask these questions as an option on their application form, but they cannot be asked in an interview. You will only find out this information if it is volunteered, and you must not let it affect your hiring decision.

4. **Ask about expectations:** Find out what the candidate's future career goals are and how long they see this position meeting their needs. Then ask what they expect of you as an employer. Then tell them what you expect of an employee. Ted, a highly successful entrepreneur, has always asked these last two qualifying questions and found them to be most helpful in the final selection process. Discuss salary expectations, benefits, and how you see the candidate fitting in long-term.

THANK APPLICANTS

Once you have selected an employee, please contact all the unsuccessful applicants. It is a tedious chore, but behind every resumé there is a person who is seeking employment and perhaps suffering from loss of confidence. He or she has taken the time to reply to you and deserves a response.

REFERENCE CHECKS AND TESTING

The golden rule for checking references is: *Never hire a candidate without a thorough reference check.* Don't put too much stock in personal references, as it is common practice to have friends and relatives lie, or exaggerate or not know the whole story, as shown in the Real Life example 'No Check—No Money.'

<u>REAL LIFE:</u> No Check—No Money

A busy hairdressing salon owner desperately needed an employee when a stylist quit without notice. A friend recommended someone she had known for years, who was hired instantly without references being checked. It was later discovered that the employee had been liberally helping herself to the till and pocketing business income paid to her by clients.

On investigating the employee's background, a belated reference check found one business that refused to give the employee a reference, while the other had fired her for the same reason.

Eight Essential Employment Questions

Insist on business-related references where possible, then call to find out the following information. If someone refuses to give a reference, consider this a red flag. Try talking to someone in a position of authority at the same business, or do not hire the candidate. If an employee was entirely satisfactory, employers are usually more than willing to give a good reference.

1. **Employment:** Confirm the dates, position held and job responsibilities.
2. **Work habits:** Was the candidate punctual, reliable and motivated without undue absenteeism?
3. **Relationships:** How did the candidate relate to other employees?
4. **Supervision:** How did he or she cope with being supervised? If the job involved a supervisory role, was it performed successfully?
5. **Personality traits:** Was the candidate honest, trustworthy, cheerful and positive?
6. **Negatives:** Were there any negative aspects you should know about?
7. **Positives:** Were there any positive aspects that made this candidate special?
8. **Rehire:** Given the right circumstances, would you rehire the candidate?

Is Testing Necessary?

If you have carefully checked references plus performed a thorough interview, testing candidates shouldn't be necessary. However, in some situations, a basic test will put your mind at ease. Ted owns a printing business and is knowledgeable in operating all the printing equipment. During interviews, he would ask candidates technical questions, and if they were not answered to his satisfaction, he would not hire them. At times, he would ask a candidate to operate a press. His success rate at hiring the right employee has been nearly 100 percent.

IDEA

DESIGN A BASIC TEST

If the position requires preparing correspondence or using a software program, ask the candidate to compose and type a business letter or enter some data to the accounting program. Technicians could be asked to answer some specific questions and tradespeople to demonstrate their abilities. Some employment agencies offer applicant testing, usually for a fee. This may be a viable option if you are not comfortable doing it yourself.

YOUR RESPONSIBILITIES AS AN EMPLOYER

Hiring the right employee is only one part of being an employer. You need to understand all the other responsibilities involved in becoming a boss. This includes determining your hiring structure, knowing the extra costs involved, and tackling any problems you encounter.

Hiring the Self-Employed

The term "self-employed" applies to casual labour, subcontractors and self-employed commissioned salespeople. If they do not have Workers' Compensation coverage, then it is usually your responsibility to provide it, so check the labour codes and Workers' Compensation regulations in your province. You do not pay any employee benefits. Self-employed people should bill you at least monthly.

Some chintzy employers hire people on a subcontract instead of what should be—an employee basis—a common and illegal practice. Many clients have come to me for accounting sevices at year-end to report their subcontract earnings, only to discover that they have to pay large tax and CPP sums as they have worked full-time for one employer. If these people report you to the provincial Ministry of Labour, you may be liable for unpaid employee benefits, overtime and vacation pay.

Commissioned Salespeople

Whether you hire on a self-employed or salaried commission structure, you will have to decide which expenses (such as cellular telephone and auto costs) will be paid by your business. Some pay a monthly non-taxable vehicle allowance, so clearly define your expense limits. If the salesperson works only for you, they should be hired as an employee.

Employees should complete a weekly expense report, including a mileage log of all business-related trips. Normal commissioned expenses can include an automobile, telephone, clients' lunches, travel expenses and a home office. Create a policy dictating whether the employee can claim "other employment expenses" on their personal taxes. To claim this, the employer must sign a T2200 at year-end, agreeing to the expenses the employee incurred to generate a commissioned income.

Part- and Full-Time Employees

Become conversant with provincial employment standards and federal payroll requirements. Understand your obligations, including overtime, statutory holidays, vacation pay, and termination procedures. Your provincial Ministry of Labour will send you a copy of their *Employment Standards Act*.

You must maintain detailed payroll records for all employees. Payroll remittances to Canada Customs and Revenue Agency (CCRA) are due by the 15th of each month. At year-end, the payroll is reconciled and T4s prepared. It's wise to prepare a full job description outlining the employee's responsibilities, followed up by a meeting with the employee to discuss and clarify issues. An employment contract safeguards against future disputes, so consulting with an experienced lawyer is advisable.

HOW MUCH DOES AN EMPLOYEE COST?

For a full-time employee, the hourly rate is just the start of your expenses. Add a 20 percent margin to the salary to cover all mandatory costs. Figure 7.1 shows an example of a monthly salary calculation. Workers' Compensation rates will vary from province to province.

Figure 7.1	Example of a Monthly Salary Calculation

Hourly wages: $12.00 x 40 hours x 4.19 weeks =	2,011.20
One statutory holiday per month	96.00
Four percent vacation pay	84.28
	2,191.48
CPP: 3.9% (less annual exemption)	76.55
Employment Insurance: 2.4% x 1.4	75.75
Workers' Compensation (average rate $4.00/$100)	87.65
Total monthly costs:	**$ 2,431.43**

This employee costs an extra $2.50 an hour with an average of two-and-one-half days a month being non-productive due to statutory holidays and vacation pay. None of these costs—excluding Workers' Compensation—apply to subcontractors, so be fair when you negotiate their rate. They don't qualify for Employment Insurance plus pay their own CPP contributions, and receive no paid vacations.

Other Costly Factors

The cost of hiring doesn't stop at wages. There are many incidental expenses that employees generate. To help plan your cash-flow, review Figure 7.2 and check those which apply to you and estimate how much the expenses total on a monthly basis.

HOW TO MOTIVATE YOUR EMPLOYEES

There is a fine line between being "a good boss" and becoming too friendly with your staff. Unfortunately, countless employees have taken advantage of their employers by building a relationship of trust and then adversely using it. Conversely, the stories of "bad bosses" are common. Most people have experienced one during their working life. These negative experiences can sour employees and prevent them from giving you their utmost.

Figure 7.2	Fundamental Expense That an Employee Can Generate

	Amount
❏ coffee, bottled water, snacks	_____
❏ new lunchroom equipment	_____
❏ office equipment and furniture	_____
❏ computer and accessories	_____
❏ expense account items (auto, travel etc.)	_____
❏ cellular telephone or pager	_____
❏ bonuses or incentives	_____
❏ corporate clothing	_____
❏ stationery and business cards	_____
❏ telephone line	_____
❏ rental of parking space	_____
❏ medical benefits	_____
❏ staff lunches	_____
❏ training programs	_____
❏ sick leave	_____
❏ vehicle allowance	_____
Total additional costs:	$ _____

Many bosses forget to reward their employees. There are some simple formulas that cost little but will enhance your employee's performance if you apply them and work together to develop a team spirit. Remember that your employees represent your business, so their complaining can cause irreparable damage to your reputation.

Take the "Good Boss, Bad Boss" test in Figure 7.3 and see how you score. Of course, the more answers you check under 'good boss,' the better relationship you will build with your employees and the more productive their output. Now you are team-building.

IDEA

SHOW YOUR APPRECIATION

The secret to a successful employee-employer relationship is team-building. Make each employee feel an important part of the business—which they are. Use encouragement, show appreciation and caring, while still maintaining rules and boundaries. Ensure there are more rewards at the end of the day than money.

EMPLOYEE THEFT—AN EMPLOYER'S NIGHTMARE

The innovative methods that employees use to steal from employers could fill a book. The message intended here is to warn you not to be too trusting or create tempting situations. Incorporate systems that will curtail theft or keep it to a minimum. Here are some of the more common methods of stealing.

Time Theft

Employees will steal copious time from you, often without you realizing it. Those few extra minutes at breaks, lengthy personal phone calls, playing computer games on company time, sending personal e-mails, Internet-surfing, arriving late and leaving early, not using equipment correctly and causing breakdowns, taking days off for personal reasons but calling in sick, being hungover and working slower, making stupid errors, taking personal detours on company business, and using company vehicles for personal matters. Where will you draw the line?

Merchandise Theft

Employees often take things that don't belong to them. It could be as small as a stapler or as large as a sofa. Theft can be difficult to detect, such as a nibble from the deli section. Make your policies and consequences clear. Ensure you have a foolproof inventory and administrative system.

Figure 7.3	The Do's and Don'ts of Team-Building—Good Boss Bad Boss Quiz

POSITIVE: GOOD BOSS

❑ Always say thank-you for a job well done

❑ Praise and reward extra efforts

❑ Meet regularly to discuss problems and listen to employees' concerns

❑ Start an incentive system

❑ Be understanding of family crises and allow time off for urgent matters

❑ Take employees to lunch occasionally

❑ Send sick employees home

❑ Ask how the family is

❑ Discuss situations that could threaten an employee's job, such as work shortage

❑ Review performance and salaries regularly and discuss any job-related concerns

❑ Throw a Christmas party or summer barbeque

❑ Clearly define job responsibilities

❑ Share your business successes and keep employees informed of business progress

❑ Allow adequate learning and training time

❑ Give adequate warnings of potential layoffs

❑ Ask if employees will work overtime

❑ Pay overtime at the correct scale

❑ Don't penalize an employee for arriving late due to an emergency situation

❑ Keep your mind and door open

NEGATIVE: BAD BOSS

❑ Take the "that's what they are paid for" attitude

❑ Expect employees to continually give without recognition

❑ Ignore concerns because it must be done your way

❑ Complain about rising wage costs

❑ Threaten employee with loss of job if too much time off is taken

❑ Do nothing

❑ Make them stay at work

❑ Show no caring or concern

❑ Tell employees that their job could be on the line if they don't perform

❑ Give only mandatory raises and threaten layoff if work performance doesn't improve

❑ Do nothing

❑ Expect employees to do anything you ask

❑ Take all the credit and tell them nothing about the business

❑ Expect employees to learn immediately

❑ Fire or lay employees off on the spot

❑ Demand that they work overtime

❑ Pay at normal hourly rate

❑ Deduct pay for every minute not worked no matter what the situation

❑ Keep your mind and door closed

Cash Theft

If you have an efficient accounting system, cash thefts can usually be discovered. Monitor the petty cash and make sure there is an official receipt for each expense. Retail stores experience great difficulty with cash, so balance the till each night and make employees accountable for losses. Cash used from the till must have a supporting invoice. Watch for repetitive shortages during one person's shift as was the case in the Real Life example, 'Stealing With a Smile.' Know all the suppliers that you write cheques to and review the disbursements once a month.

REAL LIFE: Stealing With a Smile

A sales assistant I once heard of insisted on taking the lunch shift and sending her boss out to "make sure she ate well and had a break." When merchandise was sold during this period, she would ring up the sale, then ask the customer if they needed a receipt. If they said no, she later voided the sale, pocketing the cash.

Finally becoming suspicious, the owner monitored the till tapes closely, discovering the consistent lunchtime voids. The employee was fired, but the estimated loss over a period of time amounted to thousands of dollars.

Computer Theft

Files and programs can be copied onto disks in seconds and slipped into a purse or briefcase. Installing computer security systems may be necessary. One enterprising young lady working in a large payroll department created two fictitious employees, prepared computerized cheques, opened false bank accounts, and regularly cashed the cheques. She also gave herself a few hundred dollars a month raise. Because of the large volume of cheques, the employer signed them quickly and didn't get suspicious for quite a few months. The total documented theft amounted to over $10,000.

Reputation Theft

A disgruntled employee can do significant damage to your reputation. This can be effected by maliciously gossiping to other employees and undermining their working relationship, or by "bad-mouthing" you to friends, clients and business associates. Either way, your hard work is being destroyed by one malcontent. Watch for subtle warning signs of a troublemaker and keep an open line of communication with your employees.

White-Collar Crime

Examples of this nature are referred to as white-collar crime. In many documented cases, theft from an employer seems not to be taken as seriously as crimes involving violence or even shoplifting. It is difficult to prove unless accurate accounting records are maintained and evidence carefully documented.

Having worked with the Commercial Crime division in both Canada and the United States, I was sickened over a case that caused the closure of a large company due to money laundering and inventory theft of well over $100,000. The men involved were never charged. All you can do is install theft-proof systems and monitor your employees' actions closely.

YOUR HIRING CHECKLIST

If you are ready to take on the responsibility of becoming an employer, use Figure 7.4 to ensure that you follow all the right steps. If you need more detailed information, read *Hiring, Managing and Keeping the Best* by Monica Beauregard and Maureen Fitzgerald in the McGraw-Hill Ryerson SOHO series. It is packed with valuable information not only on the hiring process, but also on how to motivate and keep your employees.

You Need More Than Good Help

You now have some hiring guidelines, and when your new team is in place, you are ready to take a giant step forward—nearly. You now need to increase sales to justify your hiring. Before you can effectively market and sell, you need to better know to whom you are marketing. Chapter 8 shows you how to better define your customers and how to revise your marketing plan.

Figure 7.4	Your Hiring Checklist

	YES	NO
1. I feel that I possess the required skills to direct an employee.	❏	❏
2. I have defined a need for an employee.	❏	❏
3. I have prepared a detailed job description.	❏	❏
4. I know under which terms I will hire.	❏	❏
5 I have prepared my job priority list.	❏	❏
6. I know which methods are best to locate an employee.	❏	❏
7. I know the benefits I will offer.	❏	❏
8. I have read and graded the resumés.	❏	❏
9. I have made a list of questions for the interviews.	❏	❏
10. I have written out my expectations of an employee.	❏	❏
11. I have checked three business references.	❏	❏
12. I have performed a basic test.	❏	❏
13. I understand my responsibilities as an employer.	❏	❏
14. I have calculated the additional payroll costs.	❏	❏
15. I have calculated the additional associated costs.	❏	❏
16. I understand what constitutes a "good boss."	❏	❏
17. I am aware of theft and have taken steps to prevent it.	❏	❏
18. I can afford to pay an employee.	❏	❏
19. I have read and understand the provincial labour act.	❏	❏
20. I understand the Workers' Compensation requirements.	❏	❏

....

CHAPTER 8

How Do You Grow Your Customer Base?

ARE YOU MISSING YOUR MARKET?

"I can't seem to find new customers," many frustrated entrepreneurs lament. "My advertising isn't working for me!" Although not an uncommon dilemma, lack of focussed marketing means inadequate sales. If you don't know where or who to promote your business to, telling the world how great you are can be a costly and futile experience.

There are many effective, low-cost marketing methods you can use, although they all require commitment and capital. If you have a specific target market, the results will be far superior.

Change Marketing Techniques

You are confronted by a vast selection of marketing tools, and each day, the choices grow as technology progresses. The Internet is a classic example of how most businesses are being forced to change their marketing strategies. Seems that now if you don't have a Web

IDEA

BIG

TRY *NOT* MARKETING

Few customers are going to knock on your door to give you business. *You* have to make it happen. The minute you stop promoting a new business, business stops. Sourcing potential sales, finding avenues for promotion and follow-up should be part of your daily routine. Try an experiment. Stop calling and sourcing out business for a week or two and see how quiet your phone becomes.

site, you are hardly taken seriously. The key to successful marketing is to keep up with these changes and focus your strategies on the direction that consumer trends are taking.

So how do you increase your customer base? Where are they? Who are they? You need many of your eight essential entrepreneurial skills to feel comfortable with the challenges that marketing poses. If you use "hit and miss" techniques, these costly adventures usually have minimal return for a maximum outlay. There are better ways to market that will guarantee you long-term business, and these are described in Chapters 11 and 12.

UNDERSTAND THE COMPONENTS OF MARKETING

There are many misconceptions about what marketing really means. Marketing is not selling—selling is selling.

Marketing Is...

Marketing is informing potential clients about your products or services. Before you start to plan your marketing stategies, you should have defined who and where your market is. To market, you have to advertise and promote to specific consumers using various methods.

Your next goal is to increase your client base. "Targeting your market" refers to finding out who needs your business and narrowing your marketing focus toward these people.

Promotion Is...

Promotion refers to the various techniques that you use to attract customers. You can network, communicate with potential clients, go to a trade show, hold an open house or grand opening, and advertise. Other methods include sponsoring a community organization, entering parades, speaking to groups, or holding workshops or seminars.

Advertising Is...

Advertising is using the various media to carry your message. These include radio, television, the Internet, coupons, flyers or other printed media. Many people mistakenly think that printed advertising is the only way to get their name known, as is evident by the number of advertisements in newspapers and magazines and by the piles of flyers delivered to your mailbox. Consumers are overwhelmed with advertising, so before you spend expensive dollars, research the success of these methods.

IDEA — PLAN WELL AHEAD

You should try to plan up to a year ahead, regularly reviewing the results to monitor both the cost and effectiveness of your strategies. Like most plans, it will be subject to change. You may try a type of advertising or promotion that doesn't reap the expected results. Conversely, you may find that one form of promotion or advertising works better than others and have to adjust your strategies accordingly.

REVISIT YOUR MARKETING PLAN

A marketing plan is an integral part of your business plan. If you are experiencing difficulty increasing sales, revisit, reevaluate and revise your plan. It is a necessary guide to marketing your business, which methods you will use, when you will use them, and what the cost will be.

REEVALUATE YOUR MARKETING PLAN

If your original marketing plan isn't reaping the desired results, it's time to reevaluate why. Many factors affect how consumers view your business and how and when they will spend their money. You may have found that your products or services need modifying to keep up with changing economic or technological trends. Study your past methods of reaching out to consumers and ask yourself these questions:

1. Is what you thought would work still working?
2. How has it changed?
3. What methods are succeeding and producing profitable sales?
4. What isn't working?
5. Has your original market focus changed?

6. Why?

7. Is this a long or short-term change?

8. Are you spending enough time and money on marketing?

Evaluate Changing Trends

Realize that trends will directly affect your business. Is the market growing, consistent, or slowly declining? Are prices becoming more competitive? Is technology changing to a point where it may affect your sales in a year's time? Are consumer trends changing? People often become so consumed with their business that they are ignorant of the rapidly changing world around them.

Evaluate Finances

There is no way around it. Money is necessary for increasing your customer base, so you have to calculate how much you can afford to spend on marketing each month. Under-budgeting is an expensive mistake. Most businesses start on a shoestring budget, usually leaving little room for continued marketing costs. By preparing an annual cashflow projection, your figures will indicate how much room there is in your budget for marketing. To reiterate—no marketing equals no sales.

REVISE YOUR MARKETING PLAN

To revise your marketing plan, you need to realize that there is more to marketing than just advertising and promotion. This section will guide you through the various components of reevaluating and revising your plan, with suggestions for improvement.

These components are divided into four categories:

1. Your business image
2. Identifying your market
3. Your marketing budget
4. Your marketing techniques (see Chapters 11 and 12).

1. Your Business Image

Businesses are judged on first impressions, so ensure that yours is always professionally presented to customers. There's no time like the present to assess your image and fine-tune it if it is a little scruffy. Start by revisiting these five important areas.

Name: People remember businesses with clever or easy to remember names. Does your name aptly describe what you do? One curbing company named their business Perimeter Curbing Ltd. They promoted their business in such a way that people called and ask for "some of that perimeter curbing stuff." How many people ask for "Kleenex" instead of tissues?

MAKE YOUR NAME WORK FOR YOU

One woman who sells therapeutic mattresses calls her business Sleep Matters. Another woman named her mattress store Sleep Depot—short, snappy and easily remembered. It certainly beats E.D. Enterprises. What is E.D. Enterprises anyway? Make your name market your business and work for you. It's the beginning of low-cost marketing magic.

If you have a registered name and don't want to change it, retain the original name and create a "byline" name. As an example, my business started in 1983 as Eastleigh Management Services, as it was located on Eastleigh Crescent. My Web site domain is www.smallbizpro.com. I am now changing my marketing technique to utilize Smallbizpro, but will retain the original business name, which appears on all corporate stationery.

Logo or slogan: If you don't have a logo or slogan, consult with a graphics professional to design you a corporate image. Everyone recognizes the K-Mart and McDonald's logos. One Canadian moving company named their business "Two Small Men With Big Hearts Moving Co." Their name became their slogan and is easily remembered.

Others use simple but easy-to-remember slogans. I use "The small business specialist." Your logo or slogan can work hard for you if you are creative. A little naughty but never forgotten is the scaffolding company whose slogan found on their tee-shirts reads "Call us for an instant erection." Say no more.

Mission statement: A mission statement is a few sentences that reflect your business goals and commitment to your clients. Seeing this written statement always reminds you of why you are in business, and indicates to clients that you care. It can be short and simple but should capture the spirit of your business. For a service business, it could be a sentence such as: "To always be there for our clients in times of emergency, and to never keep them waiting." This simple statement really says to the consumer: "I care about you."

IDEA **SPLASH YOUR MISSION STATEMENT AROUND**

Writing down your mission statement makes you more committed to excellence. Splash it on brochures and promotional material. This reflects a professional attitude to clients. Many businesses hang their framed mission statement in offices or reception areas where clients can see them.

Staff and business appearance: Take a complete inventory of the physical appearance of your business, including the office, vehicles, staff, and your personal appearance. What looks untidy, dirty, or badly-organized? See it from a customer's point of view on their first visit. Would they be impressed?

A dirty or untidy store reflects to customers that perhaps this business is unorganized or doesn't care. Ensure that you and your employees are well groomed. Even a mechanic can wear clean coveralls. Remember—first impressions are critical.

Corporate theme: Have your logo and name printed on hats, tee-shirts and coveralls. Counter staff or representatives should have corporate shirts, sweaters or golf shirts. Make sure they are regularly laundered so that employees always present a clean and professional business image. The investment in corporate clothing will more than pay off.

If you don't have a "corporate theme," develop one. Your theme should incorporate all of the above: a snappy name, logo or slogan, and mission statement, with clothing, vehicles, promotional material and stationery all proudly bearing your corporate image.

2. Identify Your Market

Perhaps you didn't start with a researched knowledge of where and who your market is. As an example, a fashion boutique proprietor felt that her market was all the women in her community, but it wasn't. Her clothes were expensive, and she was located in a small strip mall in a middle- to lower-class community where the average person couldn't afford to pay her prices. There were more accessible fashion stores in a nearby larger mall. The business closed in under a year.

A new landscaping business felt its market would be anyone who owned a house and garden, particularly as the business operated in an area with many new houses. This was a wrong assumption. Most of the houses in this middle-income estate had small garden lots. It didn't take much effort for the owners to prepare the garden themselves using bark mulch, a few rocks, plants and turf. A few used the landscaping service, but nowhere near as many as was expected.

Understanding the demographics of your consumers—that is, who and where they are—allows for focussed planning of your marketing campaign. How do you find this information? Find the answers to these questions:

- What are your market demographics?
- What age groups use your business?
- Where do they shop?
- Are you catering to residential or commercial consumers?

Define your market demographics: Are you familiar with the demographics of your marketing area? Different methods are needed to target consumers who live in different types of residences. Where people live will determine how and what they buy. An apartment dweller has no use for a sit-down lawn tractor. Does your area consist of detached houses, townhouses, apartments, small or large farms, industrial areas or commercial offices?

IDEA   STUDY THE POPULATION

Study your area, breaking it down into the above categories, and note where the main concentration of each type of dwelling or business is. What percentage of the population is transient or seniors? This knowledge is helpful for planning your marketing focus. Your municipal hall can help you with many of these statistics.

Know the age of your average consumer: What is the average age group of people who use your business? Are you in the right location to service them? Many communities have concentrated populations of certain age groups, such as townhouse complexes. Your marketing should be designed to attract the main age group that you are targeting.

For example, stores such as Bootlegger and The Gap specifically cater to teenagers as they spend a tremendous amount of money on "looking cool." The stores are located in busy malls because "hanging out at the mall" is one of their favourite pastimes.

Understand consumers' shopping habits: If you understand how and where the average consumer shops, you can better target your marketing to accommodate their needs. Most people don't have time for shopping anymore, so you have to know how to make your business readily accessible to customers. Supermarkets now gear to our "too busy" society by offering Internet shopping—my personal dream come true. Use the marketing survey found at Figure 8.1 to research this information.

Residential or commercial consumers: Are you targeting residential or commercial business? Which portion of your business generates more profits? Some janitorial companies focus on commercial buildings yet will clean the occasional house. Some make the mistake of taking anything that comes along, losing their focus and not specializing in one area.

Determine which type of market you are catering to and focus on it. You can diversify later when you are more established. Remember—it is better to become known as the expert in one area than to bounce from pillar to post and be master of none.

Use these avenues to conduct your market research:

- Visit your municipal offices and ask for any information they may have on local demographics—many have access to valuable information that will shorten research time.
- Research your competitors using the Yellow Pages. You could pretend to be a consumer and phone competitors to ask questions. Study their advertisements in the local papers to see what they offer.
- Visit your local chamber of commerce and talk to the business information centre representative. They work closely with the

business community and have a membership list. If you are a member, this list will give you an indication of similar businesses in your community.

- Go surfing on the Internet and browse competitors' Web sites. You may find some new and innovative marketing ideas.
- Visit trade shows that attract businesses similar to yours to see how competitors and other businesses market their wares. You will come away full of new ideas and also be on top of what the competitors are offering.

Physical boundaries: If you are a retail outlet, most of your business will be generated from the local community. Therefore, it's useless to advertise outside of this geographic area unless you are a specialized business. If this is the case, your advertising could extend well beyond your community.

STUDY PREVIOUS CUSTOMERS

Look at past sales records and see where your business has come from. If over 60 percent is local, then your marketing should focus locally. However, if your service can be offered outside of your community, calculate what physical boundaries are practical. Take into consideration travelling time and your hourly billing rate. Is it profitable to travel farther afield? Or could your networking contacts help you to build your reputation and hence your business closer to your home-base?

Competition: In a society where dollars mean everything and disposable incomes are shrinking, customer loyalty is often dictated by their wallets. Investigate your competitors regularly. Study pricing, product lines, advertising and promotion techniques, and customer service policies.

Find out: How long have they been in business? Do people travel a distance to their location? Why? How busy are they? How do they treat their customers? Study their displays to see what appeals to the customers. Think of innovative methods that will allow you to compete without resorting to price-cutting.

IDEA BIG

DON'T MAKE CUSTOMERS WAIT

An Angus and Reid poll conducted recently in Canada asked 1,500 consumers about service. The average person will not wait more than two minutes in a lineup before leaving the store, and they want to be served by knowledgeable people. Forty percent stated that they did not return to stores when these problems were experienced. Being an expert is important to the consumer, as is prompt service. Compared to your competition, are you currently offering the same or better service and expertise to your clients? If your answer is no, then get to work to remedy this.

Consumers' incomes: You won't sell antiques to people living in a low-income area, nor will you succeed in selling cheap products to affluent people. Define the income bracket of the majority of people in your marketing area. If it is 60 percent middle-income and 30 percent low-income, your marketing methods, product mix or service should be geared to accommodate these people.

Changing trends and spending habits: Consumers spend in cycles dictated by the time of year, their financial position, changing trends, and the time they have for shopping. Families with two working parents are usually looking for the quickest way to obtain the best product or service at the cheapest price.

Talk to as many people as you can, telling them about your business, and ask them their expectations of an ideal business. Listen to their answers—you may find some innovative ways to market that will fulfill these needs.

IDEA BIG

CAPITALIZE ON TRENDS

Keep abreast of current and predicted consumer trends. If the economy is suffering, how could you address the fact that people have less disposable income? Unusual situations such as the Year 2000 predicted chaos saw a surge in sales for products such as freeze-dried, canned and packaged foods, camping equipment, earthquake preparedness kits and computer upgrading. How could you capitalize on these situations?

Service the home-based businesses: Don't discount the home-based business sector. How could you service these people? One large retail office store offers home delivery within 24 hours for orders over a certain amount. The local dairy now carries a variety of foods for their home delivery service. In-home dry-cleaning pick-up and delivery service, personal coaches, massage, vehicle repairs and personal chefs all cater to the millions of people working from home who need convenience, so why not your business too?

Take a market survey: The best way to evaluate if you are providing what your customers need is to ask them. Prepare a small marketing survey with a list of questions pertinent to your business. Ask consumers about your products, prices, what they expect, and how regularly they would use your business. See Figure 8.1 for a sample survey.

IDEA · BIG ·

REWARD SURVEY PARTICIPANTS

Spend time talking to a cross-section of people who live in different community areas. As a thank-you, present them with a gift certificate or a small gift from your business, along with a business card. If you don't have time to do this, pay a college marketing student to do it for you, although you will get more information if you do it yourself. You could encourage people to fill out the questionnaire by offering a chance to win a draw prize for completed surveys.

Tabulate survey results: This information is invaluable for formulating your revised marketing plan. Try to complete at least 30 surveys, then compile the results. Study them carefully to see how and where you should focus your future marketing strategies.

I recently taught a horse entrepreneurship university college course at Kwantlen University College in Langley, B.C. and asked the students to survey 10 people. The results from even this small survey were surprising—some business plans were changed or even scrapped based on consumers' responses. What the students thought consumers would like or pay differed from what consumers felt.

Figure 8.1	**Consumer Market Survey**

1) Why would you use this type of business?

2) How often would you need these services or buy these products?

3) What is the final factor in making a purchase—price or service?

4) What kind of service do you expect?

5) What type of after-sales service and warranties would you expect?

6) What would you pay for a service/products such as these?

   Service _____ Price _____

7) Have you heard of this business before?

8) Where did you hear about it?

9) Where would you shop for this type of product/service?

10) Where do you do most of your shopping?

11) What services would the ideal business provide to you?

12) Which newspapers or magazines do you read regularly?

13) Which are your favourite radio and TV stations?

14) What is your age?

15) How large is your family?

16) What type of work do you do?

17) What are your hobbies and interests?

Your ideal consumer profile: After your research is completed, you will have an excellent profile of your ideal consumer. You now know your geographical boundaries, how people live, whether you should service the commercial or residential market, and what your competition is doing. You know your consumers' average age and income bracket, and where and how they shop. Even more valuable information will be what they read, listen to and watch.

You will have a better understanding of whether consumers will use your business and what their expectations are. Now you can plan how to target this market without wasting valuable dollars.

3. Your Marketing Budget

Before you plan your marketing budget, read the following two marketing chapters to define the most effective methods that will work for you. You will need to plan ahead, identify the techniques that will work for you, and monitor the results.

Plan ahead: Timing is crucial for planning and implementing your marketing ideas. There are times when it doesn't even pay to advertise. Do people really want their furnaces serviced in summer? No— but they are thinking about it in the fall, so you should start a strong marketing push when children return to school. You can offer specials during the slow season, but don't expect overwhelming results.

IDEA **BIG** **BOOK SPACE EARLY**

If you choose to advertise in newspapers or magazines, be familiar with their copy and camera-ready art work deadlines. Magazines usually require copy two months ahead of printing. If you are booking a trade show or mall display, obtain their annual program of events, as many of the spaces are booked up to a year in advance. Newspapers and magazines supply annual schedules of publishing themes, and you can usually obtain a copy by phoning.

Set a budget: If your business is still new, you may have to spend 10 to 15 percent of projected sales to get and keep your name recognized. A marketing budget should never be less than four percent of gross sales.

If your business grosses $5,000 a month, you should be spending between $200 and $750 a month on marketing. Some of these costs have to be paid in advance, such as trade show deposits, so have the available funds. You have to spend money to make money.

Review annual sales figures month-by-month to decide which months need an advertising push. Capitalize on special events and seasons such as Christmas. Your name needs to be consistently in consumers' eyes, so have funds available each month for some form of promotion. If you can't afford to spend the money, consult your accountant for some advice.

Combine techniques: One strong push won't bring long-term business, so as you plan your budget, allow for using a combination of techniques. This may include a trade show, seminar or workshop, coupled with a small advertisement in the local paper, or a press release. Set out an annual schedule and use a mix of techniques that will have their most powerful results during your peak selling seasons.

Figure 8.2 shows an example of a four-month marketing plan for residential air purifiers, using a marketing budget of five percent of projected sales. The owner plans to use a well-rounded, low-cost yet effective mix of marketing techniques.

Monitor results: No doubt you have tried various marketing methods and have some idea of what is working for you—and what isn't. The key to evaluating each new technique is monitoring the results. When customers call or come into your store, politely ask them where or how they heard of you, then tabulate this information.

IDEA BIG

USE A SIMPLE LEAD MONITORING SYSTEM

For phone enquiries, keep a two-copy message book by the phone, noting how the caller heard about your business. Add a line "referred by" to your sales invoices and then transfer the information to your invoice. You now have a permanent record of how sales or leads were generated. You can review the invoices and messages each month to monitor the results. This is necessary information for formulating future marketing plans.

To recap, when you revise your marketing plan, you should:

- always present a professional business image
- design an effective name, logo, slogan and mission statement
- know your consumer demographics intimately

- be familiar with competitors' products and prices
- be aware of current and future consumer trends
- know how much you can afford to spend each month on marketing
- know the seasonal trends for your business
- know which marketing methods will work for you
- monitor all calls and record where the leads came from.

Figure 8.2	Marketing Plan

PERFECT AIR HOME FILTRATION SYSTEMS
JANUARY 20__ TO DECEMBER 20__

SALES AND BUDGET	JAN	FEB	MAR	APRIL
Projected sales	$10,000	$12,500	$15,000	$16,000
5% marketing budget	500	625	750	800
MARKETING METHODS				
Spring home trade show		385		
Chamber business-after-business			70	
Conferences	80			130
Community newspaper, weekly small display ad	120	120	120	120
Mall display, home show weekend				200
Networking luncheon	15	15	15	15
Chamber monthly dinner	25	25	25	25
Press releases re-new product	0	0	0	0
Product evaluation	180		180	
Web site hosting	30	30	30	30
Newsletter to clients and prospects			250	
Coupons, cards, gifts, promotional aids	50	50	50	50
Brochure printing				230
TOTAL COST:	**$500**	**$625**	**$740**	**$800**

HOW DO YOU BETTER TARGET YOUR MARKET?

The big question still remains unanswered—how do you reach these consumers now that you know who and where they are? There is no magical formula—you have to work this one out for yourself. The marketing chapters will give you some innovative ideas.

Once you understand your consumers' needs, you will be able to eliminate expensive marketing methods. The more paper you print, the more you are going to spend on advertising. If your consumer market is teenagers to college students, think about where these people spend most of their time. Could you introduce your business to schools or colleges? If your market is senior citizens, how could you introduce your business to seniors' complexes, rest homes or recreation centres?

IDEA **BIG** : | **WEAR THE CONSUMER'S SHOES**
Identify the marketing techniques that you have responded to as a consumer. Note the ones that persuaded you to purchase a product or use a service. Would any of these methods work for you? How can you apply them to your business?

A simple fridge magnet is a permanent reminder of your name and telephone number. These magnets are a *must* for service businesses. Most fridges sport an array of them. Consumers always use them and they are useful for pinning up children's artwork.

Marketing is a continued mix of "keeping your name out there." Some methods are short-lived and temporary in their effectiveness, such as newspaper or radio advertisements. Make sure you find the right balance and combination for your business.

Have you ever listened to the radio in your car and wanted to write down a telephone number in rush-hour traffic? It's logistically impossible. Therefore these techniques should always be complemented by other long-term methods such as joining networks or delivering regular workshops—coupled with that little fridge magnet waiting quietly for the moment when it is most needed.

WHERE CAN YOU IMPROVE?

Part of revisiting, reevaluating and revising your marketing plan is to assess where you are now and how you can improve. In Figure 8.3 use the checklist and for each question, think whether you are satisfied with this area of marketing, or whether you could make some improvements.

If you are completely satisfied, tick the "satisfied" column. If there is absolutely nothing more you can do, then tick the "completed" column. If you find areas needing improvement, tick the "needs work" column. When the checklist is completed, you will have a plan ready to put into action. As you complete each stage to your satisfaction, tick the "completed" column. This plan may take some time to implement, but each baby step is a step in the right direction.

Learn to Communicate Your Message

Once you are more focussed on where and who your market is, you have to step up your marketing plans. To grow any business, you must become a competent communicator. Chapter 9 demonstrates how to present a professional written image to your clients, and then use these skills to your advantage.

Figure 8.3	Improving Your Marketing Plan: A Checklist

	COM-PLETED	SATIS-FIED	NEEDS WORK
1. I have set long-term goals for the business.	❏	❏	❏
2. I have set short-term goals for the business.	❏	❏	❏
3. I have set personal long- and short-term goals.	❏	❏	❏
4. My business name aptly describes what I do.	❏	❏	❏
5. I have an excellent business logo.	❏	❏	❏
6. I have a snappy slogan.	❏	❏	❏
7. My mission statement reflects my business goals.	❏	❏	❏
8. My office or reception area is clean and organized.	❏	❏	❏
9. My work area is clean and well organized.	❏	❏	❏
10. My staff and I are well groomed.	❏	❏	❏
11. My staff wear clean uniforms or company clothing.	❏	❏	❏
12. All company vehicles are cleaned regularly.	❏	❏	❏
13. The company name is on the vehicles.	❏	❏	❏
14. I am familiar with how people live in my community.	❏	❏	❏
15. I know the average age of my ideal consumer.	❏	❏	❏
16. I understand my average consumer's shopping habits.	❏	❏	❏
17. I know where and when they like to shop.	❏	❏	❏
18. I know the physical boundaries of my business.	❏	❏	❏
19. I am aware of my larger competitors.	❏	❏	❏
20. I am aware of most of my smaller competitors.	❏	❏	❏
21. My prices compare favourably with my competitor's pricing.	❏	❏	❏
22. I offer better service than my competitors.	❏	❏	❏
23. I have recently visited my main competitors.	❏	❏	❏

Figure 8.3	Continued

	COM-PLETED	SATIS-FIED	NEEDS WORK
24. I treat my customers as Very Special People.	❑	❑	❑
25. I keep informed of changing economic trends.	❑	❑	❑
26. I tailor my business to accommodate these trends.	❑	❑	❑
27. I keep informed of changing consumer trends.	❑	❑	❑
28. I tailor my business to accommodate these trends.	❑	❑	❑
29. I have conducted a market survey for my business.	❑	❑	❑
30. I have set an adequate monthly marketing budget.	❑	❑	❑
31. I monitor the results of all marketing methods.	❑	❑	❑
32. I ask all new clients how they heard of my business.	❑	❑	❑
33. I know the seasonal trends of my business.	❑	❑	❑
34. I attend industry trade shows at least twice a year.	❑	❑	❑
35. I am connected to the Internet.	❑	❑	❑

CHAPTER 9

Are Your Written Presentations Professional?

COMMUNICATION IS YOUR KEY TO SUCCESS

By now it should be obvious that you need more than technical and financial skills to be an excellent entrepreneur. You also have to learn to become an engaging speaker and a witty writer. "Oh no!" you sigh. "No one told me this when I started my business." Growing your business will depend on your ability to communicate a variety of messages to a variety of people using a variety of media.

If you are shy and lack enough confidence to openly communicate with people, you will have infinite difficulty in taking your business to the next level. The next two chapters are devoted to the art of improving both your written and verbal communication skills.

Think about the variety of people that you communicate with: customers, potential customers, suppliers, associates, the competition, bank managers, government agencies, accountants, lawyers, and members of various associations, to name a few. Each time you communicate with someone, they are formulating an opinion about you, so your competence as a business person is always being judged.

First Impression—Last Chance

We are bombarded with countless methods of communication in our fast-paced, electronic society and some people get sloppy in both their presentations and responses. How many times have you received a letter or some form of advertising, only to toss it aside because the content was grammatically incorrect or it was unprofessionally presented?

Do you use that business, or have you already judged them as unprofessional and filed them in the recycle bin? We are quick to judge others on first and often fleeting impressions. Each time you communicate in business, do so professionally—remember, you are being judged on everything you write, say or do. Scary thought, isn't it?

Communication Overload

The age of speed and cyberspace has changed what was a simple business world into a complex clutter of paper, electronic and technical gizmos. These include:

- **e-mail:** personal, business, broadcasts, spam-mail
- **faxes:** personal, business, broadcasts, junk-mail
- **letters:** direct mail, advertising, business and personal
- **direct mail:** advertising campaigns, charitable solicitations
- **brochures:** advertising businesses and special events
- **advertisements:** newspapers, magazines, TV, radio, Internet
- **stationery:** business cards, letterhead, envelopes, promotional material
- **media releases:** newspapers, magazines, TV and radio
- **telephones:** conference calls, speaker phones, cellular phones, tele-marketing, pagers
- **voice mail:** replacing receptionists, call-waiting, call-forward, phone soliciting
- **video and audio**: tapes, compact discs, overhead presentations
- **Web pages**: with graphic, audio, visuals and banner advertising.

There is infinite power in both the pen and the ability to hold an impressive and informative conversation. If you lack these skills, start working on them now. Remember—YOU are your business, and of the Eight Essential Entrepreneurial Skills mentioned in Chapter 2, the ability to communicate is near the top of the list.

THE ART OF WRITING PROFESSIONAL LETTERS

Composing a letter is like any other work of art—just as an artist carefully plans each masterpiece, so should you plan each letter and know exactly the message you want to convey. Address the five "Ws"—who, what, why, when, and where—and don't forget "how." What tone do you want to set with each letter? Your letters should be composed to generate the desired responses.

Improve Your Written Skills

You will need to use the written word every day of your business life. Some of the more common business letters you will need to compose are:

- letters of introduction
- follow-up letters to potential and existing clients
- quotations
- thank-you letters
- overdue account reminders.

IDEA **LEARN HOW TO WRITE**

If writing is not your forte, take an evening course on how to write business letters. A course on creative writing is extremely helpful as you will be able to prepare your own press releases, compose arresting letters, design your own advertising materials, and contribute articles to magazines. Becoming "published" is an effective, long-term method of increasing your exposure and credibility as an expert.

HOW TO SET OUT A SMART LETTER

Each situation requiring a letter deserves some careful thought before composition. There are some standard requirements for any letter to appear professional. Starting from the top, each letter should contain these 10 components:

1. date and correct business title
2. correct professional title of addressee
3. correct spelling of all names
4. appropriate opening address
5. suitable opening paragraph
6. comprehensive and concise body of letter

7. grammatically correct text
8. suitable closing paragraph
9. correct closing address
10. your business name and writer's title.

Figure 9.1 gives an example of a follow-up letter sent after a customer service manager met with a potential client.

TWELVE TIPS FOR WRITING WINNING LETTERS

Your letter will either hold the attention of the reader—or it won't. People are busy, so you have to write letters that quickly catch their attention. Here are some tips to help you compose that brilliant masterpiece.

1. If your letter is a "cold call," research the company and the correct title of the person you are addressing the letter to. Show him or her that you have taken time to learn a little about their business.

2. Use professional letterhead. Avoid large logos or heavy, bold print as this detracts from the letter and screams your name to the reader. Keep it tasteful and simple, using good quality paper.

3. First plan your letter in point form, then take each point, numbering them in the order you want them to appear. Next compose your letter around these points. This way, you will not miss any pertinent information and the letter will flow well.

4. Take advantage of the many tools a word processing program offers. Don't rely completely on the spell checker as it accepts any word that is spelled correctly. You can change your language preference to Canadian-English as the default setting is usually American. Use the grammar check for those finer details.

5. When the letter is completed, carefully edit it for rambling sentences, correct punctuation, long paragraphs and readability. If you stop as you are reading, reread the sentence to discover why. Re-word the sentence until it flows.

6. Study the physical aspects of the letter. Use one-inch margins and plenty of white space, as busy letters are difficult to digest.

Figure 9.1	Sample Follow-Up Letter

June 3, 20__

Pacific Northern Overnight Express ← **1**
9331 - Suburban Avenue
Toronto, Ontario
M5X 2W3

Attention Mr. Peter Casey: Operations Manager ← **2 & 3**

Dear Mr. Casey, ← **4**

It was a pleasure meeting with you on May 27th to discuss the potential of Mainline Truck Service Ltd. becoming your fleet maintenance contractor. After reviewing both the condition of your fleet and your current rates, I am excited at the opportunity to submit a quotation for your consideration. ← **5**

I believe that our company can increase the life of your fleet by implementing a comprehensive service schedule that will not exceed your budget. Your vehicles are the lifeline to your profits and we are committed to being always available for immediate repairs and service. ← **6**

We pride ourselves on going that one step further by offering the services our clients both need and have come to expect. For example, to start we thoroughly inspect each vehicle free of charge and prepare full maintenance reports, along with the cost and a suggested maintenance schedule. I shall include this information in our quotation.

Please do not hesitate to contact me with any further questions regarding our discussion. I will prepare a detailed quotation by June 15 and will courier it to your office. I personally guarantee you that we will go out of our way to meet your needs. ← **7 & 8**

Yours truly, ← **9**

David Johnson

David Johnson
Customer Service Manager ← **10**
Mainline Truck Service Ltd.

Use shorter paragraphs in long letters, and make the content interesting. Use a standard font, such as 12 point Times New Roman. Avoid using large, small or fancy fonts.

7. Keep your letters positive unless circumstances dictate otherwise. Start with a pleasant greeting, keep the tone upbeat yet professional, and close with an appropriate salutation. Avoid standard closers such as "looking forward to hearing from you in the near future." Try something different: "...I wish you a successful and enriching year and will follow up with you within 10 days." By noting that you will follow up, the reader is prepared for your call.

8. Avoid using block capitals and exclamation marks to stress a point. Capitals "scream" at readers and exclamation marks look childish. If you must emphasize a point, use italics, but sparingly. Refer to books such as *Write Right* by Jan Venolia for quick reference.

9. Your letterhead should contain all forms of contact including phone, fax and cellular numbers, e-mail address, and if available, your Web site address.

10. For a first-time contact, include your business card. Where letters may get filed away, most people keep business cards and will look for a card before looking for a letter.

11. Although labelled envelopes look neat, if your letter is of a personal nature or a thank-you card or letter, hand-write the envelope—it adds a nice personal touch.

12. Don't write a letter if you are in a negative mood. Wait until you can concentrate all your positive energy on the content, as your mood is often reflected in your writing.

SAMPLE LETTERS FOR ALL OCCASIONS
Letters of Introduction

Introductory letters can be mailed or e-mailed, and are a low cost method of introducing your business to potential clients. They can be effective marketing tools if they are not aggressive and don't contain a strong sales pitch. Letters should be well-written, friendly and informative, telling the reader who you are, what your business is, how long you have been in business, where you are located, and the services you provide.

Many people think that e-mail is a less formal method of communication, and therefore spelling and grammatical errors are acceptable. They are not. Sloppy e-mails are acceptable between friends, but not for business.

IDEA **BIG**

SAVE TIME

Using the copy and paste menu, you can send personalized introductory e-mails without using the broadcast method, which is unprofessional and liable to be instantly deleted. Address the e-mail personally by including the name of the manager of a specific department rather than just addressing the e-mail to "The Operations Manager." To not include a person's name is like getting a letter in the mail addressed to "The Occupant."

Figure 9.2 shows an example of a computer repair and maintenance business introducing their services to a potential client. It can be sent either by e-mail or on your company letterhead with the appropriate address.

Letter of Quotation

The opportunity to submit a quotation means you are over the first hurdle, so a professional presentation is the next step to closing the sale. If you don't use quotation forms, type the letter, as handwritten ones look amateurish. Having done your research, you know your client's needs and what extra services you can provide.

Try to offer an edge over the competition so that your quotation stands out from the others. Include all terms of payment, as attention to these finer details is important. Your client doesn't want any surprises once you develop a business relationship. Figure 9.3 gives an example of a quotation for janitorial services.

Thank-You Letters

Always say thank-you. My personal philosophy is this: If you aren't sending out at least two or three thank-you cards or letters a week, your business is suffering from your lack of gratitude. Did a supplier go out of their way to deliver a sudden, urgent order? Did

Figure 9.2	Sample Letter of Introduction

Attention Mr. James Connor: General Manager

The Internet has created many exciting opportunities for businesses to apply their creativity and expertise in serving the millions of new cyberspace customers. Your Web page design business is important to these people and no doubt relies heavily on the ability of your equipment to remain functional at all times.

Our company has been in business for six years and our purpose is to keep you operational. We understand that time is of the essence when breakdowns occur. We come to your premises to maintain and repair all computer equipment, offering a unique 24-hour emergency service. We have the latest diagnostic equipment and pride ourselves on keeping up with technology.

Our rates are competitive and our service exemplary. We offer free telephone support and are happy to provide testimonials from satisfied clients. I have enclosed my business card and brochure, and should mention that we offer a 25 percent discount for your first service call on presentation of this letter.

I wish you a successful year and am happy to answer any questions you may have.

Yours truly,

Robert McMillan

Robert McMillan
President
Hi-Tech Performance Service Ltd.

a friend refer a new client to you? Did you complete a job for a new client? Did a newspaper print your press release? Don't ever take these things for granted—it's common courtesy to say "thanks." A thank-you letter also gives the client an opportunity to contact you if there are any concerns. Figure 9.4 and 9.5 offer some short examples.

Figure 9.3	**Sample Letter of Quotation**

June 19, 2001

Professional Personnel Services Ltd.
Suite 203A,
19947 Springfield Avenue,
Edmonton, Alberta
T0K 1J0

Attention Mrs. Janet Phillips: General Manager

Dear Mrs. Phillips,

I enjoyed meeting with you on May 26th to discuss the janitorial requirements for your premises. We understand the need for your offices to look clean, bright and professional at all times. Based on our discussion, I am pleased to submit the following quotation.

QUOTATION FOR JANITORIAL SERVICES:
203A-19947 SPRINGFIELD AVENUE

The following quotation is based on an annual contract fee, which is subject to renegotiation for any additional requirements.

Cleaning of all offices and staff areas five days a week (Monday to Friday):

1. **Janitorial services provided:**
- daily dusting of all furniture and fittings plus waste disposal
- sanitizing and cleaning telephone receivers once a week
- daily vacuuming of all carpets, shampooing every three months
- washing and polishing all linoleum and floors
- cleaning and sanitizing washrooms
- stripping linoleum every six months
- removing marks from walls and doors.

2. **Cost of services:**
   Monthly fee: 875.00
   Plus GST: 61.25
   TOTAL: **$936.25**

Figure 9.3	Continued

3. **Hours of service:**

Service commences at 7:00 p.m. each evening and will be completed by 10:00 p.m., excluding evenings when shampooing and stripping are scheduled. Please note that we are fully bonded and insured.

4. **Payment terms:**
   a. Services will be billed weekly and payable within thirty (30) days of invoice.
   b. A 2.5% discount is applicable to invoices paid within seven days of invoicing.
   c. A monthly 2% service charge will be applicable to overdue accounts.

We shall contact you the next business day with problems needing attention and I guarantee that we will take professional care of all your janitorial needs. I shall call you within two weeks, and in the meantime, please contact me with any further questions. We would be happy to supply you with testimonials and references.

Yours truly,

Peter Saunders

Peter Saunders
Sales & Service Manager
Corporate Cleaning Services Ltd.

Account Reminders

They key to successful collections is to have clients respect your terms and pay on time while still retaining the clients' respect and business (unless you don't want their business anymore). Your first letter should be polite, as there are often circumstances that you may not be aware of, such as a family emergency, illness, or a lost invoice. Figure 9.6 offers an example of a first reminder letter.

IDEA

BIG

RETURN A FAVOUR

A thank-you card is usually appropriate, but in some cases, a letter is better. Not only does the recipient appreciate you remembering and thanking them, but your letter can be used as a testimonial or reference when the recipient needs it. One good turn deserves another.

Business letters don't have to be stiff or formal. Make your customers feel that they are important to you by conveying the message that you will bend over backwards to accommodate them. Most people enjoy the personal touch that a letter conveys. Make yours outstanding and express your message personally yet professionally by using creative penmanship.

Figure 9.4	Sample Thank-You Letter

Dear Gerald,

Many thanks for designing such an appealing and professional Web site for my consulting business. After only a couple of months, I am receiving wonderful feedback from people visiting the site. It loads quickly and the graphics make it more interesting. Not only is it a great advertisement for my business, it also contains information which people can download and use.

As these were mostly your suggestions, I compliment your professionalism. The price was quite reasonable for the complex work involved. I shall gladly refer you to anyone who needs a professional site that is in itself a work of art. Thank you once again. I am thrilled at both your work and the response from visitors.

Jane Smith

Jane Smith, President
Corporate Consulting Ltd.

Figure 9.5	Another Sample Thank-You Letter (#2)

Dear Mrs. Johnstone,

Thank-you for using Neat N'Trim Landscaping to prepare the garden for your son's wedding in July. I am pleased you called us in plenty of time, as together we were able to make your ideas become reality. The plants we suggested you add to the garden will produce a mass of perennial colour each year.

I shall call you two weeks before the wedding to inspect the garden to ensure everything is in order. This is part of our follow-up service and is free of charge. In the meantime, please call us if you have any questions. Thank you once again for the opportunity to work with you, and I hope the wedding is a wonderful success.

Kevin Brown

Kevin Brown
Neat N' Trim Landscaping

HOW TO WRITE A POWERFUL MEDIA RELEASE

Don't overlook one of the most powerful promotional tools available to businesses—a well-prepared media release. Print media such as newspapers and magazines, and electronic media such as radio and television are always looking for newsworthy stories that will interest their readers, listeners and viewers. All it takes is that creative and well-written "hook" or idea. A "hook" is usually what attracts the initial attention of the reader. It could be the way you word the headline or opening paragraph, or an innovative approach to an issue that encourages the reader to continue on.

Editors receive hundreds of media releases each week—by fax, e-mail and post. Because they work under constant deadlines, ploughing through piles of poorly-prepared releases becomes a tedious job. One community newspaper editor commented, "I receive hundreds of press releases a week; some are hand-scrawled with no

Figure 9.6	Sample of a First Overdue Account Reminder

Dear Mr. Waterhouse,

We realize that sometimes accounts are overlooked for various reasons. On reviewing your account, I have noticed that your April invoices still remain outstanding. As they are now 60 days overdue, I am writing to see if there are any problems with your shipment. Please contact our office if you need a copy of the invoices or if there is a pricing or shipping discrepancy, and we will attend to it immediately.

Your business is important to us, and we value your business. If I haven't heard from you within 10 days, I shall call to discuss this matter. If your cheque is in the mail, we thank-you and look forward to serving you in the future.

Tara Keffer

Tara Keffer
Accounts Representative
Cougar Import/Export Ltd.

contact numbers and incomplete information. I throw them away," he stated. "I don't have the time nor the inclination to read them."

A media release must capture the interest of the editor or producer within the first few lines, and this is accomplished by a professional and powerful presentation. A truly newsworthy story, written to appeal to the audience of the media you are sending it to, is your best bet for success.

If your story is used, nothing beats the credibility that this type of publicity generates. If your media release and the story it tells are interesting enough, the editor or producer may assign a reporter to "do a story" on you as was done in the Real Life example, 'Wonderful Publicity.' This is an added bonus as the publicity is an invaluable asset to building your media kit and widespread credibility.

The media's concept of what is news will vary throughout Canada. What is the newsworthy to B.C. media may have no interest to the Toronto media. Your reception by the press will be based on where you live, its size and population, its focus, the timing, space, and the amount of competition from other newspapers. For a community newspaper, an article should relate specifically to that community. In areas where the media is not so receptive, your creativity will have to work overtime to design that compelling hook or unique angle.

REAL LIFE: *Wonder*-ful Publicity

Two energetic women attending a lunch seminar I presented on low-cost marketing took my advice and approached the community newspaper about their product. They had recently become distributors of a new environmentally-friendly "Wonder Cloth" that cleaned anything and everything, without using toxic cleaners, two ideal hooks that sparked the interest of the news reporter.

On reading the local newspaper 10 days later, I was thrilled to see a full-page story about the women and their new business. On calling to congratulate them, I asked how they did it.

"We did what you told us to," was the excited reply. "We went to the newspaper, hopeful of a few lines, but look at this—a whole page!" They were thrilled. You can't put a monetary value on this type of positive exposure and the credibility it adds to your business.

Know Seasonal Trends and Keep Informed

The media work to a schedule of seasonal themes and most will make this schedule available to you. Look at the topics to decide how you can tie your business to them. At the same time, keep abreast of what is happening internationally, nationally and locally. There may be a "hot" subject that your business can tie into, such as "should you dot.com or not dot.com?"

As an example, a computer consulting company with some timely information on this subject could host a free seminar for small businesses, or submit some controversial or educational material on the subject. This would make interesting news and increase their credibility as experts.

Some of these seasonal trends that may be appropriate for your business include:

- Christmas, Easter, Mother's Day, Father's Day, Valentine's Day, Halloween
- back to school, school vacations, travelling, camping, hiking, fishing
- Small Business Week, Secretary's Day, National Women's Business Week
- spring gardening, summer vacations, fall clean-up, winter recreation.

How to Prepare a Media Release

The print media is the most common media used by businesses, so learn how to prepare a professional media (press) release. Once again, your creativity is needed. Media releases follow a standard format, and the rules are:

1. Head the page "MEDIA RELEASE."
2. Use the appropriate sub-heading: "FOR IMMEDIATE RELEASE" or "HOLD UNTIL..."
3. Include all contact information upfront.
4. Include the date.
5. Prepare a subject headline (this will undoubtedly change if printed).
6. Double-space the text; limit your information to two pages.
7. Start the text with the place of origin e.g., Vancouver, B.C.
8. Include some quotations from a key staff member in the text where possible.
9. Answer the six essential questions—who, where, what, when, why and how.
10. Close with appropriate symbols (either-30-, ### or [end]).

Figure 9.7 gives a short press release written for a local community newspaper, using an example of a realty company that specializes in selling rural properties. By holding this free seminar, they convey to the public that they care about buyers being well informed before purchasing acreage.

A local newspaper would usually print this is the type of release because it is of community interest and not too lengthy. The people attending the seminar will become potential clients and think of

Figure 9.7	Sample Media Release

MEDIA RELEASE ← **1**

FOR IMMEDIATE RELEASE ← **2**

CONTACT: Brian Phillips   **PHONE:** (604) 532- 6336 ← **3**
Country Estates Realty   **FAX:**   (604) 532-6338
DATE: March 19th, 20__ ← **4**   **E-MAIL:** bphillip@netcom.com

**FREE SEMINAR FOR FIRST-TIME
HOBBY-FARM PURCHASERS** ← **5**

Langley: ← **6 & 7**   Spring is here and many suburbanites dream of changing their lifestyle by moving to rural hobby farms. If you purchase the wrong property, this beautiful dream acreage can become a nightmare. Country Estates Realty Ltd. is sponsoring a free seminar to help first-time hobby-farm purchasers make informed decisions.

"Many buyers are not aware of the unique considerations in purchasing rural properties," says Brian Phillips, an award-winning realtor with 20 years' experience. "There are many factors to consider, including transportation, schools, neighbours, well water problems, government legislation concerning land usage, flooding and manure handling, to name a few. We want to help people realize the factors and pitfalls to consider before rushing into signing a purchase agreement." ← **8**

The seminar will be held in room 112 at the Langley Community Centre on Saturday, March 25th from 10.00 a.m. to 12.00 p.m. Coffee and refreshments will be served. For more information or to RSVP, please call Brian at 532-6336. ← **9**

← **10**

Brian's company as "the experts." If you think hard enough, you should be able to generate several story ideas around your business.

HOW TO PREPARE A PROFESSIONAL MEDIA KIT

To gain more widespread media exposure you must use the right tool, commonly known as a press or media kit. As the media is deluged with enquiries, make your kit stand out by its professional presentation. Use a high-quality twin-pocket portfolio that contains as much pertinent, well-organized information as possible. It should include the following items:

- a cover letter outlining your topic and confirming your call
- biographical information about yourself and your business, including awards, nominations, and committees you represent
- testimonials or letters of reference
- articles demonstrating your credibility on the subject, or a need for your story
- corporate information (brochures, videos, photos)
- published articles you have authored
- anything that validates you or your business's credibility
- a press release.

Pitch Yourself to the Media

Before sending the kit, call to ask for the name of the producer of the show or editor of the section you want to contact. Ask for the correct spelling of their name and full postal address. Then ask to be put through to him or her. Introduce yourself and your business—making the call as exciting and as positive as possible—and ask if the

IDEA **PREPARE A DYNAMITE COVER LETTER**

Prepare a cover letter confirming your conversation. Thank them for the opportunity of submitting your material, detail the pertinent information, and confirm that you will follow up in 10 days to ensure safe delivery. Make the cover letter positive and intriguing enough to capture the reader's interest, ensuring that it answers the six essential questions. Send the kit and follow-up by telephone in 10 days.

person would like you to forward a media kit. If your pitch is intriguing, you will be invited to send in your information for review.

The Follow-Up Phone Call

Editors and producers are busy people so keep your follow-up call short and to the point. Don't even ask if they have read your material at this stage—they will tell you if they have. Figure 9.8 gives an example of a follow-up conversation.

Keep a copy of the cover letter in your follow-up file and call back within two to three weeks. Keeping in touch without becoming a pest is called persistence, and it pays off. One reporter commented to me that I "was persistent," but she appreciated it as she was so busy that things often got shoved to the bottom of the pile. Now she calls for small business resource information, which has resulted in further press coverage without even asking for it.

Build a Relationship

The media need resource people whom they can contact for information when they need it. Once you are on file, you may well be asked to provide input for articles or shows. Let your media contacts know that you are always available to help them. There are various media organizations who are always interested in newsworthy stories, particularly if they tie into their publishing or production themes. Consider the following associations:

- local, provincial and national television and radio shows, newspapers and magazines
- specialty, trade and free magazines
- trade newspapers and journals
- Internet publications
- association and chamber of commerce newsletters
- government training organizations
- college and university newsletters.

| Figure 9.8 | Sample Follow-Up Call Conversation |

"Hello Jennifer, Marlene James calling. I'm following up to ensure that you received my media kit safely in the mail (or by courier or delivered to the front desk)... You did? Please contact me if you need more information, and thank-you once again for taking the time to review my package. I look forward to hearing from you and have a wonderful day."

How to Source Media Leads

Who has the time to spend countless hours doing research? If you're not already on-line, then get plugged in. The amount of information you can gather by surfing the Net is amazing. You save on travel, time, postage and long-distance calls.

To quickly locate a contact, find the media you are interested in through the search engines and go to their Web page "contact us" link or staff directory. Peruse their site to become conversant with their focus, format and content.

IDEA BIG · · · · ·

KEEP A DATABASE

Print out your search results to keep track of those people you have contacted and those to be contacted. You can do this either manually or by using a contact management program. The Internet will give you lists of newspapers, magazines, radio and TV stations. If your business appeals to a specific market, such as students at post-secondary institutions, there is no better tool than the Internet to locate this information in the geographical area you require.

Use E-Mail

Try an introductory e-mail, and if you don't get a reply within a week, follow up with a phone call. E-mails get lost and forgotten, but in most cases, you will receive a reply. You have the contact's name and can phone the main company switchboard to be put through.

You have a legitimate reason for calling—to see if the e-mail arrived. This can be a comfortable opener to the conversation after you have introduced yourself. If the e-mail was not received, be ready to capture the attention of the listener by having a positive and creative spiel ready. Keep your media release handy as a reference.

CAN YOU IMPROVE YOUR WRITTEN SKILLS?

This chapter demonstrates how using you written skills can help you market your business and increase your profile as "the expert" in your field. Complete the checklist in Figure 9.9 and use it as a guide to plan how you will achieve this goal.

You are Halfway There

Competent and creative writing skills coupled with a professional presentation can be one of your most effective and inexpensive marketing tools. This is half the battle. Now you have to continue the communication process by having the ability to express yourself verbally and concisely. The next chapter will help you to increase those all-important verbal skills.

Figure 9.9	Written Communications Strategies For My Business

1. Currently, I use the following written methods to communicate in my business:

   ❑ personalized e-mail   ❑ fax

   ❑ e-mail broadcasts   ❑ fax broadcasts

   ❑ letters of introduction   ❑ press releases

   ❑ direct mail   ❑ follow-up letters

2. I experience difficulty with the following:

   ❑ replying to faxes   ❑ writing promotional copy

   ❑ replying to e-mail   ❑ replying to letters

   ❑ account collections   ❑ follow-up letters

3. ❑ I could improve my written communications by:

   ❑ making time to send letters of introduction

   ❑ sending follow-up letters after meeting potential clients

   ❑ sending more thank-you letters and cards

   ❑ sending regular collection letters to clients

   ❑ using e-mail to introduce my business

   ❑ using e-mail to correspond with business associates

   ❑ keeping hard copies of important e-mails for reference

4. I could improve my communication skills and increase my profile by:

   ❑ learning how to write effective media releases

   ❑ marketing my business using the media

   ❑ taking a course on writing business letters

   ❑ taking a course on creative writing

   ❑ submitting articles to magazines, newsletters or newspapers

   ❑ using the Internet to locate e-magazines to submit articles

   ❑ gathering written testimonials and evaluations

   ❑ informing the community newspaper of my business

   ❑ hiring some part-time help to allow me to focus on the above

Figure 9.9	**Continued**

5. Every business is unique in its own right. Write down what sets your business apart from others.

    _____

    _____

    _____

    _____

    _____

6. Now think of various ways to use the information above to promote your business utilizing your writing skills. Which trade publications, newspapers, magazines or e-magazines could you write for?

    _____

    _____

    _____

    _____

    _____

7. Research courses, seminars, books or programs that will teach you how to improve your writing skills. Note the pertinent details and put a timeline on completing them.

    a. _____

        I will complete it by: _____

    b. _____

        I will complete it by: _____

    c. _____

        I will complete it by: _____

Do Your Verbal Skills Need Enhancing?

TELEPHONE TALK

The telephone is a most valuable asset to your business, so use and treat it with respect. It is your responsibility to always be reachable. If your business requires that you regularly be absent from your office, designing a reliable communications system is a priority so that you don't lose business, as was the case in the Real Life example, "The Too-Big Bank."

For a micro-business, ideally you require two phone lines: one for calls and one for the fax and Internet. Use either a cellular phone to forward calls to when you are out of the office, or voice-mail or a pager. Whichever you use, let callers know that messages will be returned promptly. People are impatient and don't like lengthy waits for return calls.

Your Communications System

Telephone companies offer a variety of packaged services for a monthly fee. Use these to remain in touch with your callers and to always know who called and when. Some of the options that can enhance your communication are:

1. **Call display:** keeps you informed as to who is calling
2. **Call forwarding:** to other numbers when out of the office
3. **Call alert:** lets you know when another call is coming in
4. **Call display for second caller:** displays phone number of second caller
5. **Toll-free line:** can be connected to your main number for a nominal fee

6. **Voice mail:** to take a message if you are on the line or absent

7. **Cellular phone:** for call-forwarding, retrieving and returning messages

8. **Conference calling:** to talk to multiple parties at once.

Answer Your Calls Professionally

There is no substitute for a professional voice answering the telephone. If you operate a home office and have children, connect a second "smart ring" number for them, which rings with a different tone. This warns you that it is not a business call and you can choose to ignore it. Teach your children not to answer the business telephone during working hours. Even though a polite child sounds cute, it does nothing for your business image.

IDEA **RETAIN THE PERSONAL TOUCH**

Train employees to be polite, cheery and helpful when they answer the telephone, as it is often the first form of contact by a potential client. Ensure clients feel they are being treated as VSPs. If you are looking to update your communications system, avoid the electronic directory system. People are sick and tired of being electronically directed to more voice mail boxes and recorded messages. They tolerate it with large corporations but don't expect it from a small business. The personal touch goes a long way in this electronic era.

REAL LIFE: The Too-Big Bank

A client tried to phone a local bank to confirm a fax number to send some information to a loans officer. On looking up the number, there was only one central listing for all branches, which she dialed. She was asked whom she was calling. She gave the name and branch and was informed that the person she wanted wasn't listed.

"But I know she's there," said the client in frustration.

"Well why are you calling?" asked the receptionist.

"Because I need her fax number!" Now the client was angry. This was none of the receptionist's business. "Please give me the branch number."

"Well alright then," answered the receptionist reluctantly, as if she was doing the client a favour.

On calling the bank, a recorded voice answered.

"Thank you for calling the Too-Big Bank. Please leave your name and number and someone will get back to you within two hours." The client was now completely disgusted with this run-around and vowed that she wouldn't deal with a bank that couldn't be communicated with. She cancelled her loan application and went elsewhere.

TEN TIPS FOR TELEPHONE ETIQUETTE

Whether you are calling to collect an overdue account or making a cold call, follow a few basic principles and you will generate productive conversations. The art of telephone etiquette can be easily learned. Here are a few pointers to help.

1. Write down the important points before calling.
2. Always know whom you want to talk to—don't just ask for "the manager."
3. Prepare a suitable opening, body and close for your conversation.
4. Don't call anyone if you are not in a positive mood.
5. Make follow-up and sales calls before lunch when people are more receptive.
6. Don't call right on opening or before they have had time for that first coffee.
7. Open with a pleasant salutation and talk on a personable level, as if you were face-to-face.
8. Don't waste people's time—try to strike a balance between being both friendly and professional.
9. If the other party appears unreceptive, ask if it would be more convenient to call back at a more suitable time.
10. Close with a friendly salutation, letting them know when you will be in touch again.

Professional Greetings and Messages

First impressions are important for building relationships so always answer the telephone professionally and positively. "Good morning, Doncaster Plumbing and Heating Services, this is Jonathan speaking. How may I help you?" Greet your caller first, give the company name, and let them know whom they are talking to. You won't go wrong using this professional and courteous greeting.

Many home-based businesses make the mistake of leaving unacceptable messages on their voice mail. "Leave a message after the beep," or "you have reached the Smith residence and Bonny's Gift Baskets, we're not home so leave a message" doesn't cut it.

CHANGE YOUR HOME-BASED GREETING

Home-based businesses should leave a professional greeting on their voice mail. Try something like: "Thank you for calling Doncaster Plumbing and Heating Services and the Janson residence. Your call is important to us, so please leave a message and we shall return it shortly. For emergencies, please call our cellular number at 555-9987. Thank-you for calling and have a wonderful day."

CALLING WITH CONFIDENCE

Most people shudder at the thought of making cold sales calls, the main reason being fear of rejection. No one likes a telephone slammed down in their ear. It takes a certain personality to be a salesperson because they face rejection every day and still motor on, undaunted and unruffled. The art of successful cold calls is to develop your confidence and communication skills, coupled with a professional, friendly, non-aggressive approach.

Warming Up Cold Calls

No doubt you have received numerous cold calls from people selling anything from carpet cleaning to crematorium plots. These companies usually use telemarketers for soliciting business, relying on volume and the numbers game. Small businesses don't have this luxury, so the key is to target your leads and not use "hit-and-miss" methods.

Use the 10 tips outlined earlier and remember—you are offering a valuable service and people need you. You are calling only to introduce your business. If people are interested, you can follow up with either a letter, fax, or an appointment. Figure 10.1 gives an example of a landscape company making a cold call.

IDEA **TRY A SPECIAL OFFER**

A special time-limited offer, such as "no GST" or "a 10 percent discount," can often help to speed up the telephone sales process. Start with a friendly "opener" to the conversation. This allows you to feel out the mood of the person you are calling. If you sense reticence or impatience, keep the call short or ask if they prefer you to call at a more convenient time.

Follow-Up Calls

This conversation allows the caller to politely follow up in a couple of weeks before the season for tree-spraying ends. Even if no business evolves from the call, the recipient is now aware of the business, has a brochure, and can be added to a mailing list for newsletter or promotional mailings.

Figure 10.1 Sample of an Introduction Cold Call

"Hello, is this Mrs. Wilkes? I am William Cleary of Gorgeous Gardens Ltd. What a lovely day to be in the garden. I hope you're taking advantage of the good weather. I'm calling to let you know that we are a new local business offering a variety of gardening services, including yard cleaning, landscaping, tree pruning, spraying, topping and lawn maintenance. Do you ever have a need for any of these services?... Occasionally? I would be happy to send you a brochure detailing all our services and prices. It's actually time for dormant sprays for your fruit trees, and we are offering a special this month. We also offer free quotations... Send you a brochure? With pleasure. If you give me your address, I shall mail it tomorrow. Our number is on there if you would like more information. Please feel free to call us with any gardening questions as we are more than happy to help...Yes, I'll enclose some information about the dormant sprays. Thanks for your time and enjoy your garden."

<table>
<tr><td>

IDEA

BIG

• • •
</td><td>

MONITOR FIRST-CALL SUCCESS RATE

Many people keep brochures, cards and information and will use them later or refer your name to others. It's important to follow up your sales calls for any potential sales, and you need to monitor your progress to know which strategies are working and which are not. Keep a written record of your progress for future reference.
</td></tr>
</table>

William's follow-up phone call with Mrs. Wilkes should sound like the conversation outlined in Figure 10.2.

Figure 10.2	Sample of a Follow-Up Call

"Hello Mrs. Wilkes, it's William Cleary again from Gorgeous Gardens. I spoke with you two weeks ago and am just following up to ensure that our brochure arrived safely. It did? Good. Can I help by answering any questions about your trees or garden? Some people aren't sure about using pesticides and sprays when they are on well water so I wondered if this was a concern of yours...No, our sprays are all environmentally friendly as we cater to people living on rural properties. Are you going to spray your fruit trees this year? The season is coming to a close...Well, if you missed last year, I would suggest it now as it certainly reduces the risk of damage to your fruit crop. Yes, I'd be happy to drop by and give you a quotation. What day and time would suit you?... I'll look forward to meeting you next Tuesday at 2:30 p.m. Mrs. Wilkes. I'll bring some free fertilizer spike samples for you too—your trees will love them. Take care and enjoy your day."

How to Tackle Tardy Accounts by Phone

Calling clients to ask for money has to be the worst possible chore. Many procrastinate hoping that the cheque arrives in the mail, which it usually does. But when it doesn't, you have to call to find out why. Cash flow is the lifeline of your business, so grit your teeth, grab your aged receivable list and start phoning. Easier said than done, isn't it?

First gauge the client's receptiveness. There are many reasons why people don't pay. The old adage about the squeaky wheel holds true, particularly in collections. Those who don't squeak don't get the oil. Start your conversation by taking the guilt away from the customer and placing a little on yourself—it will break down their barriers and make communication easier. Try adapting the sample conversation in Figure 10.3 to make your calls.

Figure 10.3	Sample of a First Collections Call

"Hello John, this is Eva from Office World Stationers. Are you enjoying the sunshine?... Yes, it is too nice to be working today. John, I was calling because I was concerned that there may be a problem with your account. Are any of our invoices missing or incorrect? Your account seems to have slipped into ninety days...Yes, I'll hold while you have a look.

You're waiting for a credit on one invoice? Please give me the details and I'll fax a copy over to you immediately. Perhaps it got lost in the mail. Could you clear the account for payment when it arrives? We'd appreciate it as you usually pay so promptly. Please don't hesitate to call me if there are any future problems. Thanks for attending to this promptly."

Persistence Pays Off

Customers often experience cash flow problems so you need to be persistent. Remember that businesses go broke overnight and trade suppliers are usually the first ones to suffer. If you know that a business is experiencing difficulties, you need to take a firmer stand on your collection calls.

Figure 10.4 gives an example of a call to a good client whose payments have slipped behind for the second time. This account should be watched closely, and if promised payment terms are not met, stronger action must be taken.

SPEAKING OF BUSINESS...

Public speaking isn't everybody's cup of tea, although this skill can be learned. Business doesn't come to you—you have to go out

Figure 10.4	Sample of a Second Collections Call

"Good morning Mrs. Pearce, this is Richard Whalley from Fine Oak Furniture. How are you today? …Yes, business is slow during summer unless you own a resort, but it'll pick up when the children are back at school. Mrs. Pearce, I'm calling to discuss your overdue account. I'm reviewing our receivables and noticed that your payment didn't arrive as promised. Some invoices are 90 days overdue. Your credit record is usually excellent and I see there are orders waiting to be shipped… Yes, I understand how slow this time of the year can be, and we don't want to put your orders on hold as you have been a good customer…

The overdue balance is $3,500 in 60 days and $4,225 in 90 days. Could I make a suggestion? As your order quantities are currently small, could you pay C.O.D. for the current orders and divide the balance of $7,725 into four cheques, one payable this week and the others payable every two weeks? You could then keep buying product while reducing the account…That would work? Good, but if there are any problems with the cheques clearing, please let me know immediately…It's my pleasure Mrs. Pearce and thank-you."

and get it. This is achieved by communicating. If you love what you are doing and are an expert in your field, you have the basis to learn public speaking, a skill that will enable you to successfully talk in any situation.

Speak Your Way to Success

A person who develops excellent speaking skills is always in demand. Groups and associations are continually seeking good speakers. The more you speak, the more your skills increase and your name becomes known as an expert.

Think about how you can apply your business knowledge to developing a twenty-minute keynote address and a couple of three-hour seminars. If you work at getting your name known, business will come to you. Here are some of the organizations that are always seeking speakers:

- chambers of commerce
- radio and TV stations

- networking groups
- business associations
- church groups
- colleges and universities
- government and private training programs
- schools
- events requiring a master of ceremonies
- special community events
- corporate training programs
- speaker bureaus
- local council committees such as Economic Development
- corporate, private and government conferences
- trade shows, home shows, career fairs
- adult education classes.

IDEA · **BIG**

NOTIFY THE PRESS

Before you speak, always send press releases to local newspapers. This serves many purposes: you could have more press coverage to add to your media kit, and more people see your name in print, attend the event, and network your name to others. One speaking event can generate multiple contacts.

HOW TO DELIVER A DYNAMIC PRESENTATION

What makes a successful speaker? First, you have to enjoy people and be interested in them. A sense of humour is a wonderful asset. If you have listened to any good speaker, you will probably have remembered them by their delivery, not just the content. Most good speakers have the ability to laugh at themselves, inject humour into their presentation, interact with the audience, and tell stories that the audience can relate to.

The dynamics of a successful delivery include:

- body language—using hands, expressions and your body to convey messages
- using the floor space and not standing still at the podium
- using notes as little as possible
- being energetic, changing tones, using pauses for effect

- maintaining eye contact throughout the room
- using props such as white boards, overhead projectors and visual presentations
- quoting examples and case histories that people can relate to
- involving the audience
- answering questions from the audience
- ensuring all equipment is in working order before the presentation
- using quotes and humour
- speaking in a language that the audience can relate to
- knowing who will be in the audience and tailoring the speech to suit
- delivering your speech without using frequent "ums" and "ahs"
- keeping to time
- providing handouts for the audience to take home
- changing voice speed and tone to drive points home.

Know Your Audience

Delivering a successful speech requires you to understand the audience and their intellectual level. Develop an opening that makes them feel comfortable. This is often achieved by either telling a joke, a good story, or by asking the audience a question.

By asking a question, you can then gauge their receptiveness. Are they quiet, shy, or sombre? If they are quiet, you will have to use more interactive methods to draw them out and warm them up. Once you get the audience smiling or laughing, they will be more receptive.

Be Remembered and Enjoyed

Your speech should contain an informative body and close that leaves the audience feeling inspired, happy and educated. People retain only a small percentage of what you say, so if you leave them with a few inspiring or helpful ideas, then you have done a good job.

Include a handout covering the main points of your speech, as people not only refer to it, they pass the information on to others. Have other informational handouts available—if you are a hit, they will quickly disappear. After your speech, you may receive other invitations to speak, thank-you cards, e-mails or phone calls. These are the satisfying rewards of a good presentation.

IDEA **START SMALL**

An excellent way to gain experience is to offer to speak to smaller groups or school children. There are numerous community associations that would enjoy hearing a guest speaker, particularly if you don't charge. The thank-you cards, e-mails or letters can then be used as testimonials. Also you can ask the group to supply you with testimonials or feedback for future use.

Published press releases and positive testimonials are valuable additions to both your credibility and media kit. It doesn't matter if you are a landscaper, metal worker or financial consultant—there is sure to be a subject you could talk about. Look at the course programs for adult education and you will see a myriad of subjects. One unusual course offered in Seattle is the art of cigar smoking. Now get creative.

NETWORKING—BREAKING THE ICE

The average person suffers from lack of confidence and shyness in a room full of strangers, but this can be easily overcome by allowing someone else to speak first. At most networking events, people wear name tags. Approach someone looking alone and uncomfortable, read their name tag and say: "Hello Susan, my name is Jennifer Scott. What does your company Safe and Secure do?"

Let's be honest, everyone likes to talk about themselves, and Susan will happily launch into a description of her business. Ask a few questions and be a good listener. Of course, ask for a business card and present the listener with yours. This is a networking rule.

The Twenty-Second Infomercial

No matter who you talk to, the question, "What do you do?" invariably arises. Be prepared and practise your twenty-second "infomercial." There is nothing worse than asking someone what they do and then have to listen to an unstructured, rambling spiel. The professional will have a concise answer that is informative and will not bore the listener.

When Susan has finished her spiel, the first thing she will ask Jennifer is: "And what do you do Jennifer?" Now a relationship has been established. You both feel more comfortable, and you can deliver your infomercial. Work on the script carefully and learn it off by heart.

Figure 10.5 gives the text of Jennifer's infomercial. She has managed to describe her business in detail, mention prices and her success—all in twenty seconds.

Figure 10.5	Sample of the Twenty-Second Infomercial

"Susan, I'm a personal chef and I cook up a storm for busy professionals who don't have time to cook nutritious meals. I come to your home, consult on your meal preferences, shop, cook and prepare up to four family meals. I also cater and serve dinner parties for up to twelve people and my romantic dinners for two are a hit! My prices are very reasonable and I ease the guilt of serving regular junk food meals."

Build Relationships

Selling is all about building relationships, and this is what you are building the minute you start a conversation. Before consumers decide to purchase from you, they are first looking for someone who is trustworthy, experienced and personable to help them make the right decision. Whether you are networking at a seminar or displaying at a trade show, it is *you* who will sway the consumer either way.

Use Non-Threatening Openers

Appearance, presentation, body language and your ability to be a good listener work hand-in-hand with your communication skills to win consumers over. Dress smartly, smile, be attentive, and focus on the needs of the person you are talking to.

If you are at a trade show and someone stops at your table, don't launch into a sales pitch straight away. First feel out the person's mood—remember—they are just looking and are going to be wary of a strong sales pitch. Here are some example openers:

- "How are you enjoying the show today? There's some interesting new products here. Have you had a chance to see the kitchen composting system in aisle three?"
- "Hi, my name is Richard. It's a beautiful day to be out of the office isn't it? Have you attended this show before?"
- "Hello, would your child like one of the candies and a balloon?"
- "How are you today? Can I help you with any particular information?"
- "I see you are an exhibitor also. What is your business?"
- "Hello, I'm Gerry Taylor of Taylor and Associates Accounting. Would you like to fill in an entry form for our draw prize? It's this beautiful gourmet basket."

Once a comfort level has been established, you can then progress into some business patter:

- "This is our second year at this show. It's a wonderful venue for meeting people and keeping up with technology. Is there anything I can help you with? Our company has just become the Canadian distributor for this new accounting software. Have you seen it before?"
- "We're very excited about being here today. We've just launched an exciting new product line. Do you have an older dog?... You do? Would you like to try a free sample of our new flea control product? You don't have to push pills down their throats or apply sprays or powders. I have a brochure that you could take home."
- "Do you have a garden? ...Don't you get sick of edge-trimming and the lawn growing into the garden beds? My husband always damages my flowers and it's like World War Three. This concrete edging landscape curbing allows you to run the mower along it and keeps the beds neat and tidy—and it lasts forever if you don't run a truck over it."

You have now broken the ice and should be able to gauge the person's interest. You can then describe what you do or show them your products. Ask lots of questions to let the listener know that you care about their needs and are interested in them. Make sure they leave your table with a card or brochure. If there is a real interest, make a note on their card or offer to contact them the next week. Follow-up is where the sale will transpire, so be diligent in this process.

IMPROVE YOUR COMMUNICATION SKILLS

Now it's time to review how you can apply the information found in this chapter to enhance your verbal communication skills and build better relationships with clients. Ultimately, you will have to rely on your ability to communicate, market, sell, administrate and take your business to the next level.

This requires a combination of being available to your customers by using the right communications system, writing professional correspondence, and by feeling confident enough to deliver the right words at the right time.

Study and complete the checklist in Figure 10.6. Use it as a guide to identify where and how you can improve your communication, using some of the suggestions. Then make a commitment to become a top-notch communicator.

USING EFFECTIVE COMMUNICATION

Now you can apply these communication skills to enhance your marketing and selling. The next chapter focuses on using these skills to promote, publicize, and advertise your business at a minimum cost with maximum expose.

| Figure 10.6 | **Verbal Communication Strategies for My Business** |

1. Currently, I use the following methods to communicate in my business:

    ❑ telephone   ❑ cellular phone

    ❑ voice mail   ❑ pager

    ❑ follow-up phone calls   ❑ telephone

    ❑ networking events   ❑ meeting with clients

2. I could improve my communications system by:

    ❑ installing an additional telephone line

    ❑ using voice mail

    ❑ call-forwarding messages to my cellphone

    ❑ using a pager

    ❑ using a cellular phone

    ❑ using e-mail

    ❑ hosting a Web page

    ❑ using a fax machine

3. I experience difficulty with the following:

    ❑ returning messages   ❑ being away from the office

    ❑ expressing myself clearly   ❑ follow-up phone calls

    ❑ talking to strangers   ❑ selling myself and my business

    ❑ speaking confidently   ❑ making time for any of the above

4. I could improve my verbal communication by:

    ❑ making regular introductory telephone calls

    ❑ following up by telephone after meeting potential clients

    ❑ trying some sales calls and monitoring the results closely

    ❑ following up with after-sales service calls

    ❑ attending to messages more promptly

    ❑ making weekly collection calls

    ❑ hiring some part-time help to allow time to focus on the above

Figure 10.6	**Continued**

5. I could improve my communication skills and increase my profile by:
   - ❑ joining Toastmasters to improve oral and presentation skills
   - ❑ designing short workshops and speeches
   - ❑ speaking to schools and associations
   - ❑ joining more community and networking associations
   - ❑ circulating my name as a speaker to related organizations
   - ❑ contacting TV and radio stations for interviews

6. Now think of various ways to use these ideas to promote your business. Where could you present seminars or deliver a keynote address? Which TV or radio shows are relevant to your field? Jot down some possibilities.

   _____

   _____

   _____

   _____

   _____

7. Make a time commitment to tackle two of the ideas in question 5 and put a timeline on them.

   a. _____

       I will start on _____

   b. _____

       I will start on _____

8. If you have checked off any items in question 2 to improve your communication system, list these below and research the cost. Then commit to a date for implementation.

   a. _____ Cost: $ _____ Date: _____

   b. _____ Cost: $ _____ Date: _____

   c. _____ Cost: $ _____ Date: _____

Figure 10.6	**Continued**

9. If you are not already a member of networking groups or business associations, list three that would be of interest to you. Write down their telephone number, next meeting date, location and cost.

    a . _____ Telephone: _____

        Date: _____ Location: _____ Cost: _____

    b. _____ Telephone: _____

        Date: _____ Location: _____ Cost: _____

    c . _____ Telephone: _____

        Date: _____ Location: _____ Cost: _____

CHAPTER 11

How Do You Apply Communication Skills to Marketing?

USE LOW-COST NO-COST MARKETING MAGIC

As you develop your written and oral communication skills, you can apply them to some of the most low-cost successful marketing techniques that will increase both your profile as an expert and your income. If you study highly successful people, you will find that they use many, if not all of these methods.

You can't just sit back, hoping that customers will come to you. This is not recommended even for an established business, but it is deadly for a new, small business competing with dozens of others. The winner in this race is the one who goes out and makes it happen.

Practise Your Entrepreneurial Skills

You will need to harness most of your eight entrepreneurial skills for marketing, particularly motivation, communication, confidence, expertise, passion and persistence. It's always difficult trying something new, so you will have to set your goals to get motivated. To make the most of the leads you generate, you will need sound communication skills. Once you start trying some of the suggested methods, your confidence will build with each new success.

Although the methods outlined in this chapter sound easy, they all take some thought, commitment and planning to implement. Success will be long-term, creating many ongoing and beneficial contacts. By tackling all of these ideas during my business career— more so in the last three years after putting time limits on my goals—

the results have been overwhelming. I even had to take my own advice and enlist extra help.

BUILD YOUR COMMUNITY PROFILE

Most small business sales are generated from the local community. Your market research should have confirmed this. No amount of advertising can replace one-on-one contact for building the personal relationships necessary to promote and grow a small business. So your first step is to become an active member of your community.

Join Community Organizations

Coach a little league team or join a drama group or service organization such as Big Brothers. When you give to your community, you receive many benefits: an outlet for your individual interests—which you need to relieve the stress of overwork—a sense of accomplishment, personal development and social and business contacts.

If you are a mechanic and someone in the group needs a vehicle repaired, there is a good chance they will turn to you for advice. If you give them an expert answer and show that you care about fulfilling their needs, you will probably get the work. If you take good care of them and don't overcharge, word-of-mouth referrals will bring you more customers.

IDEA **BIG**

JOIN FOR THE RIGHT REASONS

Join a group that will give you personal satisfaction. Don't be obvious and join for business reasons only, and don't push your business onto people—you will push them away. Be subtle and non-aggressive when business is discussed. Radiate that passion, confidence and expertise. Don't forget to take an interest in other people's work and lives. The golden rule of networking is to care about and help others besides yourself.

Join Networking Groups

With the growing trend towards small and home-based businesses, networking groups are springing up everywhere. What is a networking group? An association of business people who meet for the common purpose of making contacts, exchanging leads and referrals, and to reduce isolation.

Networking groups meet at various times—some weekly, others monthly. Some restrict membership to one of each type of business, such as one representative of an accounting company or realtor. Some are for professionals only, while others cater to a focussed membership, such as women's groups or trade associations.

Networking *Works*

Many networking groups feature speakers and design meetings to help promote members' businesses. There is no tool more powerful than learning the art of networking as is shown in the Real Life example, 'Immediate Community Recognition.' As an example, in April 1995, a Valley Women's Network chapter was formed in Langley, British Columbia. Fourteen women started the group, which was a sister group to three other networks in the Fraser Valley. The network grew so large that currently, four other chapters have formed, with a combined membership of well over 300. More new chapters are being organized.

Network members develop long-term friendships and business relationships, turning to others within their network to fulfill their consumer needs. The meetings encourage members to increase contacts and try a little public speaking. Members leave these meetings feeling positively charged, no longer alone, and ready to tackle the world.

As one member of a Manitoba network stated: "The network is inspirational and uplifting. It reduces home-based isolation, establishes outside contacts and is wonderful for brainstorming and fresh

IDEA

BIG

PARTICIPATE

When you become involved in a networking group, don't expect to sit there and have business come to you. It won't. Join a committee, help out, introduce yourself to people and exchange business cards. Give to other members and they will give back to you. The time spent will reap rewards. If there are no networking groups in your area, start one and gain immediate community exposure.

ideas." To learn everything there is to possibly know about the art of networking, read *Networking is More Than Doing Lunch*, by Larry Easto in the McGraw-Hill Ryerson SOHO series.

REAL LIFE: Immediate Community Recognition

Barb Rees lives in the coastal town of Powell River in British Columbia, and had always wanted to start a women's network. In September 1998, the Langley chapter of the Valley Women's Network helped her to organize the network. Just two months after launching the group, she was asked to become a director for the local chamber of commerce.

Barb was soon known by all the businesses—and the local press— for her hard work and efforts in establishing the network, which currently has nearly 50 members. She has been asked to sit on various boards and has gone from being just another of the area's 22,000 residents to a well-known and well-respected member of her community. Her business has also grown and she is on track for reaching her goals.

Join Your Chamber of Commerce

Chambers of commerce exist to promote the economic health of your community. Don't join and merely read the newsletter and wait for it to happen. Attend their events and introduce yourself to other members.

You may feel intimidated when you attend your first few meetings as traditionally, representatives from many larger, well-known

IDEA

BIG

JOIN A COMMITTEE

Get involved by volunteering your services on a committee. If you let it become known that you are interested in the organization's activities, you will be asked to help out. The membership will soon get to know you and what you do. By being involved, you are showing that you care about your community. The chamber may recommend your services when people call for referrals, and members will turn to you when they need your services.

businesses attend, as do local politicians. Don't feel out of place, as small and home-based businesses represent the largest percentage of membership. Use the "breaking the ice" technique as described in Chapter 10.

Reap the Many Benefits

You will learn valuable information about your community and how it operates plus have an opportunity to contribute directly to decision- and policy-making. You may have some fresh and innovative ideas that will benefit your community. As an active committee member or director, you can have direct input in formulating and implementing these ideas.

Chambers of commerce receive regular media publicity through local newspapers, as will you if you are an active member. Most chambers offer membership benefits such as medical plans, advertising opportunities, business networking sessions, and the chance to attend many diversified events and educational seminars.

INCREASE YOUR SPEAKING EXPOSURE

As you develop enough confidence to speak to smaller groups, there are some exciting opportunities available and the networking benefits are excellent. Each time you speak, someone will tell someone else about your presentation, and so it goes on. Your credibility as the expert builds until you are in demand and able to command reasonable fees for your presentations. Here are some ideas on how to achieve this.

Teach Adult Education Classes

If you are an expert at what you do—for a living or even a hobby—why not pass this knowledge on to others? There are many benefits to teaching adult education classes and most communities offer a variety of subjects. Classes are usually small, ranging from eight to 25 participants. This is an excellent training ground to practise your speaking skills. Smaller groups are usually friendly and quite forgiving if you are a little nervous. Once you survive the first class, it becomes easier.

Preparation involves planning the course material so that you teach within a given time frame. Courses can be as short as two hours or as long as a term. Your basic requirements are handouts, overhead transparencies, and a presentation that is both interesting and informative. Initially, you will spend time in preparation, but materials can be repeatedly used.

IDEA **GET PAID TO NETWORK**

You are paid to teach adult education classes, with hourly rates ranging from $20 to $70. What an added bonus! Your students all are potential clients, so this is a win-win situation. When the course is finished, you have developed that necessary relationship of trust with your students. If they need help, who will they call first?

After teaching a ten-week evening bookkeeping course for three years, business blossomed from regular classes of 25 to 30 participants, until I finally employed a full-time bookkeeper. When that business was sold, it paid off the house mortgage. Most of the increased business came from the evening classes and community exposure as a weekly business columnist for a local newspaper.

If you think about it, we would all rather use a business where we know and trust the owners. When you become known in your community, people refer you to others. Teaching is satisfying and rewarding, and a way to give something back to your community. The most successful business people give generously of themselves.

Become a Speaker

It is said that only five percent of the adult population can comfortably face a crowd with a microphone in hand and speak with ease. Of that five percent who do appear to speak effortlessly, probably four out of five have experienced butterflies, sweaty palms, and a good attack of nerves before speaking. Given time and experience, this nervousness is replaced by feelings of excitement and anticipation. As Chapter 10 explains, speaking is an art that *can* be learned.

Eight Terrific Benefits of Being a Speaker

Master the art of public speaking and all these benefits can be yours.

1. You are considered an expert in your field.
2. Listeners become clients.
3. The more you speak, the more your confidence grows.
4. Your new skills can be applied to sales and public relations.
5. You can earn excellent money as you become more professional.
6. Organizations network your name to other groups.
7. Organizations are always looking to hire good speakers.
8. You can receive excellent press coverage through media releases.

IDEA **BIG**

JOIN TOASTMASTERS INTERNATIONAL

Public speaking skills can be learned by joining Toastmasters International. Local groups usually have small memberships who encourage you to learn in a supportive and non-critical environment. I have seen nervous wrecks develop into excellent, confident and informative speakers in a short time with Toastmasters training. You also learn other valuable skills such as more articulate word usage, setting agendas, chairing meetings and time-keeping, which are all invaluable assets in business.

Speaking Opens New Doors

Previously closed doors will open wide once you polish your speaking skills. There is no better feeling than being in demand for the knowledge which you professionally impart. Speakers can earn $3,000 to $5,000 a day—and then there are the exceptional ones who command up to and over $20,000 a performance. Your enhanced communication skills will enable you to express yourself competently and clearly in a variety of scenarios.

Present Workshops and Seminars

A major benefit of becoming an expert in your field and polishing your communication skills is putting these skills to work for your business. Take your expertise and offer it to the public in the form of workshops or seminars. By building a selection that address a variety of topics within your field, you can offer your services to numerous organizations.

To gain confidence, start locally and ask for written references, then market your seminars to other organizations. Expect to give some of your time free of charge or for a small honorarium. Wherever you appear in public, you usually receive free publicity, and people will network you without you even asking them.

IDEA **OFFER FREE SEMINARS**

Offering a free seminar on a specialized subject will attract potential customers to your business. As an example, a travel agent could offer free seminars on different vacation hotspots, such as Australia. The same travel agent could design a seminar about travelling to different countries, with information, tips and advice to keep vacations safe, interesting and cost effective. Those in attendance are qualified leads, because they wouldn't come if they didn't have future travel plans.

Get Creative

A Web page designer could present a seminar on what appeals to "surfers" on the Internet, or how to market using a Web page. A retail fashion store could host seminars on wardrobe coordination for business women. A vitamin store could deliver a seminar on the benefits of using natural supplements during pregnancy.

There aren't too many businesses that couldn't offer some form of public education relevant to their field. You just have to be creative and make the effort, work hard at increasing your communication skills, and market yourself with passion and persistence.

DISCOVER THE POWER OF THE MEDIA

What are newspapers and magazines comprised of, excluding advertising? The answer of course, is news—generated by people and events. How does the news get there? Reporters have to find interesting stories to inform and attract the readership. Who generates these stories? People like you.

Contrary to popular belief, it isn't usually hard to get your name in the news, although it is more difficult in some cities such as Toronto. Newspapers are always looking for interesting stories about local people. You need to creatively find a unique angle of interest pertaining to your business—or something timely or of interest within your community or industry—that will capture the interest of an editor or reporter like in the Real Life example, 'Front-Page News.'

REAL LIFE: Front-Page News

On attending a seminar called "Getting Your Name in the News," we learned of a warehouse storage company that landed a whole front page of publicity in the business section of a large Seattle newspaper. How? By using a unique story angle.

The company rented one storage locker to a writer, who couldn't find peace and quiet at home. At the other end of the complex, another locker was rented to a young rock band, who couldn't find anywhere to practise because of their noise.

Get Your Name in the News

Think about the reader appeal in such a simple yet unusual story. You can't put a price on this type of publicity. Not only is it free, but readers are influenced by what they read in newspapers, and your credibility is immediately enhanced. I had the honour of a whole page in the business section of the *Vancouver Sun* and it has been an invaluable addition to both my media kit and credibility.

Compare what you pay for a small advertisement in a newspaper to the benefits of media coverage. How many small but interesting businesses have you seen publicized in local newspapers? These people have found a way to get their name in the news. You won't find a reporter beating down your door to interview you, so you start with a professional press release. If you can't write one, hire an experienced writer to prepare it for you.

IDEA **CONTACT RADIO AND TV SHOWS**

Exposure on television or radio greatly adds to your credentials and credibility. Once you have polished your speaking skills, approach producers with an idea for a segment that is related to your business that will pique their interest. Is there some controversy within your industry, or a new product that listeners or viewers need to know about? Is it time-saving or environmentally friendly? Could you educate people with this information? To reiterate, be creative in your thinking and find that appealing "hook."

DEMONSTRATE, EDUCATE AND NETWORK

An integral and necessary component of networking your business is exposure. You must never stop learning how to better manage your business, and must keep up with industry changes. The best way to achieve these goals is to attend industry trade shows, conferences and seminars—seriously networking at the same time.

Participate in Trade Shows

Trade shows are invaluable for exposure and networking contacts. Not only do you have an opportunity to physically display your business, but you can also see how others organize and promote theirs. You can assess the competition and leave with some new creative ideas, clients or leads.

IDEA **TARGET THE RIGHT SHOWS**

If your business caters to residential consumers, focus on home shows. If you cater to businesses, attend shows organized by chambers of commerce, business and entrepreneurial fairs. If your products are agriculturally related, attend spring and summer fairs and agricultural events. There are shows for every interest—books, gardens, homes, vehicles, technology enthusiasts—you name it, there is a trade show or fair for it. There is no better opportunity to meet new clients one-on-one in a targeted environment.

Trade shows are well worth your investment in time and money although they require that you use many of your entrepreneurial skills. If you are shy, attending shows will help to increase your confidence as you talk to more people and "get your lines down pat." Use them as practice grounds for polishing these skills as the young man did in the Real Life example, 'Discovering Trade Show Success.'

REAL LIFE: Discovering Trade Show Success

A shy young man had been operating a motorcycle store for two years. His business was growing but he was still struggling to make ends meet. At his first trade show he was thrilled at the outcome, generating $6,000 in sales and handing out over 600 business cards. His only regret? "I should have done it sooner!"

Shopping Malls

Retail malls are excellent local venues for promotion and exposure as is demonstrated in the Real Life example, 'See it, Feel it, Touch it.' Malls usually work to a schedule of theme weeks, and the managers will send you an annual schedule of events. The few hundred dollars invested will give you more publicity than a dozen full-page advertisements.

REAL LIFE: See it, Feel it, Touch it

A landscape curbing company had difficulty finding the best method to promote its products, so they tried a mall display during Home Week. Using a colourful but inexpensive display with samples, plants, pictures and bright signs, shoppers were interested in this attractive, labour-saving product and delighted in touching and feeling the samples. The opportunity to demonstrate their product was exactly what was needed. They generated more leads in a week than they could handle, and now use these venues regularly.

IDEA

BIG

-
-
-
-
-
-

KNOW WHAT TO EXPECT

Don't have the wrong expectations of trade shows. People are usually just browsing and comparing prices. You are a living advertisement informing consumers of the benefits of your business. People stopping by your table are interested, so use the opener tips found in Chapter 10. Welcome, inform, and give them brochures and cards. Offer free quotations but don't pressure to close a sale. It's not always the time or place. If you leave with a few leads each day and your brochures are being distributed, you have done well. The secret to a successful trade show is immediate follow-up.

Trade Show Tips

To ensure a successful trade show or networking event, here are some important tips to remember.

Use a draw-card: Attract people to your booth using a combination of methods. Candies, pens and novelty "freebies" never fail, in fact, people look for them. Demonstrations always attract a crowd. Have you ever noticed the people watching cooking or make-up demonstrations?

Perhaps you could use a skill-testing questionnaire, offering a prize for the winner. I used one of these at an entrepreneurial trade show, offering a free consultation for the worst score. This piqued people's interest plus it was a comfortable opener for a chat about their business problems.

Converse professionally and politely: Don't pounce on people as they approach your table. Use the appropriate opener. Ask if they would like to fill in an entry for your draw box, and whether they would like to take some information with them. Be professional, polite and interested in their questions.

Offer draw prizes: No table is complete without a competition, if legal in your province. Most people love to enter competitions, so splash lots of "win" signs around your booth. Provide a space on the entry form asking if the contestant would like a free quotation or more information. This qualifies leads for follow-up. Check federal competition legislation at *http://competition.ic.gc.ca*, and provincial legislation through your Ministry of Consumer Affairs Office to ensure that your draw or contest is not illegal.

Follow-up: Sometime during the next week, contact the people you met or those who were interested in your business. Tell them that it was a pleasure to meet them and ask if they need more help or information, to please call. Let them know who won the draw prize. If you don't follow up after a trade show, you will lose valuable business.

Expect calls from other exhibitors if you deposited cards into their competition boxes. Be polite—they are just following up. Listen to their approach and use ideas that appeal to you. If you feel their call is too aggressive, this is a reminder not to use this approach on your potential clients.

Distribute brochures and handouts: Count your cards and brochures before you put them on the table so you can monitor the level of interest. Display informative handouts for people to take home as this enhances your credibility as an expert. As an example, a garbage disposal company could prepare handouts about the benefits of composting or recycling. Make sure all your contact points are printed on the handouts.

Dress presentably: Always dress to suit the occasion at these venues. Remember, first impressions *always* count. Tee-shirts or golf shirts with your printed logo look smart, and convey the silent message that you are a professional. If you don't have corporate clothing, wear a suit or smart casual clothes. Jeans and sneakers are out unless you sell jeans and sneakers.

IDEA **GIVE YOUR BRAIN A BOOST**

Participating in these events takes you away from the day-to-day routine of doing business and reduces isolation. It is a mini-mind-vacation. Learning new information and meeting new people will help to re-motivate you. Even if you learn only one or two pertinent facts to apply to your business, the time has been well spent. Touch base with any new contacts soon after the event, express your pleasure at meeting them and suggest getting together for coffee or lunch.

Attend Conferences and Seminars

The main benefits of attending conferences, seminars and workshops are education and the invaluable networking contacts and exposure. Attend events pertinent to your business or that will help to increase your management skills.

You must keep current with industry changes and will always learn something. Even if you are technologically up-to-date, there are bound to be other areas you can explore. Learn about new products, marketing on the Internet, changing marketing and selling techniques, or motivating employees and yourself.

START A "BRAG BOOK"

Few people realize the value of using evaluations, testimonials, and "brag books" as marketing tools. Have you ever seen an interior decorator's brag book or a model's portfolio? These are their most important selling tools. Start a "brag book" as there are always satisfied clients who will give you written testimonials. Where practical, include "before and after" photos.

BUILD CREDIBILITY USING TESTIMONIALS

When people choose a book, one of the main factors that influences their purchasing decision is the testimonials. When people hire staff, references play an important role in the final selection process. There is power in the written word, just as printed media exposure informs and influences readers.

How to Obtain Testimonials

Satisfied clients shouldn't mind preparing a testimonial for you. Ask your client: "Gordon, were you happy with the work I did for you?... You are? Would you mind doing me a great favour? I would really appreciate a testimonial from you to use for promotional purposes."

Obtain a Letter of Permission

When you receive the testimonial, send a thank-you card along with a nice note, asking for their signed permission to use the letter.

Enclose a permission form and a self-addressed stamped return envelope. The permission form should read as in Figure 11.1:

Figure 11.1   Sample Letter of Permission

October 19, 2001

Competent Computer Repair Services
19307 – 148th Street,
Maindale, Ontario
L3W 5E6

PERMISSION TO REPRODUCE TESTIMONIAL LETTER

I, *Gordon Miller* of *The Accurate Accounting Company* hereby give permission for my testimonial letter, dated *September 21, 2001* and written to Competent Computer Repair Services, to be used in part or in full in written or oral media promotions, brochures, and any other form of promotional material. This permission shall remain in effect until rescinded in writing.

Signed: *Gordon Miller*   Date: *October 19, 2001*
Title: **PRESIDENT**
Business: *The Accurate Accounting Company Ltd.*

How to Use Testimonials

Testimonials can be used to enhance a variety of promotional materials. They can be printed on brochures and handouts, used in media and press kits, advertisements, and used to show to new or potential clients. You can even frame them to display in your office or reception area. Over a period of time you will be able to build up a good selection.

Evaluations

If you are introducing a new product or service, try obtaining written evaluations from well-known companies by offering them a free test period. As an example, you may be in the business of marketing new computer security products. Offer to install a security system into a large corporation's computer network, free of charge for a three-month period, in exchange for a written evaluation. Once introduced to your product, the corporation may want to purchase it. A positive evaluation carries a lot of punch when you are pitching your products to potential clients.

GET PUBLISHED

Nothing helps to build your reputation as an expert more than getting published. If you enjoy writing, why not try your hand at preparing some short columns, 400 to 1,200 words in length and shopping them around? Many e-magazines, local newspapers, trade magazines, free newspapers and magazines are always looking for new material. Often, you can trade the article for an advertisement.

As your penmanship improves and your credibility grows, you will be paid for these articles. They are an excellent addition to your resumé, brag book and media kit. You can also earn a little extra income. The publicity from being a published writer is far superior to any form of advertising.

APPLYING COMMUNICATION SKILLS TO MARKETING

Before you tackle any of the suggestions in this chapter, think about how using these methods could apply to you, and how you can apply them to growing your business. Research and complete Figure 11.2: Where and How Can I Use Low-Cost Marketing Magic?

Use All the Techniques

These low-cost marketing magic techniques are more effective than traditional advertising. You will increase your exposure, expertise and credibility. Use these techniques with a combination of methods described in the following chapter. To formulate an effective, economical and long-term marketing plan, complete Figure 12.1 "Marketing Strategies for My Business" questionnaire at the end of Chapter 12.

Figure 11.2	Where and How Can I Use Low-Cost Marketing Magic?

1. Which community organizations could you join that are of interest to you?

   _____

   _____

   _____

2. Which networking groups or business associations would be most beneficial to join?

   _____

   _____

   _____

3. If you are not a member of your chamber of commerce, note their phone number and the date by which you will call them for information.

   Phone number: _____ Date: _____ Cost: _____

4. Think of some topics related to your field of expertise that you could design a short speech or a workshop around.

   _____

   _____

   _____

5. Question 5 in Figure 9.9, Chapter 9 asked you to identify what is unique about your business. Now think of some hooks or unique angles that could be used to write a media release or that would interest the media.

   _____

   _____

   _____

Figure 11.2	Continued

6. Research annual trade show events and note those that would be suitable for your business to exhibit at.

_____

_____

_____

7. Note which clients you could ask for written evaluations or testimonials.

_____

_____

_____

8. Research the free magazines and Internet e-magazines. Which ones could you approach to write articles for? Note all contact information.

_____

_____

_____

What Else Should You Know About Marketing?

DEVELOP A MARKETING MIX

Marketing using your communication skills is a highly successful technique, but you can't be everywhere at once. You need to develop affordable yet effective methods of keeping your name in the marketplace in order to grow your business. The methods you use will be dependent on both your type of business and budget. Because consumers are fickle, what works one time may not work the next. This means trying different techniques, changing with trends, and of course, carefully monitoring your results.

This chapter explores marketing on the Internet, advertising using more traditional methods, their advantages and disadvantages, plus some low-cost marketing tips. It advises you on how not to upset consumers, and includes a marketing planner. The rest is up to you to put everything you have learned into practice.

MARKETING ON THE INTERNET

Every time you open a newspaper or trade magazine, they are filled with "e-articles" to the point of overkill. E-commerce is still in its infancy stage compared to traditional business, with trends changing overnight. Technological stocks on stock exchanges roller coaster and "dot-com" businesses are experiencing unforeseen volatility.

A report by Forrester Research Inc. in July 2000 stated that most Web retailers will be out of business by 2001 due to weak finances, competition, and investor flight. This adverse publicity gives them a bad reputation. By the time you read this, the reverse may apply.

Still, there's no getting away from it—if you aren't using the Internet for your business then it's time to get with the program. If you need more in-depth information, there are countless reference books available on this subject. However, the benefits of marketing through a Web site are as follows.

Design and Cost

If you are not Internet-savvy, a Web site consists of one or more pages of information which is accessible by being connected to the Internet. Because people who surf the Net are impatient at the time it takes for a Web page to "load" or appear on the screen, your site should be designed to load quickly.

Extras such as audio, complex graphics or video clips frustrate the average surfer. They won't wait for information to download unless they are extremely interested in what you have to offer. A small business doesn't need massive amounts of information on their site, just enough to inform and educate.

IDEA **BIG**

MAKE YOUR SITE INFORMATIVE

People look for information on the Internet so your site should contain more than just advertising. Include helpful and educational material that can be printed out and used by visitors. It's another way of getting your name out there. If you are a restaurant, include some of your special recipes. An automotive dealership could include some helpful road safety or vehicle maintenance tips. Or try a quiz that can be completed on-line and offer support by e-mail for people with questions.

Hire a reputable designer to put your site together, because it requires both graphic and computer programming talents. You can pay as little as a few hundred dollars for a basic site to many thousands of dollars, depending on the bells and whistles. Once it is up and running, a monthly fee is paid to your Web designer to "host" or look after the site.

Your designer can amend and add to your pages as required. You will pay approximately $75 U.S. to have your domain name registered annually, your monthly Internet Service Provider (ISP) fee runs about $20–$30 a month, and the hourly rate for your designer to make any changes to your Web site can vary from $30 to $75 an hour.

Make Surfing Easy

The home page should be easy to navigate, with clear directions to the rest of the site. Pages shouldn't be cluttered, as people need a certain amount of white space to make comprehension easier. Use a readable font in a size that will readily adapt to a variety of computer monitors. If the font is too small or too light or the background is too busy, it will be difficult to read. People will give up and go elsewhere. Many Web-users appreciate a site that is "searchable," which allows them to retrieve the information they need easily, rather than waste time perusing page after page.

IDEA **MONITOR SITE VISITORS**

Make sure your contact information is on every page, and for monitoring purposes, ask your designer to include a "hit" counter. Every time someone loads your home page, the counter will register their visit. This count does include your own visits, but you can also obtain a log of site visitors, which is a more accurate record than a hit counter. Ask your Web designer how to access this log.

What's in a Name?

Your domain name is critical as it has to be easy for people to find. Many companies use their business name, so they are easy to find—for example *www.microsoft.com*. Others prefer to use a name relevant to their business. My domain name is www.smallbizpro.com. It's getting harder to register popular names because of the millions in use, so you may have to be creative.

What are the Advantages of a Web Site?

Most businesses use a "www.com" address, just as they have telephone and fax numbers. There are numerous advantages to developing a Web site and using e-mail. Many people prefer to correspond by e-mail rather than use the telephone, and surfing is here to stay. You may start by just having an e-mail address and venture into a Web site later.

You can use your site for economical marketing. Once said, it will get lost among the millions which already exist, so if you want to be at the top of the search engine listings, you will have to pay a company to make this happen. Otherwise, *you* have to promote your site. As rates and pricing packages vary, search the Internet putting "Web site promotion" in the search engine site and compare prices.

IDEA | PROMOTE YOUR WWW SITE

A Web site gives your business greater visibility and conveys the message that you take your business seriously. Many people launch their site then sit waiting for "hits." It doesn't always happen that way. However you must actively promote your site by including your Web address on every form of promotion—business cards, stationery, trade show signs, brochures, advertisements, vehicles, and the Yellow Pages. Tell everyone about it. Make sure there is something of interest on your site to encourage people to refer others to it.

Some of the advantages are:

1. **Credibility:** Suggest to potential clients that they visit your site to read about your business. Include testimonials from satisfied clients. Many people make their decision to use a business after visiting a Web site. Present your business professionally by including a personal or corporate profile.

2. **Global exposure:** Your business is showcased universally. Tourism is one sector that benefits greatly from being on the Internet. If you are seeking national or international business through introductory e-mails or phone calls, suggest that people look at your site for company credentials.

3. **A research tool:** The Internet contains a vast amount of information for research on any subject. You can keep up with world and industry news, technology and your competitors. Look at other

sites that appeal to you and incorporate some of the better ideas into yours.

4. **Easy sourcing of leads:** By using search engines, you can locate businesses on the Internet that may require your services. Once located, you can e-mail them with an introductory letter and suggest that they take a look at your Web site.

5. **People finding:** If you are looking for a specific person, such as the purchasing agent for a particular business, you can locate their Web site and then correspond by e-mail. I have done extensive successful marketing on the Internet this way—it sure beats calling directories or looking in the Yellow Pages. See the Real Life example, 'Surfing for Success' for more on my partnership experience.

6. **Cost-effectiveness:** Once established, the site's ongoing maintenance costs are relatively low in return for the 24-hour a day silent marketing that it can achieve. Results will be strictly dependent on how you utilize your site.

For most businesses, a Web site is a complementary form of marketing which works in conjunction with other marketing tools. Unless your business is built entirely around e-commerce or you are prepared to devote a lot of time promoting it from your keyboard, don't rely on it for complete marketing exposure.

REAL LIFE: Surfing for Success

In July 1999, I received a call from Global Star Software Ltd. in Toronto. They had been looking for a business start-up book to combine with their new software program, *Business Plan Deluxe*. They found my book *Business for Beginners* on the Chapters.ca site and asked for a copy to review. By August, the first Canadian shipment of software programs (including the book) was in full production.

In the last year, sales have been very successful. The innovative idea of packaging a book with the program gives consumers a feeling of added value, and has made it a popular choice both in Canada and the United States. Without "surfing the Net" this partnership would not have transpired.

TEN PRACTICAL AND PROVEN PROMOTIONAL TIPS

Growing your business doesn't necessarily involve excessive spending if you use the right methods. You have to convey a message to customers that you can either save them money or fill their need, and that you are service-oriented. If you combine a selection of the ideas mentioned here and use them regularly, you will build those solid customer relationships that are lacking in many businesses.

1. **Newsletters**: Send a newsletter every three or four months to existing and potential clients. You could distribute them using the Internet for clients who have e-mail—a definite cost-savings. Incorporate informative and educational items of interest, updates about developments within your industry, and you might try a competition to monitor the response.

2. **Discount cards:** It's surprising just how many people use discount cards, whether it's for pizza or photofinishing. There is a certain attraction to getting something free in return for being a regular customer. The "buy ten get, one free" technique brings people back to your store, and there is always the hope that they may purchase other items.

3. **Say thank-you:** As discussed in Chapter 9, send thank-you cards regularly. People who take the time to write a personal thank-you note are always remembered, and chances are your name will be referred to others. Show your clients that you care—what goes around comes around.

4. **Special occasions:** Send clients seasonal greeting cards with a personal note. Some retail stores use a birthday club and send birthday cards to clients, offering a special discount during that month. People often bring in their card to receive their discount. Once again, you are showing clients that you care about them and introducing the personal touch.

5. **Draws and competitions:** Use special occasions such as Canada Day, Halloween and Thanksgiving to offer a customer draw. People *love* to enter them. Many stores offer colouring competitions for children. Our local independent supermarket always has coffee, draws, and a suggestion box on a table where receipts

are deposited for prizes. Customers appreciate these special touches.

6. **Complimentary coffee:** Have the coffee pot brewing. You could even be generous and offer cookies. Think of the harried customer running around trying to complete a dozen quick chores. There is nothing better than the smell of fresh coffee to relax them and make them feel at home. They also appreciate free candy or balloons for the children. These little touches are always noticed.

7. **Sponsorships:** Consider sponsoring a community organization or children's team. These organizations always need funding, and your name will become known along with your generosity and involvement. You can usually display sponsorship banners at events, and will be mentioned in their advertising and programs. Donate door prizes to other community events and you'll get a special mention there too. These are all effective methods of promoting your name, and besides, it feels good to help.

8. **Notice boards:** There are notice boards everywhere, so use them. If your business caters to school children, ask permission to put a notice on the school board. Corner stores, garages and some restaurants have notice boards. Put up your business card or a flyer—it's all free advertising. Those notices with the tear-off phone numbers are quite effective.

9. **Fundraisers:** Offer your services or products to schools or organizations and donate part of the profits as a fundraiser. This is already done with products such as coupon books and chocolate bars, but you, too, can be creative. An income tax preparer could offer $5 to the organization for each return referred. Your name will be out in your community as a business that cares.

10. **Suggestion box:** Provide a suggestion box for your customers. Not only will you receive some helpful feedback, but this indicates to customers that you care about them and their concerns. If you use any of the suggestions, send the customer a thank-you card along with a small gift certificate. Then you can write about this new idea in your newsletter.

"HIT AND MISS" MEDIA ADVERTISING

You have probably tried a variety of marketing methods that didn't work for you. Your chances of encouraging business using "mass media methods" are substantially lower than if you concentrate on targeting your market. People tend to place advertisements in newspapers and other printed media without carefully focussing on a "hook" or theme.

IDEA **MONITOR ADVERTISING RESULTS**

You must design an advertising campaign that will intrigue readers and capture their attention. Use a time-limited offer or clip-out coupons to monitor your results. Always ask clients how they heard about you. Seek professional help to design eye-catching copy so that your advertisement has impact on the readers.

Different methods work for different businesses, so here are the advantages and disadvantages of the more common methods of media advertising. From here, you can better assess which ones may work for you.

Direct Mail

Direct mail is the term used for bulk mailings sent to a list of prospective customers. If you use this method, be selective about who receives your mailing. No doubt you have often received direct mail letters, scanned them and thrown most of them away. Some companies experience a high rate of success because they have the resources to produce a professional product and mail in high volumes.

Advantages:
- You can target to whom you send promotional material by using selective mailing lists.
- Because you know who received the materials, you can follow up by telephone.
- Bulk postage rates can reduce mailing costs. (Call Canada Post as rates and quantities vary.)
- You can use a time-limited offer to solicit a faster response.

Disadvantages:
- The success rate of direct mail is quite low, around one to two percent response.
- Preparing a professional mail-out is expensive and time-consuming.
- You have to interest a person at a time when they need and can afford your services.

Radio and Television

The power of the electronic media is evident by the number of companies who advertise. Buying trends are created through television and radio commercials. Because of the cost—which is usually prohibitive for a small business—this type of advertising should not be undertaken without careful research, and then only as part of a comprehensive marketing plan.

Advantages:
- Commercials are seen or heard by thousands of people.
- Some businesses tend to appear more credible if they advertise through these media.
- Viewers and listeners tend to use certain channels and will hear or see your advertisements regularly.
- Costs of advertising on local stations (as opposed to national) are more affordable and target specific communities.

Disadvantages:
- The key to success is repetition, which is costly.
- You are targeting the masses.
- It is momentary advertising and easily forgotten.
- You need to carry a larger inventory of product or have enough staff to cope with a successful response.

Coupon Books

Coupon books work well for some businesses, particularly restaurants, dry cleaning and fast food outlets who offer "two-for-one" coupons. Statistics show that less than one percent of recipients respond to these offers. One woman I encountered recently responded to a coupon book offer and was told that the company did not service her area. Obviously, the company opted for mass circulation without considering their geographical boundaries.

Advantages:
- Mass distribution makes the cost per household economical.
- Once you have supplied the advertising copy, the rest of the work is done for you.
- Results can be carefully monitored if you use time-limited special offers.
- Your business is exposed to tens of thousands of people in a short time frame.

Disadvantages:
- You could be swamped with calls and be unable to meet demand.
- You could get very little response and lose hundreds of valuable advertising dollars.
- You need to repeat the advertisement in later books, because people expect to see your advertisements more than once.
- If you make "two-for-one" or similar offers and solicit a good response, you could lose substantial profits.
- You are appealing to the mass market.

Newspaper and Magazines

Local newspaper advertising is one way to keep your name in front of the community. People do refer to their community newspaper for products and services. However, consumers are extremely price conscious and may use your business during a sale, but not return later.

Be prepared to advertise regularly. To ensure your ad doesn't get lost amongst those of the competition, your advertisement must be noticed. This can be costly, sometimes with disappointing results. Magazine advertising is usually expensive, so choose one that specifically targets readers who will use your type of business. Specialized businesses often get a satisfactory response from selective magazine advertising.

Advantages:
- Your business will be exposed to your whole community.
- Service businesses can advertise regularly in the classifieds section at an affordable cost.
- Copy doesn't usually need to be submitted to newspapers until a week before publication.

- Many newspapers run special advertising features for trades or professionals. A small display advertisement is usually quite reasonable.

Disadvantages:
- People don't have time to thoroughly read all their newspapers and usually skip advertisements unless shopping for a specific item.
- Large display advertisements are expensive and often don't solicit the expected response.
- "One-shot" advertisements are a waste of time as you need consistent exposure.
- Community newspapers are usually loaded with flyers and readers receive too much advertising to physically read it all.
- Your small advertisement can get lost amongst the big display ads.
- Your competitors could advertise the same week and offer a better deal.
- You are not targeting a specific market.
- Newspapers and magazines have a short life.

Yellow Pages

Yellow Page advertising is more a hit than a miss. In fact, if you are in business, you should be in the Yellow Pages, particularly your local directory. When consumers don't know who to use, they usually refer to either the Yellow Pages or their local newspaper. The Yellow Pages are also accessible on the Internet.

IDEA **DESIGN AN AD YOU CAN AFFORD**

Yellow Page advertising works particularly well for service businesses, because very few people use them regularly and often don't know who to use. Keep the size of your advertisement affordable because you are tied to an annual contract. Even when cash-flow becomes tight, you still have to pay the monthly account. You can say a lot about your business in a few short lines, so study the other advertisements to see what attracts you to read them.

Advantages:
- People trust businesses that advertise in the Yellow Pages.
- Your advertisement is working for you 12 months a year.
- Alphabetical listings make your business easier to find.
- In many directories, you can use a cellular telephone number to advertise.
- Everyone receives a copy of their local Yellow Pages directory.

Disadvantages:
- Large display advertisement costs are prohibitive for the average business.
- There is no way out of the annual contract.
- Your competitors advertise there.

Flyers

Flyers should attract consumers by offering something special. Try using bright or flourescent-coloured paper and don't clutter the page with too many graphics or words. Use a time-limited offer to monitor responses. Circulate small quantities in a selected area and monitor the results before embarking on large flyer drops. They also make useful hand-outs at trade shows and special events.

Advantages:
- Your local newspaper will deliver them for a reasonable cost.
- You reach a larger market at once.
- You can monitor the results almost immediately.
- They are inexpensive to produce.
- Your name is being circulated in your community.

Disadvantages:
- The response rate is low compared to the number circulated.
- Consumers are inundated with flyers and advertising materials.
- Consumers have to need and be able to afford your product at that time.
- Flyer delivery can cost up to 10 cents each.

There are other ways to advertise your business, including ads on transit, benches at bus stops, billboards, posters, coupons and free samples in mailboxes, to name a few. For the average small business, many of these methods are over the budget. Plan your marketing strategies carefully and make every dollar work for you.

THE "DON'T UPSET THE CONSUMER" LIST

It seems that everyone is trying to sell everyone something, and quite frankly, consumers become tired of being solicited. Have you ever been called by a realtor and asked if you would like to sell your home? Don't you get annoyed? There are a few rules to remember as you plan your marketing campaign. Rule number one is: "Don't upset the consumer." To save bad feelings and wasted efforts, avoid these following methods:

- **Fax-broadcasting:** *Don't* send unsolicited faxes to home-based offices after hours as people are often disturbed late at night by the fax machine. Although fax broadcasts are a popular method of advertising, business people do get tired of receiving them, so be selective in who you send them to.

- **Telemarketing:** *Don't* call people after five o'clock at night or on weekends. We all dread receiving telemarketing calls at the best of times, but aggressive companies tend to solicit business just as you are taking the first bite of dinner or burning the steak on the barbeque. They know you will be at home, but few consumers respond positively to these calls.

- **Spam e-mail:** *Don't* spam people on the Internet. It's the same principle as junk-mail faxes or unsolicited phone calls. Because of virus threats, yours will be immediately deleted. I've lost count of the number of spam e-mails I receive and delete. As consumers, we resent it.

- **False offers:** *Don't* phone people with false offers such as: "You entered our competition and have just won a prize. We are in your area and would like to deliver it when both husband and wife are home..." These tactics are used by vacuum cleaner salespeople to get a foot in the door to sell an overpriced, shoddy product. If you offer free prizes, make sure there are no strings attached and don't cheat the consumer. One report to the Better Business Bureau by an irate consumer can do extensive damage to your reputation.

  Don't advertise a special deal when you have only minimum product available at the discounted price. If you make these offers, include in the advertisement: "Only 50 in stock—no rain checks" so that consumers know. Conversely, I went to purchase a television for my mother at Christmas, reserving "the last one at that price" by phone. On arriving at the store, there were piles of the same television in stock and customers buying them at the discounted price. I felt that I had been lied to.

- **Competitions:** *Don't* phone the winner of a competition informing them that they have won a prize and then try to sell them something more. Prizes should have no strings attached. If you are following up leads from a trade show, don't call people who have marked their entry form "no" in reference to further quotes or information. This is the type of aggressive follow-up that discourages people from entering competitions, and it gives your business a bad name.

HOW TO PLAN YOUR MARKETING APPROACH

These last two chapters should give you many diversified marketing ideas to ponder. Think how each one could be applied to your business, and over what time frame. Because many ideas involve only a small amount of money, you could implement some immediately. Others take time to organize, but the efforts will reap you long-term business.

If you need more marketing information, read *Smart Marketing on a Small Budget* by S.j. Ross in the McGraw-Hill Ryerson SOHO series. It is an excellent, step-by-step, comprehensive "how-to" reference book that covers all aspects of marketing.

To help you now plan your marketing, review the list of ideas in Figure 12.1. This worksheet allows you to plan up to two years ahead, so you can monitor your progress to see if you are staying on target. This information can be transferred to your marketing budget.

What is the Next Step?

Now that you have learned how to revamp your marketing plan, increase your communication skills and use effective methods to market your business, the next step is to learn how to complete the sale. Chapter 13 guides you through the selling process and helps you to better understand what consumers need and expect from you during and after the sale.

Figure 12.1	Marketing Strategies for My Business

STARTING DATE: _____

Projected Time Frame

MARKETING IDEA	Under 3 Months	3 – 6 Months	One Year	Two Years
Join a community organization	❑	❑	❑	❑
Join a networking group	❑	❑	❑	❑
Join the chamber of commerce or Rotary Club	❑	❑	❑	❑
Teach adult education classes	❑	❑	❑	❑
Become a speaker	❑	❑	❑	❑
Use press releases or radio/TV interviews	❑	❑	❑	❑
Participate in trade shows/networking events	❑	❑	❑	❑
Participate in conferences and seminars	❑	❑	❑	❑
Present a workshop or seminar	❑	❑	❑	❑
Obtain evaluations and testimonials	❑	❑	❑	❑
Market using e-mail	❑	❑	❑	❑
Launch a Web site	❑	❑	❑	❑
Produce a newsletter	❑	❑	❑	❑
Offer discount cards	❑	❑	❑	❑
Send thank-you cards	❑	❑	❑	❑
Send birthday and seasonal greetings cards	❑	❑	❑	❑
Use draw and suggestion boxes	❑	❑	❑	❑
Sponsor a community organization	❑	❑	❑	❑
Support fundraisers	❑	❑	❑	❑
Offer complimentary coffee	❑	❑	❑	❑
Advertise on community notice boards	❑	❑	❑	❑
Use direct mail	❑	❑	❑	❑
Use radio or television commercials	❑	❑	❑	❑

Figure 12.1	Continued

	Projected Time Frame			
MARKETING IDEA	Under 3 Months	3 – 6 Months	One Year	Two Years
Advertise in a coupon book	❏	❏	❏	❏
Use newspaper advertising	❏	❏	❏	❏
Use speciality magazine advertising	❏	❏	❏	❏
Circulate flyers	❏	❏	❏	❏
Design a brochure	❏	❏	❏	❏
Design informational handouts	❏	❏	❏	❏
Other: _____	❏	❏	❏	❏

CHAPTER 13

How Do You Improve Your Sales Skills?

SELLING IS AN EVERYDAY EXPERIENCE

Everything you do in life is motivated by the sales process. Think about the many decisions you make. Which house do I buy? Which trip do I take? Do I take this job? These choices involve a decision that was a result of selling yourself on the answer.

Everything you wish someone else to do is also motivated by you selling them on the idea—going for a job interview, applying for a loan, or being elected for public office. These situations all use the same techniques as selling a product or service to others.

This chapter will convey the message in simple terms, using everyday examples, that the concept of selling is not foreign to you. In fact, we use it each day and are already quite effective at the technique. If you understand the overall sales concept, how the consumer thinks, and the more formalized sales process, you will feel more confident in your selling abilities, which will help you in growing your business. You will need to harness your passion, communication skills, confidence and expertise to help build your sales skills.

What is "Selling"?

Selling is an integral component of the marketing mix. But what does "selling" mean? Selling is the process of transferring goods or a service from one person to another. Other definitions may include "for the transference of money." Almost everything we do involves the sales process.

You Can Already Sell

Most people have the ability to sell, and use it all the time. For example, in the morning you have two choices—you can get up or stay in bed. We automatically condition our minds to "sell" ourselves on one of the two choices. Whichever choice is appealing is the choice we make. You may decide that you need to go to work so you won't be fired, or that you have put in extra time and can afford to stay in bed. Either way, you have sold yourself on this choice.

Dispelling the Sales Myth

Many salespeople make the mistake of trying to sell something to someone who really doesn't need or want it. This is referred to as high pressure sales, the type of stereotypical sales process that we all detest. No doubt certain salespeople come to mind when "high pressure" is mentioned. Some have earned their bad reputation.

Have you been pressured at a holiday time-share presentation or been hounded by an aggressive appliance salesperson? You probably didn't use or return to these businesses. Hopefully you vowed not to use those tactics on your customers.

IDEA

BIG

DEVELOP WINNING SALES QUALITIES

Learn to recognize and develop the qualities of a winning salesperson. An ideal salesperson can emphasize with customers and is sensitive to their needs. They are dedicated, competitive, energetic and usually self-driven. They are quick thinkers, good communicators, understand figures, are loyal team players and are usually outgoing and charismatic. They are willing to learn, can work independently, but above all, are honest.

A good salesperson's goals are to assist clients in making the right decision that will fulfill their needs and expectations or solve their problem. The key phrase here is "solve their problem." There is no place in business for the stereotyped salesperson. Always look upon your job as one of helping people, which is the real goal behind this cooperative or nurturing selling style.

CONSUMERS ARE FILLING A NEED

Think of selling as filling a need, because fundamentally, that is what selling is about. People buy because they have a need at that time, whether it is physical or psychological. When partners argue, one may go on a shopping spree or buy comfort food. Why? Because they are filling a need for some positive reinforcement.

Few people want and need a hydraulic jack, but if their car had just broken down, the story would be different. Knowing your customers' needs and wants—and the difference between the two—will help the aspiring salesperson to make a successful sale.

Your aim is to develop a positive relationship with your customers. A happy customer will tell their friends and acquaintances about your business and will return in the future. An angry customer will also tell everyone about your business but not in the manner that you would like. Everyone has a dissatisfied sales story to tell.

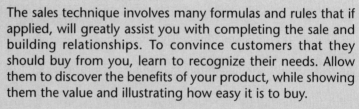

IDEA **USE THE SALES CRITERIA**

BIG

The sales technique involves many formulas and rules that if applied, will greatly assist you with completing the sale and building relationships. To convince customers that they should buy from you, learn to recognize their needs. Allow them to discover the benefits of your product, while showing them the value and illustrating how easy it is to buy.

USE THE SIX-STEP SALES PROCESS

To effectively sell, it helps if you understand the six-step sales process, which works integrally with the "Five Ws" of selling which follow. The sales process follows this sequence.

1. **The Prospect:** finding and identifying potential customers
2. **Planning:** knowing how you will approach the presentation and which sales strategy to use
3. **The Presentation:** presenting your sales strategy to the prospect
4. **The Problems:** being ready to competently handle customers' objections

5. **The Purchase:** knowing the right technique to use in closing a sale

6. **Public Relations:** following up after the sale to ensure customer satisfaction.

THE FIVE "Ws" OF SELLING

You need to understand and use the five "Ws" of selling. Ask yourself these five questions before you attempt to close a sale. You will be pleasantly surprised at how much easier it is to complete the sale.

1. Who is buying?
2. What do they need and want?
3. Why do they need it?
4. Where do they need it?
5. When do they need it?

1. Know Who is Buying

Don't assume that the person standing in front of you is the one making the buying decision. Many salespeople try to convince a prospect that an item is exactly what they need, when that person isn't the actual purchaser. Ask who is the decision-maker and who is the user.

For example, a husband often accompanies his wife when she shops for plants. He is approached by a salesperson who informs him that the tree he is looking at is low maintenance and beautiful when it blooms. The husband doesn't need this information.

If the salesperson had asked the husband what he was looking for, he would have been told that his wife was the purchaser. The wife would appreciate the service, the husband would appreciate being left alone, and the salesperson would appreciate the sale. Know who is buying before you start your sales presentation.

2. Know Their Needs and Wants

The difference between needs and wants can only be ascertained by asking the prospect. There is a distinct difference between the two that cannot be evaluated any other way. You may decide that you need a vehicle to get to and from work. A poor salesperson will decide that a certain vehicle is the one that you need and start the sales process for that vehicle. A good salesperson will question you to find out your exact needs and build the sales process around them.

You *need* a vehicle that gets excellent mileage as you drive 60,000 kilometres a year. You also need a good sound system, plus air conditioning due to your asthma. Unless you were asked about these requirements, the salesperson wouldn't know. You may *want* a vehicle with cruise control and that looks sporty. You don't necessarily need these, but if the price was right, you may consider them in you purchase decision.

3. Why Do They Need It?

Now you must be more specific and ask for what purpose the goods are to be used. Using an alarm sale as an example, if a customer only wants to scare off possible intruders, an alarm sign may suffice. If valuable merchandise is being stored, then a complete system would better suit their needs. By finding out why the customer needs (or wants) a certain product, you can more clearly define how to assist them.

4. Where Do They Need It?

Knowing where a product or service will be used is important sales information, as the sale may depend on other associated costs. This knowledge is especially essential to service businesses. When a project is estimated, you need to know where you will be working, as this directly affects the cost. If the work is not local, you may need to evaluate whether subcontracting is necessary. These factors will affect the final contract price.

This knowledge can also help you to determine the desired product or service quality. A customer will pay a higher price for a premium product if the situation warrants it. For example, a department store alarm may suffice for the average home owner but may not be suitable for a business, which will pay a higher cost for a more dependable alarm. Where the alarm is to be used is an important factor in this sale.

5. When Do They Need It?

Most people research before they purchase and enjoy the browsing process. Ask the customer when they need the product or service. This information can assist you to specifically fill the customer's needs. If a customer was going to buy a computer next month, you could inform him or her that it will be on sale then, or that a new model will be available. The customer appreciates your honesty and concern, will not feel pressured, and will most likely return to purchase from you.

For example, a couple may start house-hunting three years before they want to move. If the realtor didn't know this information, she could waste valuable time showing houses. By asking when they planned to move, she could develop a strategy of showing only suitable houses. When the couple were ready to purchase, they would have developed an excellent rapport with the realtor and would most likely purchase from her.

Always Ask

These examples demonstrate why you must ask customers these five questions. By being better informed before attempting to close a sale, you won't make the mistake of under- or overselling them. Customers will appreciate your attention to detail and the fact that you listened to their needs and didn't try to sell them something they didn't want or need. If you are still unsure of any facts, ask— customers are usually happy to tell you.

THE "SIX Ps" OF SELLING

Now that you better understand how to assess a prospective client's needs, the next step is to continue with the sales process— referred to here as the "Six Ps" of selling. This enables you to better understand how to recognize your prospect through to after-sales service.

1. The Prospect

People new to selling often ask: "Who is a good prospect and how will I recognize one?" The simple answer to this is that everyone is a prospect. Not everyone will become a customer but everyone is a prospect.

Webster's dictionary defines a prospect as "a potential client or customer." To elaborate, a prospect is anyone who has the ability or opportunity to use your products or services. This doesn't mean that they *will* use you, but only that they have the opportunity available to them.

As an example, a grandmother shopping for clothes mistakenly could go into a children's store. She doesn't need children's clothes, but the salesperson doesn't know this. At this point, the grandmother is still a prospect, because she may be looking for her grandchildren.

The salesperson should approach the grandmother, and on being informed of the error, direct the grandmother to a woman's clothing store. The grandmother now ceases to be a current prospect. By assisting her, she may become a future prospect. The old adage of "you can't judge a book by its cover" applies to understanding who is a prospect.

GENERATE MORE LEADS

You have to use your creativity to continually generate sales leads. Be organized and keep a lead file of both prospective, current and old customers. Contact old customers, and ask people for referrals, such as neighbours and friends. Use business and personal groups and associations to generate leads. Try advertising, using mailing lists, and when you feel comfortable, try cold calling.

2. Planning

Before you launch into any sales presentation, you need to plan your approach and the sales strategy to use. Every customer is different and many will present you with unforeseen challenges. The secret is to know what constitutes a successful presentation and how to handle diverse situations.

Your confidence and expertise will build with practice, so rehearsing various approaches and sales demonstrations will help you to feel more at ease. Have the appropriate sales aids ready and ensure that the setting is comfortable for the customer. Know how to handle different cultural and ethnic values.

Planning which approach to use involves some standard sales techniques. Learn how to be personable, appeal to the customer's emotions and senses, and how to involve them in the conversation. Strike a balance between demonstrating the product and relating its features and benefits. Explain each feature slowly and thoroughly. These factors are all necessary to ensure a successful presentation.

IDEA **USE THE "FEATURES AND BENEFITS" TECHNIQUE**

Study any advertising flyers from large stores and you will notice that they stress the features and benefits of their products. This is a strong sales tool that must be used. A feature is a *characteristic* of a product or service. A benefit is the *value of the feature* and what it does for the customer. One feature of a gas dryer is the self-timer. The benefits are that it turns itself off and conserves energy.

3. The Presentation

Once you have identified a prospect and believe that there is an opportunity for him or her to become a customer, you start your sales presentation, extolling the virtues of your product or service and why a buying decision would be in the prospect's best interests. Never deceive a prospect into believing that your product is infallible. A good salesperson will tailor the presentation to meet the prospect's needs while emphasizing the benefits and downplaying the drawbacks.

Your sales presentation is the process of influencing your customer, and starts the moment he or she enters your doors. It continues until the sale is either made or lost, or a decision to return is

IDEA **DELIVER A DYNAMIC PRESENTATION**

A dynamic presentation takes preparation, so do your homework and know your product or service thoroughly. Use effective sales tools and have brochures or take-home information readily available. Spend time getting to know your customer and dress smartly. Remember those first impressions. If you need others to help, ensure they are available, and have any paperwork accessible and ready.

made. It includes planning and after-sales follow-up, which sometimes means going that extra mile to ensure a successful presentation.

The problem of perception: One problem you may experience is clarifying the difference between a business's physical appearance, what it can do, and what you say it can do. Let's use an automotive repair business as an example. You drive into a garage to be faced with rusted vehicles, beer bottles and garbage piled against the wall, and a dirty ill-kept shop. You are starting to make a decision about the quality of service that can be delivered.

On entering, you step in some old oil. The filthy washroom has no tissue paper. A scruffy, unkempt mechanic with nicotine-stained fingers approaches you. He uses language unfit for children's ears. Would you trust this man with your vehicle?

Contrary to these external appearances, he is recognized as one of the best, award-winning mechanics in the region. His abilities are unquestionable yet his presentation appalling. The message to this analogy? How customers perceive your business on first impressions is how you are being judged. Ensure that your sales presentation is exactly how you want the customer to perceive it.

4. The Problems

It is surprising how many salespeople struggle to prevent their customers from voicing their problems or concerns. You need customers to voice their problems before you complete the sale. It is your job to ensure that all problems or objections are satisfactorily answered before you try the closing process. Objections are defined as reasons why clients feel that they should not buy your product.

As a prospective buyer, if you mention to a salesperson that a vacuum cleaner is too expensive, yet they can demonstrate how it can save you money over the years, is it still too expensive? Was this really your objection, or was there another underlying problem that you didn't mention?

Clarify the objection: Objections voiced by customers often don't truly express the real problem. You must clarify the true objection and have suitable answers. Although this sounds impossible, it isn't as complicated as it sounds. How do you achieve this? Quite simply, be prepared. Before you can deal with the objection or problem, you must fully understand what the problem is, so ask the prospect.

After your wonderful presentation to a customer who wants to purchase a vehicle, he or she answers you with: "I'll think about it." Then ask them: "Why? Is there anything I have missed or that you are not sure of?" If the prospect answers, you can be sure there is something holding them back. Your job is to now work with them to identify that objection. Once identified and dealt with, you are in a position to close the sale.

If the customer doesn't answer your question or reiterates the first answer, you probably failed in your first attempt to complete the "Five Ws". If he or she was the decision-maker, wanted and needed a reliable vehicle immediately, and your suggested vehicle filled this need, plus you negated other problems, the customer should purchase the vehicle, providing he or she had the financial ability.

If finances were the only reason that the customer needed to think about it and you could offer a suitable financial arrangement, then the sale would be finalized. Sometimes people just want to browse. In the "Five Ws," you should have identified this and geared your presentation to suit. By helping now, you will encourage the customer to return when he or she is ready.

If the purpose of your presentation was to bring them to the point of making a buying decision, you must now handle all the objections. They have usually decided by now to use someone else, so you need to tell them why that someone should be you.

Use the "Feel, Felt, Found" Technique

There are many ways to handle objections, and two winning techniques are the "Feel, Felt, Found" and "Averting" techniques. The "Feel, Found, Felt" technique is helpful when you are dealing with an emotional customer. People like to know that you have been listening to them and that you empathize with them. This technique demonstrates that other clients have expressed similar concerns with satisfying end results.

As an example, your customer is at the point of making a buying decision, but mentions that the suit they are looking at is too expensive. You can reply using the "Feel, Felt, Found" technique, only with the utmost sincerity. If the prospect feels that you are not sincere, this method will backfire and you could lose not only the sale, but the customer. It's very effective when used correctly. Try empathizing with your customer using something like the following:

"I can understand why you *feel* this way, yet many of our long-term customers *felt* the same way when they first shopped here. What they have *found* is that by shopping here and buying top-quality workmanship suits, the suits have lasted and kept their appearance for twice as long as our nearest competitor. It really depends on what you want." (This should have been identified during the "Five Ws" stage.)

Use the "Averting" Technique

This second technique is more a pre-emptive method to use before an objection is even raised. When a salesperson repeatedly hears the same objection, they can then incorporate the answer into their presentation, thus completely averting the objection. If you sell computers, you might use the following:

"…even if the speed of computers doubles in the next six months, this computer allows you to use this installed software for many years to come. If an upgrade is necessary, we can easily do that for you, it's no trouble at all and we can do it free of charge when you buy the unit."

By using the "Averting" technique, you have circumvented this common objection about the speed of technological change while allowing the client to focus on the features and benefits. A competent salesperson can time the averted objection to minimize the effect of the objection and maximize the benefits, then continuing on to stress how this software will help to solve the customer's problem.

5. The Purchase

The purchase, or the close, is the most important part of the sales process, because if you don't close the sale, your efforts were in vain. This section explores what a trial close is, how to use it, why people find it difficult to close, how to overcome these problems, and when it is time to close.

What is "Closing a Sale?"

"Closing a sale" is the specific point during your presentation that confirms a buying decision by your customer. It only occurs after all your prospect's objections and concerns have been satisfactorily answered. Closing the sale is the question that you ask to complete this part of the sales presentation. Remember—once closed, don't continue to close.

How Do You Close?

To demonstrate how to close, imagine a salesperson who is making a presentation to a customer about a trip to Mexico. They have given a detailed account of what the customer can expect, places to go, and things to do. There is not much more to say.

Before closing the sale, the salesperson may ask questions such as: "Will we book an early September or a fall departure?" or: "Will we be booking a reservation for you alone or will you be travelling with a friend?" Trying to close a sale by asking these questions is called a trial close.

Use Trial Closes

You are attempting to solicit a positive response from your prospect on their intent. A trial close looks to use phrases that should always imply a close. Questions such as "Would you prefer the metallic colour or something a little more adventurous?" "When did you need this by?" "Will you want Picture in Picture in your new television?" are all examples of trial closes.

They do not specifically ask for the sale, but give the salesperson an indication of how close they are. During a sales presentation, try to use as many trial closes as possible. It's not uncommon to use between 10 to 15 trial closes before the actual close. The more trial closes you use, the easier the sale becomes.

Red Flag

A common mistake made by salespeople is to believe that the trial close can replace the actual close. If you don't ask for the sale, it's likely that your customer will walk away and buy from someone else. They have already made the decision to buy based on your presentation, they just haven't decided from whom. It's not enough to believe that the close will happen—*you* must make it happen.

When Do You Close?

Gauging the right time to close is difficult because only you can sense this from your conversations. Generally, it's time to close when your customer shows a genuine interest in your product. If he or she nods affirmatively, agrees with your answers, or if there are verbal or body language indications that your customer is ready to get down to business, this is the time to close.

Salespeople must continuously observe the customer for subtle signs that a purchase is imminent. Salespeople are often better talkers than listeners, thus missing these most important signs. If a customer is ready to make a purchasing decision, stop talking, start observing and listening, and close the sale.

IDEA

IMPROVE YOUR LISTENING SKILLS

There is a vast difference between hearing and listening, and successful selling requires that you listen to your customer's needs. A good listener treats each customer as a VSP and tries to think like that customer. The salesperson listens for ideas and makes notes, concentrating on what the customer is saying without interrupting. A good listener is polite, asks questions, limits talking, and is sensitive to the customer's concerns.

6. Public Relations

The message has been stressed throughout this book that follow-up and service keep your customers returning. Once the sale is completed and the satisfied customer leaves, how will you follow up to ensure that he or she stay happy? My car dealership always calls within twenty-four hours to ensure that the vehicle is operating properly, plus they send regular service reminders. I not only appreciate it, I have come to expect it.

You have many options to choose from, depending on your type of business. Letters, thank-you cards, or a follow-up call all build relationships. For some products or services, a further follow-up call may be in order to ensure long-term customer satisfaction. By building these relationships, customers will refer you to others.

CAN YOU IMPROVE YOUR SALES SKILLS?

If you learn to use the basic sales strategies and principles as outlined in this chapter, combined with a winning marketing plan and your excellent communication skills, your sales will increase by leaps and bounds. Learning all these skills may take some time and practise.

Figure 13.1 provides a checklist for you to complete to ensure that you don't miss one important step. If you have sales staff, let them take the test as well. Can you answer "yes" to these twenty questions?

What if...

This book has taken you from assessing where you are now right through to operating more efficiently and profitably. It has explored all the important factors that contribute to growing a strong, successful and healthy business. If you use all this advice, you will become a multi-faceted, entrepreneurial success.

But what if you feel that there is still no solution to your problems? Chapter 14 guides you step-by-step through how to operate in crisis mode and explains the available options. It includes a detailed worksheet and checklist to help you to assess your current situation and make a decision on your next course of action.

Figure 13.1	Can I Improve My Sales Skills?

	Yes	No
1. I avoid using high-pressure sales tactics.	❑	❑
2. I am sensitive to my customers' needs.	❑	❑
3. I am always honest with my customers.	❑	❑
4. I understand the importance of recognizing customers' needs.	❑	❑
5. I use the "Five Ws" of selling when assessing these needs.	❑	❑
6. I maintain a customer leads file.	❑	❑
7. I contact old customers and ask for referrals.	❑	❑
8. I first plan my sales presentation.	❑	❑
9. I often rehearse my sales presentations.	❑	❑
10. I have a variety of sales tools available.	❑	❑
11. I always dress appropriately.	❑	❑
12. I understand how to clarify objections.	❑	❑
13. I use the "feel, felt, found" technique.	❑	❑
14. I use the "averting" technique.	❑	❑
15. I use the "features and benefits" technique.	❑	❑
16. I use trial closes during my presentations.	❑	❑
17. I am a good listener and ask the customer many questions.	❑	❑
18. I allow the customer to talk and don't interrupt.	❑	❑
19. I understand and use the six-step sales process.	❑	❑
20. I always follow up each sale to ensure customer satisfaction.	❑	❑

CHAPTER 14

How Do You Operate in Crisis?

THE GREAT ENTREPRENEURIAL DREAM

Every year across the nation, thousands of microbusinesses start with the universal dream of success. You hear of the success stories through media and from friends. Rarely do you hear of the failures. There are hundreds of self-employment programs, seminars and courses, and an abundance of resources to help businesses through start-up. So no one really likes to think about failure—and most people don't.

Unfortunately, statistics tell us that 80 to 90 percent of new businesses don't make it. This book was written with the hope of making a minuscule dent in these depressing figures by analysing the main causes of failure in the first fragile years and offering workable, practical solutions. If you put the systems and suggestions in this book to work for you, your chance of failure will be well diminished—if not erased—and you will be on your way to growing a healthy micro-business.

"LET'S NOT TALK ABOUT FAILURE"

"What if your business doesn't make it?" I have asked many clients. "What will happen to the financial stability of the family and the family unit?"

"Let's not talk about failure," has been a standard reply, "I didn't go into business thinking about not making it. I haven't even considered the consequences of failure."

"Perhaps you should think about it," would be my reply.

Someone has to talk about the 80 percent who don't make it, so please read this chapter and take the information to heart. After consulting to many struggling businesses since 1983, the failure stories far outweigh the successes. Perhaps what breaks my heart the most is seeing the resulting divorces and innocent children suffering.

Many of the reasons for not growing a successful business are discussed in this book one way or another. Psychologically, the main reasons for failure are that people don't want to admit they are wrong, or don't like the work involved in doing it right, or think that they know it all. We all make mistakes.

One of my favourite quotes comes from an article in an old Toastmasters magazine. "Flops are part of life's menu. Everyone makes mistakes. High achievers learn by their mistakes. By doing that, an error becomes the raw material out of which future successes are forged. Failure is not a crime. Failure to learn from failure is."

IDEA **FIND A MENTOR**

Many successful people owe their success to having help and guidance from a mentor. A mentor can be anyone who is prepared to take an interest in helping you and who can offer experienced advice and support. If you don't know where to find one, ask your chamber of commerce. Explain that you business needs help. Most chambers really care about their members and will go out of their way to accommodate you.

HEED THE WARNING SIGNS

Buried in the day-to-day operation of your business, the warning signs of crisis can pass unnoticed. The more obvious signs will be there, but because no one likes admitting to possible failure, many choose to take the ostrich approach and ignore them.

On the positive side, many people have failed at one or more businesses before making a roaring success at the next one. So if this business doesn't succeed, don't feel ashamed—you will have learned some valuable lessons. Take a moment to stop and think about your business. Complete the checklist in Figure 14.1 by checking off the warning signs that apply to you.

Figure 14.1	Warning Signs That Your Business is in Crisis

❑ Your payments to provincial and federal tax agencies are behind and are incurring penalties.

❑ You cannot meet payroll commitments.

❑ Suppliers are becoming more aggressive in their collections.

❑ Your accounts payable are increasing and payments are falling behind.

❑ Sales are decreasing.

❑ Profits are not supporting overhead commitments.

❑ Inventories are decreasing.

❑ Accounts receivable are decreasing.

❑ Cash in the account is decreasing.

❑ You are reducing prices too often to stimulate sales.

❑ You are reducing the wage you take from the business.

❑ Employees are being laid off or their hours reduced.

❑ Suppliers are asking for cash-on-delivery payment terms.

❑ Banks won't give you a business loan.

❑ You keep injecting capital into the business.

❑ You are constantly depressed and irritable with feelings of futility.

❑ Consumer or economic trends are adversely affecting your business.

❑ Losses are increasing.

TEN STEPS FOR OPERATING IN CRISIS

As each business differs in their problems, there is no one-remedy-fits-all solution. In many cases, a business can be salvaged. In other situations, the most practical answer is to stop before the situation gets any worse. This is where sitting down with your accountant to review your past and current fiscal history is necessary. The ideal approach would be to devise an exit strategy on start-up. Now is the time to include an exit strategy in your future planning process.

It's no use constantly pouring money into a leaky pail if there is no way to plug the holes. On the other hand, some decisive action could well get you through this situation. There are steps that you can immediately take to ease the mental stress while you regroup and decide on a course of action.

For each of the next 10 steps, when you have assembled the required information, transfer it to the corresponding step in Figure 14.3, the worksheet at the end of this chapter.

STEP 1: REVIEW GROSS PROFIT MARGINS

As previously discussed, healthy gross profit margins are necessary to sustain overhead commitments, and it's easy for them to decrease unnoticed if they are not constantly monitored. Review your cost of goods sold and all related costs to see which ones are contributing to decreasing margins. Estimate through your accounting records how much these costs have increased this year. Review the detailed list of cost of goods expenses at the end of this chapter in Figure 14.3 and write your answers on the worksheet.

Inefficiency in any one of the areas of materials, packaging, equipment or staff will lead to lost profits. One client reviewed the discounts given for the past year, only to find that they had doubled while sales had increased by only 10 percent. Over a year, this made a difference of over $8,000. A new discount structure was put into place that satisfied the customers and reduced this expense to an acceptable level.

STEP 2: REVIEW OVERHEAD EXPENSES

If you haven't already studied your recent overhead expenses in previous exercises, now is the time to do so. Print out a detailed general ledger report for the year and look carefully through each expense account. Take five different coloured highlighters and as you review each account, use them to track the categories below.

1. One-time expenses that will not reoccur within the next twelve-month period.
2. Expenses that were unnecessary or frivolous.
3. Expenses that have increased in the last fiscal year (example: wages)

4. New and ongoing expenses (example: extra telephone line).

5. Expenses that could be reduced (example: travel).

Then complete Step 2 in Figure 14.3. You will have then identified increased overhead costs, one-time expenses and frivolous expenses. Now you are better able to prepare a "bare bones" budget.

STEP 3: PREPARE A BARE BONES BUDGET

Now you have all the information you need to calculate a conservative budget. Prepare monthly projections for six to 12 months, using statistical sales history combined with expectations from future marketing strategies to see how much profit can be generated. See Step 3 in Figure 14.3 worksheet for an example. You will need this information to negotiate with suppliers and various tax agencies. If the new budget reflects losses or little or no profit, this will be addressed further on in this chapter.

CALCULATE THE COST OF LAYING OFF

If your budget involves laying off employees, calculate the amount of severance, holiday and any other wages due, including the remittance portion to Canada Customs and Revenue Agency (CCRA). Be sure you include this amount in your cash flow calculations. Laying off long-term employees can be an expensive exercise and you need the available funds to pay out.

STEP 4: REVIEW MARKETING STRATEGIES

Although you have to be frugal at this stage, a business will not sustain sales without some aggressive marketing techniques. Review how your marketing dollars were spent and how effective the results were. Hopefully, you have been monitoring your marketing results. Complete the exercise in Step 4 of the Figure 14.3 worksheet to ascertain unproductive marketing costs.

STEP 5: REVIEW CASH FLOW

Projecting future profits doesn't take care of paying the current bills, so your cash-flow situation needs some attention. Once again,

> ### IDEA
> ## BIG
> ### SEEK MARKETING ADVICE
>
> If your methods are not working and you don't know what to try next, seek some free marketing advice from organizations such as Western Economic Diversification, your chamber of commerce, Community Futures Development Corp., Enterprise centres, or a self-help office in your community. You may have to spend some money hiring a reputable marketing consultant to help you. The Business Development Bank of Canada offers consulting services for a fee. Check their Web site at *www.bdc.ca*. It would be a shame to let a good business flounder when all that is needed is some professional advice.

your accountant should help you to interpret your financial statements or accounting records and help with your decision-making.

You will need to analyse your current cash position and determine how much of the accounts receivables are collectable and in what time frame. Inventory levels must be sufficient to meet future projected sales. Identify slow-moving items that can be turned into cash through a clearance sale. Assess whether any equipment needs repairing or if any major asset needs to be purchased in the next few months. List accounts payable, taxes, payroll remittances, and monthly loan payments. Identify those that are delinquent and the amounts. All this information should be recorded as set out in Figure 14.3, step 5.

Next calculate your current working capital position by totalling current assets and current liabilities. If current liabilities exceed current assets, you now know the amount that you are short to meet your obligations and can plan a course of action based on your sales and expense projections. This exercise allows you to plan how you will approach the various creditors and to what level you may have to further reduce expenses.

STEP 6: DEAL WITH TAX AGENCIES

If you are open and honest in dealing with agencies such as CCRA or your provincial tax department, they are usually cooperative. Your first step is to know how much you owe them and how late the accounts are. Before you contact them, prepare a budget to estimate how much you can pay each month. At the same time, you should commit to maintaining current payments.

This can be achieved by transferring the tax portion of each bank deposit into a tax savings account. In fact, always use this system to ensure that tax monies are available. Don't put suppliers ahead of taxes—you collect taxes in trust and CCRA makes this quite clear. On Step 6 of the Figure 14.3 worksheet, list the agencies you owe, the amounts, and their phone numbers.

IDEA **CONTACT TAX AGENCIES**

If taxes are behind, call the collection department of each tax agency to explain your financial situation. They will ask for a payment plan, financial figures, and your budget. They also require that current payments be kept up-to-date. If you miss one payment or the cheque bounces, don't expect any sympathy. If you don't honour your promises, expect your bank accounts to be frozen or the money taken from them.

If you have accrued a huge sum of interest, you could write to the Special Appeals Committee to have the interest portion reduced. This has worked quite successfully for clients in the past with no appeals being denied so far. Even the tax department has a heart as shown in the Real Life example, 'Tackling a Tax Crisis.'

REAL LIFE: Tackling a Tax Crisis

Diane had worked as a subcontractor for over 10 years, although she should have been on the payroll because she worked full-time for one company. However, at that time, these were the terms of employment—take it or leave it.

When Diane became self-employed she had no prior business knowledge or experience. She came to me in a desperate state of mind—the only way she could pay the huge tax bill of nearly $140,000 was to sell her property.

A series of traumatic events over the last 10 years included a huge barn fire which killed all her breeding animals, and the death of her husband from cancer. During her 10 years as a "business owner," she had effectively lost well over $50,000 in unpaid benefits such as CPP, vacation pay and employment insurance coverage. She also had to train and pay someone to do her work when she took time off. In all the turmoil, Diane didn't quite get around to filing her taxes.

Her fear of the obvious mounting tax bill kept her from facing the situation until it seemed almost insurmountable. The actual tax bill was well under $100,000, but the penalties and interest were nearly as much as the tax portion.

I prepared a long letter of explanation, accompanied by a detailed budget and the promise that she would ask her employer to put her on the payroll. After three months of negotiating, countless phone calls and correspondence, the end result was that CCRA added the current year's taxes to the bill and reduced penalties and interest by $55,000.

Diane's employer put her on the payroll so that this situation wouldn't reoccur. The bank wouldn't supply a traditional mortgage as the house needed some major repairs, but did cooperate with a term loan. Diane was fortunate that she only had a small mortgage. Now her debt is much larger, but she still has her home, saved $55,000, and won't be faced with this situation again.

STEP 7: DEAL WITH SUPPLIERS

Suppliers need to make profits just as you do, and they are well aware that businesses can bankrupt overnight. Struggling businesses tend not to communicate with suppliers, hoping to drag payments out until "things get better." This is the wrong approach. You need to inform them that the business is suffering cash flow problems and is working on solutions.

Review each supplier's account to see what payment terms you can offer. In many cases, you will need their cooperation in maintaining your supplies to continue business. Look at the situation from their perspective—they can't keep supplying you with products or services without a structured repayment plan. Perhaps you can offer to pay a small amount each month off the old debt, with new purchases being paid for C.O.D.

If you honour your commitments and pay the overdue accounts, credit is usually restored. If you are an incorporated company, trade suppliers usually lose any outstanding debts on bankruptcy. If you are a proprietorship, they can take you to court. Your personal assets are then at risk.

On Step 7 of the Figure 14.3 worksheet, list those pressing suppliers, the amounts you owe, and the date you promised to pay them. You will need this information for your cash flow projections.

STEP 8: TURBO-CHARGE COLLECTIONS

Some of your problems may be the result of lax collection procedures. There are many cases of small businesses suffering because one large client went "belly-up." Stress to all your clients that you are tightening up your credit policy and that 30 days is your limit. Offer a discount for seven-day payments. Phone tardy clients and offer to pick up their cheques.

Be aggressive with clients who stall you with no promise of payment—they may be experiencing similar problems. Be firm but pleasant as they are still your clients. Read *What to Say When Your Customers Won't Pay*, by Judy Smith and Michael Shulman in the McGraw-Hill Ryerson SOHO series. It's an excellent publication offering a variety of solutions to collection problems.

Review your current outstanding accounts receivable, breaking them down into current, 30, 60, 90 days and over. Transfer these totals to Step 8 of the Figure 14.3 worksheet. Starting with the 90 days and over, call each overdue client—get the potential bad debts before they are not recoverable. Use the suggestions in Chapter 10. Decide which accounts need further action and start immediately.

STEP 9: ASSESS YOURSELF

Continuing a business in crisis mode is both mentally and physically exhausting. It takes great courage, determination, persistence and hard work to turn a floundering business around—but it can be done. Many growing or struggling businesses have made successful transitions because owners have made concerted efforts.

The process takes time and energy. You have to be ready to face the challenges ahead and be confident that you can do it. Without this commitment, it won't happen. You have come this far in making your entrepreneurial dream a reality. Are you ready to fight to keep your dream alive, or ready to let it go? Only you can make this choice.

Take the Test

By the time you have completed these 10 steps, you will have a better indication of cash flow, future potential, supplier relationships, and a workable time frame. Before you make any final decisions, assess whether you are ready to move forward. Answer the 10 questions in Figure 14.2 and then transfer your answers to Step 9 of the Figure 14.3 worksheet and review your score.

STEP 10: KNOW YOUR OPTIONS

Finally, you must understand all the available options. A business that has experienced sudden and unexpected growth will face different challenges than one that is struggling to survive for other reasons. A growing business with long-term future potential has many opportunities to seek external help to work through their problems.

A business heading for failure can often survive and succeed by seeking professional help before it is too late. When the worksheet is completed, meet with your accountant to discuss your situation. Your options are summarized Step 10 of the Figure 14.3 worksheet.

FAILURE OF A SOLE PROPRIETORSHIP

If the most viable solution appears to be closure of the business, you should be aware of some of the ramifications. There are alter-

Figure 14.2	Am I Committed to Continue?

	Yes	No
1. Am I ready to commit to a concentrated effort?	❑	❑
2. Do I have the support of my family?	❑	❑
3. Do I realize how long this may take?	❑	❑
4. Do I feel physically ready to cope with the extra work?	❑	❑
5. Do I feel emotionally ready to cope with the extra worry?	❑	❑
6. Am I currently feeling positive about the future?	❑	❑
7. Am I willing to follow professional advice?	❑	❑
8. Am I willing to learn from past mistakes?	❑	❑
9. Could I further endanger our financial stability?	❑	❑
10. Am I currently feeling depressed?	❑	❑

natives that should be researched before this decision is made. You can work with a Trustee in Bankruptcy who can discuss the available options for resolving financial difficulties. The trustee will advise you on:

- debt consolidation/settlement arrangements
- filing a Consolidation Order
- preparing an informal proposal for creditors
- filing a formal proposal to creditors under the federal *Bankruptcy and Insolvency Act (BIA)*
- credit counselling services
- an Assignment in Bankruptcy under the *BIA.*

Understand Your Liabilities

A sole proprietorship or partnership usually carries more liability than an incorporated business. If you have signed any promissory notes or personal guarantees for loans or guarantees with other creditors, you are personally responsible for these debts, all trade creditor debts, loans, government and provincial taxes, and leases.

Your personal assets are at risk, as creditors have the right to take you to court. Liens can be placed on bank accounts or assets, both personal and business. CCRA can freeze your bank account or take funds directly from it to repay taxes. Working with a Trustee in Bankruptcy can often negate a portion of this debt or a payment-free period can be negotiated. Note that CCRA also has the ability to register a secured interest effective January 1, 2000.

Bankruptcy—the Last Alternative

When there seems no light at the end of the tunnel, bankruptcy may be the final alternative. While bankruptcy results in the elimination of the majority, if not all of your debts, it isn't a pleasant alternative. Whenever a business or an individual files for bankruptcy, there seems to be a stigma attached for the person and family involved.

The effects of bankruptcy will vary based on provincial legislation, but in a nutshell, assets are liquidated to repay debts, with certain personal possessions being exempt from the bankruptcy order. These usually include clothing, furniture, income-generating tools or equipment, motor vehicles to a certain value, food and necessary household effects. For detailed information, see *www.Bankruptcy Canada.com.* It provides information for all provinces with extensive links to other sites that may help you.

How Long Does Bankruptcy Apply?

Subject to certain restrictions, a bankruptcy is usually discharged after nine months. If you have been previously bankrupt, you may be required to appear before a Registrar or Judge before the discharge is made. The bankruptcy will remain on the Credit Bureau's records for six years from the date of discharge for a first-time bankruptcy and 14 years for a second bankruptcy. You may apply for credit once the bankruptcy is discharged, although the decision to grant credit rests with the creditors.

Steps in a sole-proprietor bankruptcy process can be summarized as follows:

1. Contact a Trustee in Bankruptcy.
2. Attend the Meeting of Creditors, if required.
3. Attend two counselling sessions.
4. Make payments to the Trustee while awaiting discharge, if required.
5. Attend court for the discharge hearing, if required.

FAILURE OF AN INCORPORATED BUSINESS

There is more protection for an incorporated company that is experiencing insolvency problems. By incorporating, the shareholders have a degree of limited liability. Unless you have signed personal guarantees or promissory notes, trade creditors are forced to take what is left over after business assets are liquidated. Government departments and banks have first priority.

A business can be saved by filing a Proposal under the *Bankruptcy and Insolvency Act.* Filing a proposal under the *BIA* enables a debtor to reasonably rearrange their finances without the fear of creditors taking legal action. Proposal terms may allow for payment of less than 100 cents on the dollar to unsecured creditors.

What are Directors' Liabilities?

Apart from any personal guarantees that directors have signed, they are responsible for the payment of GST, provincial taxes, employee wages and source deductions. In some cases, an incorporated business has declared bankruptcy and directors have then had to file for personal bankruptcy due to their inability to personally repay these agencies.

When a business either closes or bankrupts, if there are outstanding shareholders' loans, they can be claimed on the current year's income tax return as an Allowable Business Investment Loss (ABIL). You can claim 75 percent of the loss, which is reduced by any previous capital gains deductions from previous years. You can also claim the value of shares lost in a Canadian Controlled Private Corporation as a capital loss. Your accountant can tell you more.

THINK ABOUT YOUR FAMILY

If you are reading this for informational purposes only and are fortunate enough not to be in this position, it should reinforce the message that astute business management is crucial—not just for the success of the business, but for the health of your family. Small business failure has caused a multitude of divorces. I have witnessed too many cases where a business has failed or declared bankruptcy and almost immediately, the marriage breaks down and ends in divorce.

Is any business really worth risking a marriage? It's not just the broken marriages—next come the threats, sometimes violence, the turning of children against parents, and their long-term psychological suffering.

Next comes the battles over child custody and support payments. The emotional effects are long-lived and traumatic, with no one escaping unscathed. Make a promise to both yourself and your family that you will work hard to succeed at this business—and your marriage.

What Will Your Decision Be?

Although somewhat depressing reading material, this is a necessary chapter to read. If nothing else, it should convince you to become more financially conversant with your business and committed to success. Talking of success, the final chapter is devoted entirely to this subject.

Figure 14.3	Worksheet: Ten Steps to Operating in Crisis

When you have all the available information needed for Steps 1 through 10, complete the following. The information will document your current financial position and guide you through the necessary action to be taken. Confer with your accountant. If you do complete the worksheet, then you have the right attitude and are serious about turning your business around.

STEP 1: REVIEW GROSS PROFIT MARGINS

Write down the increase over normal costs in each applicable area for this current year.

1. production systems $_____
2. raw material costs $_____
3. wages $_____
4. freight $_____
5. customs, brokerage, duty $_____
6. equipment repairs $_____
7. inefficient equipment $_____
8. packaging materials $_____
9. packaging methods $_____
10. selling costs (commissions) $_____
11. discount structure $_____
12. employee unproductiveness $_____   Total: $_____

Figure 14.3	**Continued**

STEP 2: REVIEW OVERHEAD EXPENSES

When you have reviewed the general ledger and carefully categorized each of the expenses, total each category. Add together the expenses in items 1 and 2. You have now separated one-time and frivolous costs from your figures. Re-total each general ledger account minus these expenses to give you a better indication of normal operating costs. Study this amount to see how it has affected your profits.

Then total the expenses in items 3 and 4. You will need this information to plan your revised budget as overhead increases must be properly accounted for. How can you reduce these costs? The expenses highlighted in item 5 need to be reviewed to see how they can be reduced without affecting the efficiency of the business. Calculate the total of these extra expenses to see how much they contributed to reduced profits and cash flow.

1. One-time expenses $_____

2. Unnecessary expenses $_____   = $_____ subtotal

3. Increased expenses $_____

4. New and ongoing expenses $_____   = $_____ subtotal

5. Expenses that could be reduced $_____ = $_____ subtotal

   Total extra overhead expenses: **$**_____

Figure 14.3	Continued

STEP 3: PREPARE A BARE BONES BUDGET

Prepare a six- to twelve-month no-frills budget using the sample below as a guideline. From these figures, prepare a cash flow projection to estimate cash shortages.

Sample Bare Bones Budget

	MONTH 1	MONTH 2	MONTH 3
Sales			
Purchases			
Production wages			
Freight and duty			
Packaging			
Discounts			
Sales commissions			
Other			
Gross profit: (%)			
Overhead:			
Accounting fees			
Advertising			
Bad debts			
Bank charges			
CPP & EI expenses			
Depreciation			
Employee benefits			
Fees, licences			
Insurance			
Loan interest			
Marketing & promotion			
Management salaries			
Office salaries			
Office supplies			
Rent & taxes			
Repairs & maintenance			
Shop supplies			
Telephone, fax, Internet			
Vehicle gas			
Vehicle repairs, insurance			
Workers' Compensation			
Total expenses			
Net profit (loss)	$	$	$

Figure 14.3	Continued

MONTH 4	MONTH 5	MONTH 6	TOTAL
$	$	$	$

Figure 14.3	Continued

STEP 4: REVIEW MARKETING STRATEGIES

1. Marketing strategies that did not increase sales:

   a. _____   Cost: $_____

   b. _____   Cost: $_____

   c. _____   Cost: $_____

                                          Total: $_____

2. Estimated cost of hiring a marketing consultant $_____

3. Estimated cost of increased marketing strategies $_____

STEP 5: REVIEW CASH FLOW

List the current amounts in each category.

1. **Cash in bank accounts:** $_____
2. **Accounts receivable:** $_____
3. **Inventory:** Estimated revenue from clearance sale $_____
4. **Funds required to increase inventory:** $_____
5. **Fixed assets:** Estimated repair and maintenance costs $_____
6. **Estimated new asset purchases:** $_____
7. **Accounts payable:** current month _____

                             30 days _____

                             60 days _____

                             90 and over _____ $_____
8. **Taxes:**   GST _____

                             Provincial _____

                             Payroll _____

                             Personal _____

                             Corporate _____ $_____
9. **Loan payments:** Total due in next ____ months $_____
10. **Working capital:** Current assets: $_____

                              Current liabilities: $_____

                              Working capital position: **$**_____

Figure 14.3	**Continued**

STEP 6: DEAL WITH TAX AGENCIES

List the amounts owing to each agency, and their phone number. Keep a detailed log of your conversations.

1. GST $_____   Phone: _____   Called: _____

    Person Spoken To: _____   Action: _____

2. Provincial $_____   Phone: _____   Called: _____

    Person Spoken To: _____   Action: _____

3. Payroll $_____   Phone: _____   Called: _____

    Person Spoken To: _____   Action: _____

4. Personal $_____   Phone: _____   Called: _____

    Person Spoken To: _____   Action: _____

5. Corporate $_____   Phone: _____   Called: _____

    Person Spoken To: _____   Action: _____

STEP 7: DEAL WITH SUPPLIERS

List the most urgent suppliers, the amounts you owe and the date you promised to pay them.

SUPPLIER	AMOUNT	PAY BY
1. _____		
2. _____		
3. _____		
4. _____		
5. _____		
6. _____		
Total:	$	

Figure 14.3	**Continued**

STEP 8: TURBO-CHARGE COLLECTIONS

List all current outstanding receivable totals.

1. Accounts overdue 90 + days $_____

2. Accounts overdue 60 days $_____

3. Accounts overdue 30 days $_____

Total: $_____

Start contacting the over 90 days. List the oldest debts on the worksheet and the action to be taken.

NAME	INVOICE DATE	AMOUNT DUE	ACTION
1.			
2.			
3.			
4.			
5.			
6.			
7.			
8.			

STEP 9: ASSESS YOURSELF

Complete the self-assessment test in Figure 14.2 and note your results below.

Questions 1 to 8:   Yes _____   No _____

Questions 9 and 10:   Yes _____   No _____

Ideally, you should have answered "yes" to questions 1 to 8 and "no" to questions 9 and 10. Any other answers mean that if you continue, you could experience significant problems. You need a positive attitude, total commitment, professional help and family support without further risking your financial stability.

Figure 14.3	Continued

STEP 10: KNOW YOUR OPTIONS

Discuss with your accountant the following options and check which currently apply to your business. You now have a plan of action.

		Yes	No
1.	Gross profit margins must be increased.	❏	❏
2.	Overhead expenses must be decreased.	❏	❏
3.	The budget reflects that a turn around is possible.	❏	❏
4.	The budget reflects further future losses.	❏	❏
5.	Cash flow projections show a need for a loan.	❏	❏
6.	The business can survive without a loan.	❏	❏
7.	Current loans may have to be refinanced.	❏	❏
8.	The working capital is in a positive position.	❏	❏
9.	The working capital is in a negative position.	❏	❏
10.	Marketing strategies need to be changed.	❏	❏
11.	I need professional help with marketing.	❏	❏
12.	Aggressive attention is needed for collections.	❏	❏
13.	I need the services of a collection agency.	❏	❏
14.	Inventory levels are too high/too low.	❏	❏
15.	I can currently meet accounts payable liabilities.	❏	❏
16.	I cannot currently meet accounts payable liabilities.	❏	❏
17.	I can meet all tax requirements.	❏	❏
18.	I must contact tax agencies to formulate a payment plan.	❏	❏
19.	I must contact suppliers to organize payment terms.	❏	❏
20.	I am mentally and physically ready to handle all this.	❏	❏
21.	I do not feel capable of facing all this work and worry.	❏	❏
22.	There is no viable financial solution for continuing on.	❏	❏
23.	I understand my liabilities as a sole proprietor.	❏	❏

Figure 14.3	Continued		Yes	No
24. I will meet with a Trustee in Bankruptcy.			❏	❏
25. I understand the ramifications of personal bankruptcy.			❏	❏
26. I understand my liabilities as a director.			❏	❏
27. I understand the ramifications of corporate bankruptcy.			❏	❏
28. I could lose my home and family if I continue operations.			❏	❏
29. I could lose my home and family if I declare bankruptcy.			❏	❏

CHAPTER 15

Are You Ready to Succeed?

WHAT IS SUCCESS?

Success has a different connotation for everyone. It may be as simple as enjoyably exploring your creativity with a craft business, making enough money to pay the bills, or it may mean the Silver Mercedes Coupe (slightly used) at the end of the rainbow. *Business in Vancouver* devoted their May 9th, 2000 issue 550 to success. It cited some thought-provoking comments. Here are some short excerpts.

> *"It's abundantly clear that each one has a different interpretation of 'success' and it seldom stops with the obvious tally of revenues and profits. Some find success in volunteering, others in pursuing a balanced life of work or family, and still others in their work. If we can believe what people say, money is not the ultimate goal.*
>
> *Instead, people talk about passion, about vision and about creating. They bring to life numerous cliches that just won't die:*
>
> * *Money isn't everything.*
> * *You must believe in what you do.*
> * *It's not the destination but the journey that counts.*
>
> *You get the idea.*
> *Successful people take what most of us hear in goal-setting and time-management workshops, and actually apply it. And they are determined. Setbacks are just that—setbacks. They aren't permanent. They are not the end of the line. They are, as the saying goes, learning experiences."*

Success Is...

Here are some quotes from a few of the entrepreneurs *Business in Vancouver* interviewed who have travelled the long, hard road to entrepreneurial success.

"Success is not only what you achieve, but also what you help others achieve."

> Mossadiq S. Umedaly, Chair and
> CEO of Xantrex Technology Inc.

"Success to me is getting up and being excited about what you're doing. Money's important to me. It brings a lot of freedom. But it should not be at the expense of doing something I'm not passionate about."

> Steven Pollock, Partner & Operations
> Manager, The Creek Restaurant
> (Note, Steven broke his spinal cord in an
> accident and is confined to wheelchair.)

"My personal definition of success is doing something that makes you smile. You get personal satisfaction... If you just equate success with money, that doesn't do it."

> Bob Rennie, Owner of
> Rennie Project Marketing

"Success is a state of mind... It's having a talent for what you are doing, but knowing that only with focus and hard work will you reach your goals."

> Nancy Stibbard, CEO,
> Capilano Suspension Bridge

"The real challenge for me has always been how to seek balance in my life away from the business with my family and friends. When I can do that, only then, will I feel that I have been truly successful."

> Kate O'Brien, President,
> Plum Clothing Ltd.

THE INNER REWARDS OF SUCCESS

As you can see from this small sampling of hard-working, successful entrepreneurs, the word "success" is associated with many of the positive ideals that we all strive for in life. Very few people feel that money is the true sign of success.

Following is a list of those positive values mentioned in the previous quotes. Read and absorb these wonderful words. They are the real reason—apart from making a living—that you are in business.

- achievement
- smiling
- satisfaction
- hard work

- happiness
- excitement
- helping others
- reaching goals

- balance
- passion
- freedom
- focus

If you are experiencing some or all of these feelings, then you are well on your way to building a successful business. Doesn't it feel great?

IDEA **START A "THINK" GROUP**

Being successful doesn't happen if you work alone. You need others to inspire, motivate, teach and support you. Start a group with four to five associates from varying businesses who meet each week for an hour or so. Share ideas, exchange contacts, review and set new goals, brainstorm and problem-solve. It works! That's how my first book came to be. Without this peer support, it would not have happened as quickly as it did.

WOMEN MOVE INTO THE BOARDROOM

Women have made their mark in business, with their success rate quickly increasing. Female business owners represent the fastest growing sector of the Canadian economy. In 1998, the number of women-led firms increased at double the national average.

Canadian women now hold top positions in politics and the corporate environment. There are many dynamic, successful woman entrepreneurs and it's not surprising, as women have some wonderful inherent talents that can be adapted naturally to owning a business.

WHY WOMEN SUCCEED

After working with a broad spectrum of entrepreneurs for over 30 years and observing and talking to them in depth, I've assembled some thoughts on what uniquely sets men and women apart in the business world, and the challenges they face. Included are some tips to help meet these challenges.

Women...

- are committed to seeing their business succeed as every dollar invested must work for them
- see the benefits of networking and join multiple groups to make business contacts
- take more courses, seminars, and buy more self-help books to educate themselves (70 percent of book purchasers are women)
- are budget-conscious and acutely aware of overhead costs; they can make do without the frills
- are quick to learn how to prepare their own accounting
- are willing to seek professional advice—and take it
- are multifaceted; they have innate creative and artistic talents and incorporate some brilliant ideas into their service, products and marketing
- can multi-task and are able to manage several jobs at once without losing it
- are usually organized; running a family requires fanatical time-management and juggling skills
- are better suited to repetitive tasks which are a substantial part of business management
- welcome change and growth and are eager to explore all opportunities
- are usually honest and straightforward in their approach to business.

These wonderful qualities explain why so many women-owned businesses succeed. At the same time, they face many unique challenges that often inhibit them from reaching their full potential.

THE CHALLENGES WOMEN FACE

There's no doubt that women have to work extremely hard to grow their businesses. Many feel that they must always be proving themselves in the business world—which is usually true. They have to work longer and harder to obtain recognition. Banks now realize that lending money to women isn't such a crazy idea, although it's still difficult to get financing. Most women-owned businesses are started with a personal capital investment of under $10,000.

Women usually lack funding or capital to market their business or to grow, so they go about it the best way they can. Often, there is little chance of seriously devoting themselves to taking their business to the next level as they struggle to juggle business with family life and to please everyone except themselves. By putting themselves last, they put their business last.

Some women experience guilt for attending business-related functions and meetings and will often cancel them to keep the family peace. Business owners or not, they are still expected to play the role of wife, mother, cook, nurse and chauffeur, to name a few.

Success—at What Price?

Some wonderful entrepreneurial women have succeeded in both owning businesses and in the workforce, but at what price? One woman recently informed me that her business succeeded only after a second attempt, along with a divorce. "I'm my own boss now," she laughed, "and it only took 10 years of hard work and a divorce."

More women are choosing the workplace in preference to having a family or marrying, realizing that combining the two may not bring the success they strive for. Some women are forced to become aggressive to succeed, but somewhere along the way, they have had to become more hardened and sometimes selfish. Each women must make her own choice.

TEN TIPS FOR WOMEN IN BUSINESS

1. **Choose the right business:** Many women become involved in businesses that promise low start-up costs, part-time hours, no experience necessary, with maximum financial rewards. These rarely succeed. Be sure you have chosen the right business for the right reasons.

2. **Learn to say "NO":** Women constitute a greater percentage of the nation's volunteers. Giving is an important part of owning a business, but be discriminating about how much time you give and whom you give it to. Learn to say "NO" to requests for your time and energy and focus only on commitments that you feel comfortable accepting.

3. **Build your confidence:** One of the biggest problems that women face is lack of confidence. Choosing the right business, developing communication skills and becoming the expert helps to build confidence. Let go of the old adage that men are the traditional breadwinners, as times have changed. Don't let overbearing spouses or family members make you feel guilty about owning a business. Be proud of yourself. Having the freedom and family support to do what you want to is a confidence builder in itself.

4. **Reduce isolation:** A recent study by University of Alberta sociologist Karen Hughes cited isolation as the most common problem for women in business. Join networking groups, business groups and/or special interest groups. You will make the contacts you need to bounce ideas off and to turn to when you are feeling alone.

5. **Put yourself first:** Women traditionally put themselves last, hoping there is something left on the plate for themselves. Family is of course our most treasured asset, but so is a happy, healthy and fulfilled mom who has been given the opportunity to do something she has dreamed of. So try making you and your business a priority—you will feel happier and pass these good vibrations along to your family.

6. **Don't sell yourself too cheaply:** Women are notorious for undervaluing their services. This is usually the result of lack of confidence. Know your worth and let clients know what free services you offer, what will be charged for, and what your rates are. Clients will appreciate your honest and straightforward approach. Don't hesitate to state your charges. If a client tries to beat you down, stand firm or walk away from the job.

7. **Monitor your business:** Don't become "too busy" to take financial care of your business. Learn how to read financial figures, update your books monthly and review the results regularly. Consult with your accountant and plan and know your tax position. Women excel in this area if they allow themselves the time to learn. For more resource information, visit *www.wboc.ca* (Women Business Owners of Canada Inc.) It is loaded with women-related business information and links.

8. **Stop trying to be perfect:** Does it really matter if you sweep dust balls under the refrigerator or that dinner was delivered in a box? Spoil yourself with a few hours of hired housekeeping help every two weeks. In case you didn't know, Superwoman died from overwork.

9. **Take your business seriously:** If you don't take your business seriously, then don't expect your family to. Set your goals and focus, then sit down with the family with a set of rules. Work toward demanding the respect you need to successfully operate the business.

10. **Delegate household chores:** Even if you work part-time, send younger children to a babysitter so that you have focussed time. Perhaps trade sitting time with a friend or join a babysitting co-op. Delegate chores to family members. Try involving the children, even if it is photocopying or helping with mail-outs. Remember, we work to live, not live to work.

BUT MEN HOLD THEIR GROUND IN THE BUSINESS WORLD

No one can deny that throughout history, men have been the leaders, heroes and conquerors while women have been the silent strength behind them. The last few decades have seen an incredible swing toward more equality, and in some cases, total role reversals.

A recent Australian article about Australian men explained the emotional difficulty they are experiencing in letting go of their macho image. No doubt the surge of women in the workplace has been quite an adjustment for men, and generally, they have coped admirably with this change.

In Canada and the United States, women and men now work hand-in-hand in business. Gentlemen, over the centuries you have built this wonderful world with your strength, innovation, courage, and determination to succeed, so keep up the good work. Let's look at some of the reasons why men are so successful in business.

WHY MEN SUCCEED

Men...

- excel in their technical abilities, particularly in fields such as sciences and technology

- are able to look at the bigger picture as a challenge and without fear
- are excellent at delegating tedious chores
- are able to focus on one issue and steadfastly work at it until the job is done
- are usually confident in their abilities and able to express this confidence
- run with the entrepreneurial spirit and are risk-takers
- excel at communicating their ideas with confidence
- become impassioned and dedicated to their work
- are willing to travel and spend long hours away from home
- network well in situations where women often can't (the golf course or the pub) and conduct extensive business in these situations
- can "shmooze" well with clients
- are adept at closing sales
- are competitive and aggressive at reaching for their goals
- work exceptionally well in team environments.

These qualities have won wars and built empires and huge conglomerations. Yet they take time to develop and not every man is born with them. The technician who has left a corporate environment after 20 years is often ill-equipped to face the challenges of the entrepreneurial world, and many don't succeed.

After presenting a day-long seminar on starting a business to downsized upper and middle management of a large corporation, one male participant stated to me, "But I don't want to do all that administrative and marketing stuff, I don't really like people. I just want to sit at my computer and design Web pages." He had been a computer programmer for many years and will no doubt have infinite problems adjusting to being a sole proprietor. I advised him to learn to network, take a variety of business courses, and then make the self-employment decision.

THE CHALLENGES MEN FACE

The adjustment to self-employment is a difficult transition. There are few teammates to bond with, bounce ideas off or to compete with. Because men are less able to cope with multi-tasking, many jobs are put aside in favour of being the operator. For some, doing the job and earning an income is far more important than monitoring the financial progress of the business.

Tedious chores are not given priority nor do they hold any challenge. Men often choose a business for the love of money, rather than the love of their work. They tend to make more impulsive decisions without performing the required research, and are impatient to succeed. Some men are quite inflexible to change. Others are high burn-out candidates as their stress tolerance is often lower than that of women. They are more driven to succeed—often at the expense of their personal and family health.

Image is an important consideration. I see credit card expenses from male-owned operations and they differ significantly from women's expenses. Men tend to spend more on clothing, technical equipment, socializing, and vehicle upgrades.

Men buy more toys and gadgets, often without first consulting the budget. The term "But it's a write-off!" is heard more from men's lips than from women's. These problems and attitudes often hinder business growth and are contributing factors to failure.

TEN TIPS FOR MEN IN BUSINESS

1. **Become budget conscious:** If you don't have a head for figures, learn as much as you can about budgeting, projecting, planning and cash flow. Before making a financial commitment, be sure the item is needed and that the business can afford it. Keep your cheque book up-to-date and the bank account reconciled.

2. **Work with your accountant:** If you aren't too interested in figures, find an accountant with whom you can build a comfortable relationship and make time to confer regularly. Employ a reputable bookkeeping service, and heed your accountant's advice.

3. **Pay attention to details:** Small and "inconsequential" chores are often overlooked in favour of completing billable work. Use the systems found in this book and make time for the paperwork. If you don't want to do it, pay someone to set up the systems for you and learn to maintain them.

4. **Look at the smaller picture:** You need to have the everyday picture in mind as well as the big picture of future success. Don't ignore what is happening around you as you get caught up in the moment. Small problems quickly escalate if they are ignored.

5. **Be a compassionate boss:** It feels good to be the boss, but everyone can learn from their employees. Talk to them, listen to their ideas and complaints, and implement the good ideas. Encourage, motivate and respect your staff. They often have valid concerns, great suggestions, and experience in areas that you don't.

6. **Don't forget your family:** It's too easy to become a workaholic and forget the family. When it all boils down, if you don't have a happy family life, work becomes empty and meaningless. Plan to spend quality time together—pencil time out in your organizer if you find this difficult, but don't ignore them.

7. **Include family in decision-making:** Include the family in your business. Tell them how it is going, warn them if you are stressed and tell them why. Discuss important decisions that may affect them and listen to their input. Don't let the business alienate you from your family.

8. **Be open to change:** Because old habits die hard, it's easy not to change. The older we become, the more frightening change can be. Be open to new ideas and technological changes. Learn to bend the rules and be a little more flexible and patient.

9. **Limit working hours:** Men tend to burn out faster than women as they throw themselves wholeheartedly into their businesses. Adequate sleep, a healthy diet and relaxation time are all important for keeping the work machine finely tuned. Take care of yourself if you are working continual long, hard hours and learn when to stop.

10. **Listen to your partner:** No one knows you better than your wife or partner, so if you are getting strong messages—listen. Partners don't normally say anything unless there is an obvious and serious concern. Don't ignore the warning signals.

WHAT IS GOOD BUSINESS MANAGEMENT?

A successful business is one that is efficiently managed and meets both your growth and profitability expectations. It is a combination of market and consumer awareness, cost-effective systems, productive marketing techniques, regular financial monitoring, and building a positive team environment, while *you* enjoy your work and reap both personal and financial satisfaction.

IDEA BIG

DON'T GO IT ALONE

There are many resources available to help a small business to grow, and some have already been mentioned. You won't build your empire by yourself. A mentor is a wonderful asset, so is a professional business coach, who acts as a guide and a mentor (for a fee). Cross-marketing, (working with other complementary businesses to promote each other), is another way to work with others. Work with these businesses to brainstorm and share marketing costs.

To determine if you are managing your business effectively, use Figure 15.1. On this final checklist, check "yes" to the questions about areas where you feel confident that you are operating your business efficiently. For those that you answer "no" to, you know what to do—now all you have to do is to *do it.*

PLAN TO SUCCEED

This book has been written because I have a personal passion in seeing each small business thrive and grow. Working in and with small businesses for over 30 years has allowed me to experience many successes and failures.

Although businesses experience growth problems through various stages of their life, the "make-it-or-break-it" problems are usually experienced in the first three years. The information in this book will help you to grow your business if you use it.

As you may have already discovered, the formula for success isn't simple, but the rewards are well worth striving for. There is no substitute for being your own boss, watching a dream become reality, and growing with your business. Never stop learning and always be open to change. Be organized, positive, motivated, passionate, confident, the expert, persistent and never lose sight of your goals.

You have to work long, hard hours, market aggressively, administer, account for, be detail-oriented and have control of the financial reins. There are no words for the feeling of personal fulfilment you experience as obstacles are overcome, and your business grows to the next level. Never forget to always work *on* your business, not just *in* your business.

And when it's time to turn to something else, you have a viable, saleable business that has not only given you a satisfactory lifestyle, it has supported you and your family and provided some nice "perks." You have built goodwill that can now be exchanged for dollars. You have the luxury of deciding what to do next—retire, travel, or turn your hand to another challenge.

You can do it. I wish you good luck, good judgement, sound management and great happiness.

Figure 15.1 Checklist: Good Business Management Is . . .

Check yes or no for each area of effective business management.

In my business, I feel confident that I am…	Yes	No
1. Understanding all aspects of my business and the industry.	❏	❏
2. Monitoring my financial progress monthly.	❏	❏
3. Reviewing areas of concern for solutions.	❏	❏
4. Understanding how to read financial statements.	❏	❏
5. Being organized, positive and motivated.	❏	❏
6. Maintaining controlled and affordable overhead.	❏	❏
7. Providing better service to my clients than the competitors.	❏	❏
8. Making my clients feel special and valued.	❏	❏
9. Filling both a niche and a need in the market.	❏	❏
10. Known as the expert in my field.	❏	❏
11. Performing ongoing effective marketing within my budget.	❏	❏
12. Following up regularly with clients and leads.	❏	❏
13. Diversifying or not putting all my eggs in one basket.	❏	❏
14. Aware of changing economic and consumer trends.	❏	❏
15. Changing where necessary to keep up with these trends.	❏	❏
16. Continually networking my business.	❏	❏
17. Being an active part of my community.	❏	❏
18. Keeping up with technology and time-saving systems.	❏	❏
19. Using the Internet for education, research and marketing.	❏	❏
20. Using e-mail for efficiency, cost-saving and marketing.	❏	❏
21. Increasing staff morale, developing a team spirit.	❏	❏
22. Monitoring employee costs versus productivity.	❏	❏
23. Budgeting for regular professional advice.	❏	❏
24. Utilizing government-funded employee hiring programs.	❏	❏
25 Utilizing government-funded programs for expansion.	❏	❏

Index

About the Author

Frances McGuckin is an outstanding example of what can be achieved with a home-based business. Known as the small business expert, she is a speaker, author, columnist and consultant in the field of entrepreneurship. In her 18th year of business, she is CEO of Smallbizpro, Eastleigh Management Services and Eastleigh Publications.

She has been nominated for many prestigious business awards, including the 1999 Entrepreneur of the Year and the YWCA Women of Distinction awards in 1998. McGuckin was awarded Business Person of the Year in Langley, B.C. for 1999, the first home-based business to receive this award.

Her first self-published book *Business for Beginners*, reached best-seller status in under one year. Current sales exceed 50,000 copies, and is currently being translated and published in Russia. With a passion for writing and delivering the message of successful entrepreneurship, McGuckin has developed and delivers dynamic seminars and keynotes.

She designed and teaches the first Entrepreneurial Skills in the Equine Industry accredited course at Kwantlen University College in Langley, B.C. Her clients include Telus, Canfor, Royal Bank of Canada, Community Futures Development Corp., the Surrey Writer's Conference, British Columbia Institute of Technology, and chambers of commerce, to name a few.

McGuckin has been a business columnist for *The Langley Times* for six years, and contributes to a variety of publications and Internet sites. A popular media guest, she has appeared on many radio and national television shows, and is a business resource for various B.C. and national newspapers and magazines.

A passionate believer in "giving something back," McGuckin is in her third term as a Director of the Langley Chamber of Commerce, and Chair of the Small Business Advancement Committee. Her work in the Langley small business sector helped to earn Langley a national Home-Based Friendly Community Award in October, 2000. She is the founder of the B.C. Provincial Small Business Task Force and a founding member and past coordinator of the Valley Women's Network in Langley, which has grown to five branches with a membership of over 300. For more information, please visit her Web site at *www.smallbizpro.com*.

McGraw-Hill Ryerson's
SMALL BUSINESS
SOLUTIONS
SERIES

McGraw Hill

WIRED FOR SMALL BUSINESS SUCCESS

0-07-087593-6 • $24.99 • paperback

These days, being well connected has little to do with how many people you know. Full of practical advice on making the best technology choices for your business.

SMART MARKETING ON A SMALL BUDGET

0-07-560469-8 • $22.99 • paperback

Customers are the lifeblood of any thriving business. Learn how to prepare effective, professional-looking marketing materials that will attract and keep clients—all on a shoe-string budget!

BIG IDEAS FOR GROWING YOUR SMALL BUSINESS

0-07-087874-9 • $24.99 • paperback

Your business is up and running. Now take it to the next level – make it bigger and better. Learn how to grow your business and still remain successful <u>and</u> profitable.

MAKE SURE IT'S DEDUCTIBLE

0-07-560543-0 • $18.99 • paperback

Paying taxes is a certainty in life, but it doesn't have to be a hardship. Learn little-known tips that can save SOHO owners big tax dollars —from Evelyn Jacks, Canada's most trusted tax authority.

HIRING, MANAGING AND KEEPING THE BEST

0-07-0864217 • $24.99 • paperback

You have always dreamed of being your own boss... but does the idea of being someone else's boss give you nightmares? Find out all you need to know to handle every aspect of employee matters.

Available at Bookstores Across Canada

PROVEN SOLUTIONS FOR CANADIAN SMALL BUSINESS

WHAT TO SAY WHEN YOUR CUSTOMERS WON'T PAY

0-07-560411-6 • $18.99 • paperback

Every business has to deal with accounts receivable. But collections doesn't have to rely on intimidation tactics and threats. Learn the most effective ways to get your due —and keep your customers too.

WHERE TO GO WHEN THE BANK SAYS NO

0-07-560225-3 • $22.99 • paperback

Finding the right sources of financing can be an ongoing struggle for SOHO owners. This is a road map to the many alternate methods for financing your business.

DON'T GET CAUGHT IN RISKY BUSINESS

0-07-560814-6 • $18.99 • paperback

Starting and running a business can be risky. Learn how to identify the barriers to success and use this knowledge to remove the risk from your small business.

SO YOU WANT TO BUY A FRANCHISE

0-07-560419-1 • $22.99 • paperback

How can you be sure you are buying into a successful venture and not pouring your money down the drain? Get all the information you need before signing on the dotted line.

NETWORKING IS MORE THAN DOING LUNCH

0-07-560544-9 • $18.99 • paperback

Networking is more than schmoozing! Learn how to develop and mine the contacts who can help you build, run or expand your business—and much more.

SO YOU THINK YOU NEED A LAWYER

0-07-560226-1 • $18.99 • paperback

Almost every small business owner needs a lawyer at some point. Gain the knowledge and confidence necessary for getting first-rate legal advice when you need it.

Meeting the Needs of
CANADIAN SMALL BUSINESS

AVAILABLE AT BOOKSTORES ACROSS CANADA

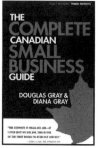

THE COMPLETE CANADIAN SMALL BUSINESS GUIDE, 3rd ed.
0-07-086495-0 • $42.99 • hardcover

From legal and accounting considerations to marketing and business plans, this book covers every aspect of starting and managing a small business.

NO GUTS, NO GLORY
0-07-086155-2 • $34.99 • hardcover

Learn about the culture of risk and reinvention that has propelled the likes of Nortel Networks, Bombardier Inc., Four Seasons Hotels, Loblaw Cos. and Magna International to global success.

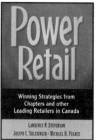

POWER RETAIL
0-07-560996-7 • $36.99 • hardcover

It's do or die in retail. Why are some retailers doing so well? Find out what it takes to be at the top... and how to stay there!

BUILDING A DREAM, 4th ed.
0-07-086271-0• $24.99 • paperback

A self-help workbook and guide to assess your business' potential for success.

THE COMPLETE CANADIAN HOME BUSINESS GUIDE TO TAXES, 2nd ed.
0-07-560160-5 • $24.99 • paperback

A Canadian guide to audit-proofing your home business and saving money.

HANDBOOK FOR CANADIAN CONSULTANTS
0-07-560101-X • $34.99 • hardcover

Learn how to turn your expertise into a successful small business as a consultant.

THE MAVERICKS
0-07-560437-X • $32.99 • hardcover

These small business trailblazers share the lessons they've learned along the way. Full of tips, advice and insight from those who've been there, struggled and succeeded.

HOME INC., 2nd ed.
0-07-551558-X • $22.95 • paperback

Full of "street-smart" tips and practical ideas to save money and avoid small business pitfalls.